ONE YEAR ON BROADWAY

FINDING OURSELVES BETWEEN THE SAND AND THE SEA

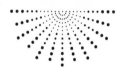

KATHRYN MCKENDRY

One Small Girl Publishing 2021

*To the creators, cast, and crew of Once on This Island
Thank you for what you do. Your work has touched our lives in
countless ways and will forever be a part of the story we tell.*

And to Jesse,

*I can't believe how lucky I am to share life with you. How is it possible
that, after twenty-seven years, I love you more today than ever?
Thank you for being my best friend, my muse, the other half of me,
and the co-author of our life story.*

Kathy

DISCLAIMER

This is a true story. While memories are never perfect, there are no intentional fictional embellishments. All dialogue is based on actual conversations, though because I initially had not intended to write a book about our journey, they are not word-for-word transcriptions but give the reader the spirit of what was said.

Most of the names in this book are the actual names of the people we met along this journey, however, to protect the anonymity of some people that we only casually came across, I have opted to change their names.

This is not a "how-to be a producer" book. We are not giving investment or tax advice, and we're not implying you should try to replicate anything we did. It is the tale of how two fans of musical theater and super fans of *Once on This Island* ignored conventional wisdom and were lucky enough to get an insider's view for one glorious year on Broadway.

There is something magical about how *Once on This Island* opens our hearts, connects us, and forever becomes a part of us.

This is our journey to the Island.

NOTES FOR THE READER

If you have not had the joy of experiencing *Once on This Island,* I've included the revival's cast of characters as a reference. I would also highly recommend listening to the Grammy-nominated New Broadway Cast Recording of *Once on This Island* before, during, and after reading as a companion to this book. Hearing the musical will bring in another, deeper layer of understanding to our story. Several times, I refer to certain special moments in the music and each chapter heading, except for chapter sixteen, is a song title from the album.

Once on This Island - **Broadway Revival Cast of Characters - Opening Night**

Asaka - Mother of the Earth: Alex Newell
Agwe - God of Water: Quentin Earl Darrington
Erzulie - Goddess of Love: Lea Salonga
Papa Ge - Sly Demon of Death: Merle Dandridge
Ti Moune: Hailey Kilgore
Little Ti Moune: Emerson Davis; Mia Williamson
Tonton Julian: Phillip Boykin

Mama Euralie: Kenita R. Miller
Daniel: Isaac Powell
Andrea: Alysha Deslorieux
Armand/Storyteller: David Jennings
Beauxhommes Narrator/Storyteller: Rodrick Covington
Beauxhommes Narrator/Storyteller: Darlesia Cearcy
Storyteller: Cassondra James
Storyteller: Grasan Kingsberry
Storyteller: Loren Lott
Storyteller: Tyler Hardwick
Storyteller: T. Oliver Reid
Storyteller: Aurelia Williams

"WE DANCE"

June 10, 2018, ~9 pm
72nd Annual Tony Awards
Orchestra Seats Aisle D Row J 311-312
Radio City Music Hall
New York, New York

*J*ESSE

"*S*ixty seconds until live," a male voice from above announced.

Guests dressed in their finest rushed down the aisles to make it back to their plush velvet seats before the live portion of the show began. The wisps of long chiffon gowns flowed behind the women in rivers of color as they whooshed past us to the front. This scene played out at every advertising break for the live broadcast of the 72nd Annual Tony Awards. The night was nearing the end, but excitement still buzzed through the air like bees in a rose garden. The biggest awards were coming up next.

"Thirty seconds until live."

The big black crane holding the television cameras swung over our heads, moving into filming position.

I looked around in wonder. This was the one and only time our son, Ryan, my wife, Kathy, and I would ever be at something this grand. The lighting around the stage bathed the whole theater in an orange glow that mirrored the warmth in my heart. I almost couldn't believe it was real. This was a once-in-a-lifetime experience. *We* were at the Tony Awards, the crown jewel of the Broadway season. I never would have dreamed it, yet somehow this was where the winds had blown us. We were surrounded by a sea of Broadway, TV, movie and music super-stars. Tina Fey, Chita Rivera, Bruce Springsteen, Nathan Lane, Robert De Niro, and countless other A-listers were among the attendees.

We sat in our seats near the back of the orchestra at Radio City Music Hall celebrating the best of Broadway. The night had already been unforgettable. Only a few hours ago, we had watched as Andrew Lloyd Webber received a Lifetime Achievement Award. We were in the same room as Andrew Lloyd Webber! I remember falling in love with *Phantom of the Opera* as a teenager and playing the cast recording over and over again. Now I was in the same room as the man who had created it.

We laughed along with the rest of the crowd when Josh Groban and Sara Bareilles made the most of their hosting duties, playing two grand pianos that faced each other and singing the words, "here's to the losers like us." We cried when the choir from Marjory Stoneman Douglas High School sang "Seasons of Love" from *Rent*. We cheered when Tony Shalhoub and Ari'el Stachel from *The Band's Visit* spoke about the beauty of bringing Muslims and Jews together on the

Broadway stage and the trials of being of Middle Eastern descent in America.

In this theater, the Broadway community had come together, unified in the belief that art and theater could bring about change in this sometimes cold and divisive world. They might be small, slow advances, but at least the arts could inspire the conversations of change.

None of that was why our little family was here. We had come to celebrate the revival of our favorite musical, *Once on This Island*, with the Broadway world. It was the moment we'd been waiting for all night.

"Ten seconds," the voice from above spoke again, and I focused on the stage.

"Ladies and gentlemen, please welcome two-time Tony winner Christine Baranski," a female voice announced.

Festive horns played, and the crowd cheered as Ms. Baranski, dressed in an all-white pant suit, walked out to a microphone at the right corner of the stage. The large screen at center stage changed from an orangish-yellow glowing "Tony Awards" sign to a blue graphic saying, "Best Revival of a Musical."

"This season's musical revivals..." Ms. Baranski began.

I looked over at Kathy and our fourteen year old son, Ryan, and smiled. They clutched each other's hands in hopeful anticipation. My heart sank as I realized they thought we had a chance to win. I knew otherwise. This moment had to be handled right.

Ms. Baranski continued, "Once again, here are the nominees for Best Revival of a Musical: *My Fair Lady*..."

The onstage screen came alive with a clip of the *My Fair Lady* cast performing "Get Me to the Church on Time," which they had performed earlier that night. Enthusiastic applause emanated from the *My Fair Lady* seating area.

I knew Ryan was going to be upset. What kid isn't disappointed by a loss? Everyone wants to be on the winning team. It was partly my fault. In my excitement about being a part of this evening, I had inadvertently conveyed to him that our show might win. I hadn't explained that while yes, it was theoretically possible for us to win, tonight's prize was almost certainly going to either the heavy favorite, *My Fair Lady,* or to the show many considered the dark-horse candidate, *Carousel.* Ryan didn't know that, though. He hadn't been following the Tony Award predictions. He was just a kid from Cleveland whose parents had gotten him swept up in all of this. He believed in *Once on This Island,* and he believed it had a chance.

Only two days ago, all of us Clevelanders had endured a crushing blow when LeBron James and the Cleveland Cavaliers had been beaten in the NBA Finals by the Golden State Warriors. I could still see the hollow defeat in Ryan's eyes from that disappointment. Now there would be this loss too. It was my duty to be a good role model. When the winner was announced, I would clap respectfully though not too heartily lest it look fake. Teenagers, I've learned, are quick to spot adults trying too hard. It wouldn't be too difficult. I was truly grateful to be a part of this beautiful celebration of live theater no matter who won.

Ms. Baranski went on, announcing the second of the three nominees: "...*Once on This Island...*"

The center screen switched to the clip of the *Once on This Island* cast with Alex Newell belting out the end run of "Mama Will Provide." At that, our entire section jumped up, cheering like crazed fans.

The stage screen changed once again as Ms. Baranski announced the third and final nominee: "...Rodgers and Hammerstein's *Carousel.*"

We watched the recap of that show's big dance number.

"... and the Tony Award goes to..." She held the black and silver envelope in her hands.

Time slowed nearly to a stop. I was hyper-aware of every

sight and sound, suspended in this moment of love and appreciation for *Once on This Island* and what it had meant to Kathy and
me throughout our lives. Now it was being showcased and
honored on this stage and on CBS in front of six million
viewers.

Ms. Baranski began to open the envelope with her left hand.

I looked over again at Kathy and Ryan. They quietly whispered to each other, "Rally Spirit! Rally Spirit! Rally Spirit!" It
was our family's good luck chant. They held tight to each
other's hands, believing in the impossible.

"And the Tony Award goes to..." Ms. Baranski paused.
Complete silence fell over this room of six thousand people as
we held our collective breath and waited for her to speak again.
"Oops, sorry."

She fumbled with the thick envelope and opened it. Her eyes
scanned the page then brightened. She took a breath and
continued...

2

"DISCOVERING DANIEL"

June, 2017
Cleveland, Ohio

*J*ESSE

J checked my inbox. My breath caught when I saw an email from Ken Davenport, the founder of Davenport Theatrical Enterprises. Not expecting to hear back at all, let alone this soon, I immediately clicked on the message. It had only been a day since I had decided to email him on a whim. It was a ridiculous notion. I didn't know anything about Broadway, unless belting out show tunes in the car with Kathy counted, but something had told me to push "send" anyway.

As I read his response, my eyes skimmed over everything except the words, "Jesse, I would love to have you come on board as an investor in the revival of *Once on This Island* on Broadway."

I read it again and smiled.

Leaning back in my chair, I thought about that cold November evening twenty-five years earlier. It had been almost a lifetime ago, but I remembered so clearly the night that brought *Once on This Island* into our lives.

November 24, 1992
Wharton Center for the Performing Arts
Michigan State University
East Lansing, Michigan

J ESSE

I t was the Tuesday night just before Thanksgiving break at Michigan State University, where I was a junior. My boss, Nina Silbergleit, at The Wharton Center for the Performing Arts had scheduled me to usher the evening performance of the national tour of *Once on This Island*, the musical.

I loved my job as an usher. Escorting people to their seats wasn't too difficult, and it was decent pay, but the real reason to work at the Wharton Center was to see the musicals that came through on tour. As an MSU student, I couldn't afford to buy tickets regularly, but as an usher, I was allowed to stick around after everyone else had been seated and see the shows for free.

That night, though, I wanted nothing more than to stay in and sleep, to forget the world around me. It had been a long, difficult semester. The weight of missing my girlfriend, Kathy, crushed me as if a large boulder had fallen on my chest. My body hurt all over, and I was exhausted. Maybe I was coming down with something. With every passing moment, I felt more terrible. Someone else should take my shift. My heart ached too much to go anywhere, and I'd never even heard of this musical.

Picking up the phone to find a sub, I started to dial the number of another usher. Then, not knowing quite why, I put the phone down and decided to go in to work. If I left the theater as soon as everyone was seated, I wouldn't have to be there long anyway. I could forget the world later.

My section that night was mid-way back in Orchestra Left. Time ticked by slowly as I escorted eager, mostly elderly patrons dressed in their Sunday best to their seats. Hiding my weariness, I feigned an air of excitement so as not to dampen the mood.

Thankfully, the house lights went down right on schedule. I waited, standing near the orchestra door in case any late arrivals needed assistance and focused on the stage. Maybe I would want to see this show the next time it came around.

Thunder crashed echoing through the cavernous theater. A flash of lightning lit up the indoor sky, and a young girl screamed as hurricane winds ripped her from her mother's arms, threatening to drag her into the sea.

But the gods who ruled her island in the French Antilles had a different plan for the little girl Ti Moune. While she watched in terror as her mother disappeared into the angry churning surf, the gods sheltered young Ti Moune high in the branches of a mango tree.

The bright morning sun brought the island to life again, and even the birds sang their praise to the god Asaka, Mother of the Earth. Their soft lilting melodies carried on the ocean breeze to two old peasants, Mama Euralie and Tonton Julian, who strolled hand in hand down the beach. Grateful to be alive, they surveyed the damage that Agwe, God of Water, had inflicted on their island through the night. Startled by the cry of a child, they looked up and spotted a little girl clinging tightly to a tree. Despite their age, poverty, and better instincts, Mama Euralie and Tonton Julian followed their hearts and adopted little Ti Moune as their own.

The stage came alive with color as women dressed in bright yellow and red skirts and headdresses joined the two old peasants and the little girl on the beach. The rhythmic beat of Caribbean drums pulsed in time with my heart. As they danced to the gods, thankful to have been spared by the night's squall, I smiled for the first time in days. The music stirred something deep within me, as if somehow, I had known this melody all along though I had never heard it. It pulled at my soul like gravity. I had to stay for a little longer.

Magically before my eyes, little Ti Moune transformed into a beautiful young woman singing, "Waiting For Life," asking the gods to reveal her purpose. What had they saved her for? Adventure? Love? Or something bigger?

In that three-minute song, in Ti Moune's pleading to the gods, I heard my own heart's prayer. I, too, wanted love and adventure, though I already knew who that love was.

The mischievous gods of the island heard Ti Moune's prayer and sent her Daniel, a young aristocrat from the other side of the island, who ran across the stage holding two flashlights until his "car" crashed and spun off the wet, slippery road. The staging here was incredibly simple, but Daniel didn't need an actual car to get the point across. It was unexpected and wonderful.

I had always loved seeing big spectacular musicals like *Les Miserables* and *Miss Saigon* with huge casts and even bigger props and sets—giant barricades, cannons, real cars, and helicopters. This was different, like nothing I'd ever seen before. There were no elaborate set designs and expensive props. The cast was barefoot, and the costumes were simple yet colorful traditional Caribbean-style clothing. *Once on This Island* was not a big flashy musical, not cotton candy for the senses. It was the exact opposite. The power was in its simplicity, drawing the audience in with the extraordinary Caribbean-flavored score and the heart-wrenching story. Nothing else was needed. It carried me away from the cold and lonely Michigan winter outside and transported me to the island. I only wished Kathy was here with me.

Then, as quickly as Daniel came into Ti Moune's life, he was taken away again, just as Kathy was whisked from mine. It struck me with the force of a wave crashing into the shore that I was watching scenes of my own story played out before my eyes. My heart hurt.

Thankfully, Asaka, Mother of the Earth, lit up the stage with her larger-than-life personality. Brazenly sashaying across the stage, she led Ti Moune on a dangerous trek through the wilderness to find Daniel. On the way, Asaka belted out the song, "Mama Will Provide." She pushed out the last note with such force it filled the air in the theater completely, like a balloon on the verge of popping.

Entirely under the island's spell, I stood mesmerized until the very end of the musical.

As soon as it was over, I ran ahead of the exiting crowd down the stairs. Desperate to see it again, I headed straight to the box office, hoping to get there before it closed. *Once on This Island* was only playing one more performance here before heading to its next tour stop, and I *had* to be there. Something had happened to me in those ninety minutes. The story and music had gripped my soul, just as Papa Ge, God of Death, had held fast to Ti Moune's. I couldn't miss the last show. It had utterly consumed me.

The lady at the ticket window shook her head. "Sorry. I'm closed for the night."

"Oh, please. I'm...I'm an usher here," I begged her. "I just worked the show, and I have to bring my girlfriend to see it before it's gone."

Pulling her glasses down the bridge of her nose, she looked over the rims and studied me for a moment. I thought she was going to shoo me away, but something must have stirred her heart.

"Okay, hun, if it's for you and your girlfriend, but don't tell no one." She grinned.

Quickly glancing left and right, she reopened the cash register and put my money in the drawer. Then she handed me two tickets under the little glass window. I thanked her repeatedly until she closed up the window and stepped out of the ticket booth through the back door.

As I looked down at the two tickets in my hand, the reality struck me that Kathy might not be able to come with me. I knew she would love the show as much as I had, if only we were allowed to see each other.

The night air outside the theater was ice cold. Luckily, my Honda scooter wasn't parked too far away. I hopped on and wound my way across campus to the house I rented with six other guys.

When I came in, Andy was on the phone that hung from the kitchen wall.

"Hurry and hang up!" I yelled. "I need the phone to call Kathy."

"Okay, okay." He mumbled a quick "goodbye" to whomever he was talking to and handed me the receiver.

I held the phone for a moment and took a deep breath. Then, I dialed her number.

*K*ATHY
The phone in my room rang. Was it Jesse? No one else would be calling this late. My heart could hope. It felt like it had been so long. I jumped to pick up the receiver before my mom could answer.

"Hello?" I said as quietly as I could, hoping she hadn't picked up the other end downstairs to listen in. When I chose to live at home for college to save money instead of in the dorms, I had never envisioned this type of scenario. Now, I was a twenty-year-old junior at MSU and regretted that decision.

"Hi, it's Jesse."

My cheeks flushed with warmth hearing his voice again. "Oh, hi," I said, playing with the twisted phone cord, nervous that my parents might hear me. "It's good to hear your voice."

"I need to see you. Are you free tomorrow night?" he asked.

"I'm supposed to be helping with Thanksgiving preparation. Why?" Maybe I could secretly meet him, but I had never done anything like that before and didn't realistically think I could pull it off. I was a terrible liar.

"I just saw the most amazing musical, and I have to take you. Can you come, please?"

"I don't know," I stalled. He and I both knew my parents wouldn't let me go, but I longed to see him again. I had to see him again.

I wracked my brain for an idea. Could I disobey a direct order from my parents? I didn't know what they would do if they found out.

"What show is it?" I asked.

"*Once on This Island,*" he said. "I've never seen anything like it." The words rushed out of his mouth with excitement. "I know you'll love it! Please, can I take you? I already bought two tickets."

I could hear him smiling over the phone. I missed that smile. "Let me see if I can get a ride." I paused. I wanted to say more but I was afraid, afraid we would get caught and afraid of my own feelings. "I'll call you tomorrow. I miss you," I added quietly.

"I miss you too," he replied.

I hung up the phone and slumped down onto my bed.

A single tear slipped down my cheek as I wondered what to do. More than anything, I wanted to see the show with Jesse. I wanted to spend tomorrow night and every night after with him. I wanted to spend the rest of my life with him.

But I wasn't allowed to *ever* see him again.

3

"WAITING FOR LIFE"

June 2017
Cleveland, Ohio

J ESSE

*T*he words on my screen hadn't changed. Ken Davenport was in fact inviting us to be investors in the show. I jumped up and walked around my small office, pacing back and forth. *Once on This Island* was the first Broadway show Kathy and I had seen together. Now we had a chance to be a part of bringing it back to Broadway. I couldn't wait to drive home and tell her, to see her face light up at the thought of us being involved. For most of the forty-five minute commute, I was thinking about how I would share the exciting news.

I pulled into our driveway just as she was parking the minivan in the garage. She must have had some figure skating lessons today. I never can remember her teaching schedule. She waited for me.

"Hi, honey." She wrapped her arms around me and gave me a kiss. "How was your day?"

"I have some great news!" I blurted out.

"What?"

As we walked in the house, I explained how I'd read an article from Playbill.com about someone producing a Broadway revival of *Once on This Island*. ("Exclusive: Broadway-Aimed *Once on This Island* Tests New Sound in Workshop"[1])

While I talked, she turned the oven on, pulled a bunch of items out of the fridge for dinner, and put them on the counter.

"Really?" She looked up from the salmon fillet that she had started rubbing with olive oil. "That's wonderful! I've missed it so much," she said. Pausing what she was doing for just a moment, she looked up as if looking into the past. "I will never forget that night."

"Me neither," I said.

Her focus turned back to dinner. A sly smile crept across my face as I picked up the plates to set the table. She dumped some rice and water into the rice cooker pot and pressed down on the switch, turning it on.

"And this time, we could be a part of it," I added.

"What do you mean?" she asked, raising an eyebrow.

"We could help bring it back to Broadway by being investors in the show." I felt like a kid waiting for Christmas just thinking about it.

Her eyes lit up as the words sank in. "Wait, what?"

I explained, "I googled '*Once on This Island* investment,' which led me directly to Ken Davenport, the lead producer. All we have to do is give him some money."

Kathy, always the more financially practical one of the two

of us, tilted her head suspiciously and asked, "Interesting...but what does 'some money' mean?"

"I'm not sure yet. Some investors put up enormous sums of money for different shows. Of course, we are nowhere near that category, but maybe there is a small piece for us, a very small piece."

I studied her expression. After almost twenty-five years of marriage, I could usually tell what she was thinking with one glance. When happy or excited, she smiles with her eyes. When unsure or nervous, she furrows her brow just a bit and tilts her head to one side. I got the furrowed brow.

I continued anyway, "Ken mentioned there is some flexibility in the amount we would have to put in, but he'll be sending me more details."

She put her forefinger to her chin, thinking about it. "That sounds amazing, but don't you think we should find out a little more about investing in a musical first? And who is this Ken guy?"

"Yes, you're right," I said, a little discouraged, and then I thought of something. "But do you remember that conversation we had on our honeymoon? On the Road to Hana?"

Twenty-three years ago, it had only been a crazy idea that had, over the years, been lost like the tiniest of mustard seeds buried deep in my brain.

Kathy turned to gaze out the kitchen window and thought for a moment. "Of course I do. Maybe the universe heard our prayer. What if we could actually do it?" she asked.

Now her eyes were smiling.

I stepped closer and wrapped my arms around her. "I know. It would be incredible."

The oven timer went off, bringing us out of our imaginations and back to reality. She lifted her head and gently kissed me then reached over to put on the oven mitts. The kitchen filled with the sweet aroma of teriyaki salmon as she pulled the pan out.

"Do you want to go up and tell the kids dinner is ready?" she asked.

"Sure."

🐚

Mid-June, 2017
New York, New York

J ESSE

A couple weeks later when I was in New York for work, I scheduled a quick meeting with Valerie Novakoff, an associate producer from Ken's office, to find out more. Posters from several musicals decorated the walls in the office—*Kinky Boots*, the revivals of *Godspell*, and *Spring Awakening*. I looked closer at the names listed under the titles. Davenport Theatrical Enterprises had been a producer for each of them.

"Hi, Jesse." Val came from around the corner of the office and welcomed me in. We sat down, and she handed me a prospective investor's packet and gave me a brief history of the company's background. "Ken has been working on Broadway for over twenty years and started Davenport Theatrical Enterprises in 2004."

Check, he was a legitimate Broadway producer.

"For *Once on This Island*, we're going to be doing some things that no one has ever done!" She quickly walked me through some of the information in the packet, pointing out a mock-up of the set. "Our stage is going to be an actual island with sand, water, fire, and even a boat." She leaned in and lowered her voice just a bit. "Lea Salonga is going to play the role of Erzulie, Goddess of Love."

Lea Salonga! I broke out in an excited sweat, my heart instantly deciding we had to be a part of this.

Then we turned to the financials.

Val pointed to a very large number on the page and said, "This is the recommended minimum amount of money that we are looking for from investors."

Alarm bells went off in my head. It was simply too much for us.

"Is there a way to put in half that amount?" I asked, hoping we hadn't lost our chance before it even started. "We might be able to find a way to do that," I added. It was still a huge amount of money for us.

"Absolutely. We can make that work! This seems like a wonderful first investment in Broadway for you and your wife," Val said.

❀

June 27, 2017
Cleveland, Ohio

*J*ESSE
Kathy and I went out to dinner to celebrate her birthday at a little Italian restaurant, just the two of us. Until recently, we hadn't made the time to do date nights very often. Not that we didn't want to, but our busy lives got in the way. For most special occasions, even our anniversary dinners, the kids came with us. We enjoyed spending those moments all together as a family. Now though, Jessica and Alyssa were twenty-one and nineteen and spent most of their time with their boyfriends. Ryan would have joined us, but he had a three-hour guitar practice nearby, so tonight, we relished a quiet dinner alone. It was a perfect time to discuss *Once on This Island.*

We sat at the little table for two by the stone fireplace and ordered glasses of wine and toasted to her birthday. I wasn't sure how to bring up the amount of money needed for the investment without having her shut down the idea. Not that she doesn't like to have fun, but she is the self-proclaimed Scrooge of the family, not to mention she gets a little hangry sometimes, so I waited for our food to come out. Then I brought it up and held my breath.

She put her fork down on her plate of handmade cheese ravioli and grimaced. "Eeeh, that's a lot. That's the minimum amount?"

"Yeah. A full-share is twice that, but they said we could split a share if that's what worked for us." I looked at her, wondering what she was thinking. This time, I couldn't read the signs.

It's not like we had an extra pile of money sitting in our checking account. We could use our investment account to do it, but we'd been saving for over twenty years, and we'd planned to use that money to buy our own business someday.

Kathy loved her career as a figure skating coach, but now that Ryan was going to be busy with high school, she wanted to take on a new challenge. Running a small local business was what she'd decided on. We dreamed of me eventually retiring from my current job. Then we would work on the business and spend all of our time making a living together.

A few months ago, we had found a potential prospect—a local pizza shop—that we were seriously considering, and Kathy was in the early stages of conducting due diligence. Now there was *Once on This Island*.

We couldn't do both.

We would have to make a choice, and relatively soon. Davenport Theatrical Enterprises wasn't going to wait for us.

Kathy leaned back in her chair and took a sip of red wine. "I *want* to do it."

"Me too. It sounds like they are being really innovative with the set design, bringing in sand and water," I added, trying to sell the idea, though I could tell she wasn't fully on board. "But?"

"But would it be smart? It's just we don't know anything about this... If it was next year, we'd have time to save up for it," she said, putting her glass back on the table.

"I know, but we'll never get this opportunity again. I don't think I would do it for any other show."

"No, you're right. No other show means as much." She paused. "Maybe you should keep searching for information on investing in Broadway. In the meantime, I'll continue combing through all the contracts and financials for the pizza place. If we decide not to go through with the business purchase, then maybe we can put the money toward the show."

My heart wanted to just go for it and tell Ken "yes" immediately, but Kathy was right. We still needed to find out more. To me, even the thought of a new challenge—learning all I could about the business of producing a Broadway musical—was intriguing. What better way to educate myself about it than having a front-row seat in the production of our favorite musical of all time?

Investing in a Broadway musical wasn't the same as making a living running our own little restaurant, though. With our own business, we would at least in theory be making a fairly steady monthly return. What kind of return could we expect from a musical? Could we even count on receiving our original investment back?

I scoured the internet for information. What I found didn't give me a lot of confidence. It didn't sound like Broadway was a great basket to put your eggs in. In fact, from a strictly financial perspective, all the data pointed to it being exactly the opposite. The statistics on Broadway investing are not stellar. While I read that Broadway returns averaged around ten percent overall, only one in five shows recoup their initial investment. Of that one in five, many provide a small gain while only a handful go on to earn large returns. In other words, if the show you chose to invest in wasn't a blockbuster, you should expect a loss of capital. This was looking like a gamble rather than an investment. If we decided to put money in this basket, the most likely outcome was that we would be out of eggs. Sure, *Hamilton* and *Wicked* have made their investors plenty of money, but how often do shows as successful as those come along?

Over the next week, we kept coming back to the same question: Can we afford to lose this money? Of course, we didn't *want* to lose it, but, worst-case scenario, if we didn't get any of it back, could we handle that?

Financially, maybe, but what about mentally? Would the possibility of losing it all be too stressful? After all, we'd worked most of our adult lives to save that money. Were we willing to let it go?

❀

1993
East Lansing, Michigan

*J*ESSE
Back in 1993, neither Kathy nor I brought *any* money into our relationship. We were young, only twenty-one and still in college when we got engaged. I didn't have the money to buy her an engagement ring, so I made a deal with my dad. I agreed to paint the interior of my parent's house, and he agreed to give me the six hundred dollars I needed to buy her a small pear-shaped diamond ring. Kathy had no idea what I was planning, and she happily spent the whole day helping me paint, not knowing she was helping to pay for her own ring.

A few weeks later, on August 26, 1993—the first anniversary of our first date—I took her out to dinner at a fancy revolving restaurant overlooking downtown Detroit. The lights were low and romantic. I was nervous. I wanted everything to go perfectly. I put the ring in its black velvet case on the ledge, and I hoped to time it perfectly so that the ring would be right beside her as soon as I popped the question.

I got up, walked around the table, and got down on one knee. I took her hand in mine. "Kathy, will you marry me?"

"Yes, of course!" she said, starting to cry before I even had time to tell her to look for the ring.

"Look over on the ledge. I think there's something there for you."

She looked and then turned back to me, confused. "There's nothing over there."

I panicked. It had to be there. I just put it there! Jumping up, I went to the ledge. "Here it is." I brought the box over, got down on one knee again, and handed it to her.

"I didn't see it. The black velvet blended into the ledge." She chuckled.

Despite the near heart attack at thinking I might have lost the ring, I couldn't have been happier. "You said yes before you even knew I got a ring?"

"I didn't think you had enough money to get one."

"Well, I didn't. You helped me paint to pay for it," I said.

She laughed and opened the box. The people at the table behind us clapped as I slipped the ring on her finger.

Now that we were engaged, we needed to focus on saving money to pay for our wedding and honeymoon, which we set for December of 1994. Both of us were still college students, and we both worked multiple jobs to pay for our rent and food. Student loans covered our last semester at Michigan State. We bought our first car from Kathy's cousin, an old Delta 88, for five hundred dollars.

Unfortunately, at the time, we didn't know how to save money. We were still just kids trying to figure things out. We barely made enough to cover expenses. Everything we earned went right back out to pay bills and, of course, order late-night pizza. Whatever money was left over, we saved for me to attend graduate school after our wedding.

Four years later, we had a two-year-old and an infant, and our budget was stretched as thin as a rubber band just before it snaps. Each month, we seemed to barely scrape by. We had just enough to pay student loans, pay rent, and buy diapers and formula, leaving little left over for groceries. A couple of months, we miscalculated our spending. A pit would form in my stomach as we neared the end of the month, and we realized we would be just short on our rent payment. What had gone wrong? I had a good job as an engineer at Chrysler in Detroit, Michigan. Why couldn't we make this work?

One night, we sat down for hours going through our finances and reviewing our spending, debt, and income. Everything laid out in front of us. That pit in my stomach felt cavernous. I wanted to throw up or cry. We'd been stupid. Every month, we were spending money we didn't have, not on anything extravagant, just an occasional dinner out at Olive Garden. We thought we were being responsible. In reality, we were getting further behind every single month. Overcoming our mountain of debt seemed like an impossible task.

I was devastated. Kathy and the girls were depending on me, and I wasn't able to provide. As soon as our youngest, Alyssa, was old enough, Kathy could go back to work, but for now, daycare was too expensive to make it feasible. Our only choice was to cut out every unnecessary expense and save every penny. We carefully laid out a plan to dig our way out of this giant hole. The problem was that the plan would take time, and we needed cash by Friday to pay rent. We skipped buying groceries, and Kathy and I got by on rice and gravy for the week, while the girls got their Gerber baby food and formula. Thursday night, we scrounged around the apartment to find all of our loose change, sorted it into coin rolls, and drove to the bank the next morning. We had just enough.

We resorted to rice and gravy a few more times, but gradually, we climbed out of that dark hole, dusted ourselves off, and looked up at the sun.

Twenty-five years later, we were in a different financial position, but the lessons learned to reach this point we had carried with us as we grew older.

The decision of whether or not to invest in *Once on This Island* could not be taken lightly. Together, we studied the materials Ken sent our way. It was fascinating to read that the creative team, headed by director Michael Arden, had gone to Port-au-Prince, Haiti to get a feel for the landscape and cultural perspectives, including taking part in a traditional Haitian Vodou ceremony. In order to create a "theater island" that felt as authentic as possible, set designer, Dane Laffrey, returned with hundreds of pictures of random walls and piles of stuff, items that would inspire the wreckage-strewn island in the aftermath of a hurricane that was about to appear in the Circle in the Square Theater. In addition to the extensive care the creative team was taking to create a real representation of Haiti, they had launched an international casting search for the right Ti Moune, beginning in Port-au-Prince and continuing to several U.S. cities.

I searched for more detailed statistics on the business of Broadway, but unfortunately, there wasn't much information available to the public. Each Broadway show keeps most of its information private, publicly providing only the weekly grosses and attendance that are published by broadwayworld.com. There was no question about it. The more I looked into it, the harder it was to justify.

But if I'm being honest, I had made up my mind.

One night, I finally said to Kathy, "This is our one shot. If we are ever going to be a part of a Broadway show, it has to be this one."

"Then let's do it," she replied.

4

"FOREVER YOURS"

November 25, 1992
Wharton Center for the Performing Arts
Michigan State University
East Lansing, Michigan

$\mathscr{K}$ATHY

I don't remember how I got there. Maybe I didn't tell my parents who I was meeting, though they surely must have known. Certainly, I didn't walk the ten miles to campus from our home. Maybe it was my brother who drove me all the way, or maybe the Gods just lifted me up and placed me at the play. I don't know. All I can say is that on the night before Thanksgiving, when I was supposed to be helping clean and bake for the holiday, I met Jesse at the Wharton Center to see *Once on This Island.*

I'd only seen one other live musical, *Les Miserables,* when I was a junior in high school. My French class took a field trip to experience the Broadway tour that came to East Lansing, Michigan. It struck me with the force of a cannon, and I was never the same. Once I had heard the music, it was forever seared into my soul, especially Eponine's song, "On My Own." My young heart, searching for my own love in vain, ached with every one of her words. I bought the cast album on CD and played it every day, singing it in my room to my books and my pet lizard, Diny. I chose it for my figure skating program for that year's ice show. I couldn't get enough of *Les Mis.* Then *Phantom of the Opera* came out, and I officially became obsessed with Broadway musicals. Most days, I listened to both cast albums one after the other. It didn't stop there. I had to see and hear every musical I could.

My dad wasn't the type of guy to go to musicals, which meant he wouldn't be buying tickets for them either, but Gramps and Grams—what my brothers and I affectionately called my mom's parents—loved them, so I would go to their house, and together we would sit and watch the classic Rodgers and Hammerstein musicals as they aired on PBS.

Other than Gramps, I didn't know any guys who even liked musicals. Especially not guys my age, and no one had ever taken me to a musical for a date before. Actually, I could have counted on one hand the number of any kind of dates I'd been on before Jesse, and they had all consisted of eating at the local pizza joint as the most exciting part of the night.

That evening felt like a real date. Jesse and I walked arm in arm through the theater lobby, Jesse in khaki pants and a button-down shirt, me in a little black dress. I was twenty years old, and I felt like a princess. It was going to be a special night, though neither of us could possibly foresee the significance it would play in our future.

As we sat in our seats, I held Jesse's hand, grateful to be there with him. My hand felt natural in his, like they had been formed for each other. The warmth of his touch radiated through my soul.

In his soft hazel eyes, I saw my future.

It didn't matter what my parents said. I wasn't a child any longer, and they couldn't keep me from loving him. I would choose my future, not them.

The theater darkened, and I tore my gaze from him to look toward the stage.

Simple and sparse. Bright island colors.

No rotating stages or falling chandeliers, and no large ensemble cast. Simple staging for a simple story, one that has been told throughout history. An all-too-familiar tale.

Forbidden love.

A test.

Loss.

Powerful because it was grounded in people's lives, in our lives.

Mesmerized, I watched as Daniel and Ti Moune, from two different worlds, fell desperately in love.

And then their parents tried to stop them.

A tidal wave of emotion threatened to drag me under like a powerful undertow, I could barely breathe. *Les Mis* was beautiful and had been my gateway to Broadway musicals, but *Once on This Island* was a version of our own story played out on stage. It both filled my heart with courage and broke it into pieces at the same time. It reached into the depths of my soul.

I could only pray that Papa Ge would have pity on us, and our journey would have a different ending.

Fall 2017
Cleveland, Ohio

ESSE

could hardly believe Kathy had agreed to invest in *Once on This Island.*

"Are you sure? What about the pizza place?" I asked.

She had spent months reviewing the contracts and talking to lawyers, lenders, and accountants on the little restaurant we'd been looking at purchasing. I would support whatever her final decision was. After all she had supported me the eight different times we had moved for me to attend graduate school or change career paths.

"Honestly," she said, "I'd rather put our money into *Once on This Island.* I don't think this is the business for us. We would have to keep looking for something else anyway. *Once on This Island* is right in front of us now."

I didn't ask twice. "Okay, let's do it!" I was so excited I jumped up from our kitchen table and started speed-walking around it.

Kathy laughed at my childish enthusiasm, but she sprang out of her chair to catch me. We stood in each other's arms for a moment.

"EEEEEE!" she squealed. "We're really going to help bring *Once on This Island* back to Broadway!" She squeezed me tighter. "I can't believe it!"

Jessica and Ryan were the only two kids home at the moment, so we called a family meeting. We would have to tell Alyssa later. After a few minutes, they came downstairs, looking confused and maybe a bit worried, probably thinking we were about to put them to work on something.

Kathy started, "So, we've decided to do something that's a bit unusual." She giggled, unable to hide her excitement.

"What?" Jessica asked.

"Driving to Alaska again? Or maybe Mexico this time?" Ryan joined in with a slightly mocking tone.

"No, no nothing like that," I said. "We've decided to be investors in *Once on This Island!*"

Jessica and Ryan looked at each other then at us. They didn't seem impressed. Jessica knew of the musical. She and Alyssa had come with us to a concert of the music performed by a local high school when she had been about eight years old. She loved the music, but we hadn't listened to it for a long time. Ryan didn't know anything about it.

Jessica seemed to sense that she should comment and said, "Oh that's cool."

Ryan chimed in, "Eh, okay... That's it? Sounds kinda crazy to me but whatever." He shrugged and headed to the kitchen, totally uninterested in our exciting announcement.

That wasn't quite the reaction we had expected. Oh well. Neither of them had seen the original or knew what it meant to us. They would understand better once they finally saw it on Broadway.

Despite the kids' lackluster response, Kathy and I were still bubbly about the idea. Later that day, I called Ken's office and told him we were in. We would invest in the revival production of *Once on This Island* on Broadway.

Now all we had to do was wait for the email, sign the papers, and send the money. Kathy and I had no idea where this decision would lead, but we were thrilled to make this leap together.

Sometime in the next couple of days, Ken contacted me again and casually mentioned that if we wanted to, there was room for us to come on board as co-producers of the show. We didn't know what being a co-producer meant, so I inquired further.

Basically, if we invested more money—a lot more money—or if we found other investors who could put in a similar amount alongside ours, then we would be co-producers. For this money, in addition to the satisfaction of knowing we were a bigger part of bringing this beautiful piece of art back to life, we would get a short bio in the Playbill listing us as a co-producer, our name would appear on the theater above the title on the billing, and if the show was nominated for a Tony Award, we would become Tony-nominated producers. Though it all sounded very exciting and fun to imagine, I laughed off the thought of us being co-producers. It was ridiculous, simply far too much money.

Saturday morning came, and Kathy and I got up early like usual. She made coffee and what I call the "garbage omelette." I nicknamed it that because she throws in all the left-over veggies in the fridge before they become garbage. It's one of my favorite breakfasts.

While we were enjoying our leisurely morning, I mentioned my conversation with Ken. I knew it was too much money for us to even consider, but for some reason, that morning, I brought it up to her.

"Well, how much more?" she asked.

I turned to her sheepishly, already knowing the answer. It was an outrageous amount.

"Uh, about six times our original investment."

She looked up from her omelette. "What? That's ridiculous!" She paused for a moment, stunned by the number. I thought egg might tumble out of her open mouth. She swallowed hard then said, "We can't do that."

"I know. Forget it. It's not possible. I already told Ken that we just couldn't do that much."

Risking that much would be everything we had saved to buy a business.

"Okay, that's good," she said, relieved.

We both laughed it off and went back to our breakfast discussing the more normal topics of the week, like scheduling issues and who was driving Ryan home from guitar lessons.

But something kept tugging at me like the moon pulls the sea. Waves of thoughts rushed back and forth in my mind asking *what if...*

May 2014
Alaska Highway, Yukon Territory, Canada-Alaska

ESSE

*O*ver the years, we had made a habit of doing a few crazy things along our journey. Searching out new experiences helped us grow as a couple and as a family. In that spirit, we decided in 2014 to take all three kids—Jessica and Alyssa were teenagers, and Ryan was eight— and set off in an RV for a month-long adventure to Alaska. We picked up the giant Winnebago we were renting in Forest City, Iowa and made our way to Anchorage, Alaska. Driving west across the country for four thousand miles with two teens, an almost tween, and no cellphone or internet service could have been a disaster.

Kathy was a little hesitant when I first brought up the idea of the trip. Maybe this was the kind of adventure she and I should take alone when the kids are out of the house.

"With all of us cramped inside a tiny space for a month out in the wilderness, what if it turned out like one of those horror movies?" she asked. "The ones where they all inevitably get on each other's nerves and then one of them snaps, goes totally bonkers, and hunts down their whole family until only one person is left standing, or they are all hunted down and mauled to death by giant zombie grizzly bears."

She has a great imagination.

"It could happen, I guess," I said, gently mocking her unrealistic fears.

She rolled her eyes. "Oh okay. Fine. We should all go."

Luckily, no horror film plot line played out on our trip. Instead, it was one of the best adventures we've ever taken. We weren't in a hurry. We had time to stop and explore whenever the trails called to us.

None of us had ever been in an RV before. We had never even taken the kids camping, but we wanted a unique experience with them. One night, camping in the Liard River Hot Springs Provincial Park at the very Northern end of British Columbia, deep in the Canadian wilderness, Kathy decided it was time to make the kids real campfire s'mores. They had only ever had the microwaved kind. These were marshmallows skewered on a stick found nearby, roasted over the campfire.

Ryan was horrified when she handed one to him. "You can't use a *stick* from the ground!" he exclaimed. "There's bugs in it!" He held onto the graham crackers, staring suspiciously at the puffy marshmallow like it was going to explode with ravenous insects. He leaned over to Jessica and Alyssa and loudly whispered, "There's bugs in these s'mores! Mom already ate one, and they took over her brain. Now they're trying to infect the world!"

I guess Kathy wasn't the only one in our family with a good imagination.

While Jessica and Alyssa ate theirs, Ryan watched them carefully for side effects. Not seeing anything out of the ordinary, he carefully took a tiny nibble of his. We all watched to see what he would do next. He shrugged as if to say, "Well this one seems okay." Then he popped the rest of it in his mouth, but he didn't eat any more.

Kathy and I glanced at each other and laughed. This trip was exactly what they needed. Our kids had become "indoor" species.

As we crossed the country, we met many more seasoned RVers, mostly older retired couples, their own children long gone, wishing they had set out sooner. Out on the road, we were grateful we had brought the kids with us.

The next evening, we camped in the Yukon Territory in Canada just off the banks of the bluish-green Yukon River, surrounded by mountain forests. The lady inside the little cabin-like building where the check-in desk was warned us not to go out alone in the dark.

"Yesterday, a bear family was spotted roaming around the campground," she said. Then as nonchalantly as if she'd just warned us about squirrels being sighted, she happily showed us where the three little shower stalls were where you had to pay for each minute of freezing cold water used.

Ryan grimaced. He was more worried about the cold water than the bears.

Despite my mocking of Kathy's fears of ravenous bears, they are a real danger up in the wilderness. There were signs posted in most RV parks and at almost every trail head giving detailed instructions on what to do in case of a close encounter with a bear. They always read something like this,

. . .

"*I*f you encounter a brown bear—the infamous grizzly bear, back away slowly unless it is charging. Then stand your ground.

If it is close enough to make contact, drop to the ground and play dead. BUT if it is a black bear, do NOT play dead. Fight him off! Oh and don't forget black bears can sometimes have brown coats too!

Never run or climb a tree. All bears are excellent climbers and can outrun humans."

*I*n other words, if you have an intimate encounter with a bear, there isn't much hope.

Throughout the night, every little noise outside our metal enclosure evoked the *Jurassic Park* scene of the T-Rex tearing apart the Jeep, only this would be a pack of hungry bears tearing through our RV. Thankfully, we made it to sunrise with no grizzly encounters.

It wasn't more than about ten minutes after leaving the campground that morning that we pulled back onto the Alaska Highway,[1] which is more like 1,387 miles of country road than highway, and we saw a family of huge brown bears meandering in the meadow just off the road. Their thick silky coats glistened in the morning sun. I pulled off onto the shoulder, where we all gazed out the RV's windows and watched them in a silent awe. With every lumbering step, you could see their powerful muscles shudder. Luckily, the bears barely noted our presence and continued searching for berries.

By the time we crossed the border and made it to Alaska, we had been changed. Together, we had experienced every one of those four thousand miles—the giant hailstones drumming on our rooftop, the bear family dining, the moose strolling down the road, the mounds of white snow and ice covering Lake Louise's turquoise blue water to Kathy's surprise and chagrin, the giant whale slapping its tail within twenty feet of our boat tour, and the calving glaciers plunging into the Gulf of Alaska. These shared encounters had bonded us even closer together. For a moment, we'd glimpsed how small and insignificant our lives were in this wide world full of wonder.

Alaska was a healthy reminder that the world takes no notice of us. At home, it was easy to fall into a false sense of importance, as if the world revolved around us. After all, each of us plays the main character in our own story. In reality, in the story of the universe, we are as insignificant as the tiny ant colony that lives at the top of our driveway. Our job is simply to make our tiny corner of the world a loving, peaceful place to be.

On one of our last mornings in Alaska, Kathy and I sat on the stony beach with the mountains on one side and the icy blue waters of Resurrection Bay in the Gulf of Alaska stretched out in front of us. We drank our coffee and watched the bald eagles soar high above us. They carried our spirits with them into the clouds.

Despite all the very sane reasons not to take three kids four thousand miles in an RV, our hearts had known which way to guide us. It seemed like every time we had taken a leap or embarked on a crazy new adventure together, somehow, our lives held more.

Despite all the very sane reasons not to become co-producers of *Once on This Island*, my heart kept asking, instinctively drawn to it like a moth to moonlight.

Fall 2017
Cleveland, Ohio

JESSE

A few days after Ken had asked me about becoming a co-producer, I received an email from his office with more details on our investment. As investors, we would be allotted two tickets to the Opening Night performance and the after-party which was scheduled for December third, 2017. Two tickets... We would need three, and you can't just buy tickets to an Opening Night. Ryan would only be thirteen. While he was more than capable of staying in the hotel for a night on his own, both Kathy and I wanted him to be a part of this special evening. This was almost certainly going to be our one and only Opening Night on Broadway. We wanted him to experience it with us, but with only two tickets, who would stay back at the hotel? Me? Kathy? No, this meant too much to have either of us miss out. We had to share this moment together. Was there any way we could get a third ticket?

I called Ken's office and got a hold of Valerie.

"Hi, Jesse," she answered cheerfully. She probably should have been annoyed with all of my questions over those months, but she never was. She always graciously answered my questions and was quick to respond. "It's possible we could give you another ticket if last minute another producer can't come, but you wouldn't know until Opening weekend," she told me.

That meant we wouldn't be able to plan either way. I wanted all of us to see it and didn't want to leave it up to chance. The only way I could ensure we all saw it together was to buy three tickets for the last preview performance.

A few weeks before a show officially opens on Broadway, the cast performs preview shows in front of live audiences. This way, they can work out small issues that may arise with costumes, props, choreography, etc, or even whether a joke or line lands correctly with the audience. Many of these issues might not be brought to light in a rehearsal, but the pressure of performing in front of a live audience has a tendency to bring problems to the surface. With weeks of previews under their belt, the cast is fully prepared for the fanfare and festivities of Opening Night.

The final preview was the matinee performance on the same day as the Opening. I decided to buy three tickets for it. Two of us would see the show twice in a row, but I figured if we were lucky enough to get three tickets to the Opening, then I would resell the matinee tickets.

A few weeks later, I was back in New York, and Ken invited me to come over to the theater and watch a tech rehearsal. I didn't know what a tech rehearsal was, but I wasn't about to miss it if I happened to be in New York City. After thinking about *Once on This Island* again for several months, I could hardly wait to make it to the Circle in the Square Theater to see how this new production was coming along.

Ken met me outside the box office. "Hey, Jesse, glad you could make it. I think you're going to love what we've done."

I followed him through the lobby's glass doors, and we headed down the escalator to the theater level. Then he opened the doors to the theater and led me into another world. As I stepped inside, my breath caught in my throat.

There was no stage. There was only sand. An island, surrounded by a sea of seats lapping up onto the shore. I had seen mock-ups of what this was supposed to look like, but now I was on the island standing right beside a little overturned fishing boat on the edge of real rippling water. How they had created a mini inland waterway in the theater, I had no idea. I half-expected Old Santiago and Manolin to appear from their long day at sea.

Ken introduced me to Ryan Conway, the General Manager of the show, and Hunter Arnold, another lead producer.

Then Ken asked me, "Hey, have you met Lynn and Stephen?" He gestured a few rows up, where a woman with bold red lipstick and short dark hair sat next to a casually dressed man.

"No, I-I can't say I have," I responded in the most relaxed, cool voice I could muster, but inside, I was freaking out, totally fangirling. *Lynn and Stephen? It can't be... Is he really about to introduce me to THE LYNN AHRENS and STEPHEN FLAHERTY, the preeminent theatrical writing team of this generation, creators of Once on This Island, Anastasia, and Ragtime? OMG!*

We made our way over to them, and Ken introduced me. Lynn, small in size but not spirit, smiled brightly.

"Hi, nice to meet you," they both said and shook my hand. Stephen went right back to studying the rehearsal while Lynn seemed more open to a short chat.

As if I'd just downed five shots of espresso, I excitedly blurted out, "I'm such a huge fan! My wife and I took the original cast recording of *Once on This Island* on our honeymoon to Hawaii twenty-three years ago." My rapid-fire rambling didn't cease. "We blasted it all over the island singing at the top of our lungs..." By the time I realized I was spewing a storm of words, it was too late.

She might have thought I was crazy, but if she did, she didn't let it show. Her smile widened, and she put her hands to her heart. "Wow, thank you. I'm so happy to hear that, and I'm glad to have you with us on this adventure."

There were maybe only a dozen people, all tied to the show, sitting in the stands. Ken and I sat down to watch some of the rehearsal. I looked around trying to burn every detail into my memory so I could tell Kathy all about it later.

They were working on a scene near the end of the show where Papa Ge, played by Merle Dandridge, threatens Ti Moune. I was curious and honestly a bit uncertain how Papa Ge

—traditionally a male role, would be performed by Ms. Dandridge. As soon as she began to sing "Forever Yours (Reprise)," chills ran up my spine, and any doubts I had vanished. She was powerful, scary, and beautiful all at the same time.

Every once in a while, director Michael Arden, sitting up in the stands, would motion for the scene to stop. He gave the cast direction as to what he wanted changed, and then they would fix it. At one point, after they replayed part of the scene, he stopped them again.

While he was directing another cast member on changes, Merle teased Hailey Kilgore, who played Ti Moune. Not breaking character, she walked around Hailey, who was still laying in the sand, and said mockingly, "Oh so you *love* him? You really, really love him?"

Hailey burst out laughing, and I was grateful to get this little peek into another world.

During the break in action, I turned to the left. That's when I saw her.

Lea Salonga.

She was playing Erzulie, the Goddess of Love. She stood on stage directly across from me! THE LEA SALONGA! Kim from *Miss Saigon*, the singing voice of Disney Princesses Mulan and Jasmine, and Eponine from the twenty-fifth anniversary special of *Les Miserables*! Was I dreaming? Were we really breathing the same air tonight?

As she sang, the faintest of whispers stirred again in my chest. *What if...*

Her celestial voice entranced me. The Goddess of Love had me in her spell.

As soon as I got back to the hotel, I FaceTimed Kathy. She was in the middle of doing something for the kids, and she carried me around the house while we talked.

"Guess what?" I didn't even wait for her to answer, still on an adrenaline rush from the tech rehearsal. "I got to meet Lynn and Stephen, and Lea was literally right in front of me!" I told her everything. I couldn't wait for her to see it all in person.

Then she put the kids on so I could say a quick "Hi" to them and to our dog Rory, who seemed mostly disinterested and a bit confused at hearing my voice but not seeing me.

Not wanting to hang up, I kept talking to Kathy. Before I knew it, we had been on the phone for over two hours, and I realized her eyes were beginning to flutter closed. She had to be on the ice by six for lessons the next morning.

"I guess I'd better let you go," I said.

Her eyes opened, wider and she smiled. "Goodnight, sweetie. I miss you. I love you."

"Goodnight. I love you too." I hung up, wishing she was here with me instead.

Neither of us liked it when I had to go on business trips. When the kids were younger, and Kathy home-schooled the three of them, we would sometimes pile into the minivan and go on my business trips as a family. We drove all over the country. While I was at meetings, Kathy would take the kids sightseeing wherever we were, whether it was Madison, Wisconsin, Des Moines, Iowa, or Birmingham, Alabama. There was always something fun for the kids to explore, local museums, historical sights, or gardens.

One time, while hiking through a botanical garden, they came upon a flock of wild turkeys. The kids decided they wanted to follow them through the gardens and see how close they could get. The turkeys started running away so the kids started chasing after them with Kathy trailing behind. Finally, the turkeys had enough. They turned behind a hedge row, and when the kids came upon them, the giant birds charged. Alyssa screamed, "Turkey!" The kids who were by then all laughing and screaming took off running back toward Kathy.

But now, the girls were busy in college, and Ryan had chosen to go back to public school. They couldn't just jump in the car with me for a week of travel anymore.

I missed those family driving expeditions. Even though I was in meetings most of the time, it was better to come back to the hotel every night to Kathy and the kids. Home was where they were.

5

"THE SAD TALE OF THE BEAUXHOMMES"

June 1992
Holt, Michigan

*K*ATHY

I had just finished my sophomore year at MSU majoring in horticulture. For the summer, I planned to dedicate every spare moment that I wasn't working in the experimental greenhouses as a lab assistant to figure skating at Munn Ice Arena, MSU's state-of-the-art college hockey venue.

I enjoyed my job in the lab, but if it was up to me, I would be on the ice from dawn until dusk. On land, I was clumsy, always bumping into things and tripping over my own two feet, but on the ice, I glided effortlessly, liberated from my terrestrial awkwardness. I was free. As soon as I walked into an arena and the blast of icy air hit me, all my anxieties melted away. Nothing else mattered on the ice. It was just me, the music, and the frozen water.

In the hot sticky summers of Michigan, there was no better place to be than in the arena where a frosty layer of fog often blanketed the ice. Sometimes, I could hardly see more than a few feet in front of me. As I skated across the frozen surface and picked up speed, the clouds of water vapor lifted and swirled around me, kissing my face with icy droplets before rising to the rafters. It was magical.

But this summer, the universe had other plans for me.

For the first few days of summer break, I thought it was just the stress and exhaustion from studying for finals, but even after a week of sleeping in, I couldn't keep my eyes open no matter how much I slept. Every day, I awoke lethargic and exhausted, like I had been drugged. My throat swelled, and every time I tried to swallow it felt like I had been snacking on shards of glass. Something was wrong.

My mom drove me to the doctor, who diagnosed me with mononucleosis and an enlarged spleen. He prescribed bed rest and a medication that it turned out I was severely allergic to. A few days later, my skin erupted in bright red hives from head to toe. It stung like I had fallen into a pit of fire ants. The relentless urge to scratch my skin off kept me awake despite my brain pleading for release.

Day after agonizing day, I slipped into sleep for seconds at a time only to wake again from the stinging. In a sleep-deprived trance-like state, my sanity waned. Fingers of darkness touched my heart, and for the briefest moment, I wished to no longer exist, for the gods to take me away from this torment, for it all to be over, not caring how. Just an end because this was not living.

How much more could I take?

Maybe if I could make a deal with God, maybe He would have mercy on me.

But what did I have to trade? There was only one thing.

Love.

Would He hear me? Was He even there?

There was nothing to lose. I breathed in deeply, trying to find some calm in the storm raging through my veins, and then a thought, a hope, came to me from somewhere, from nowhere. I made a promise in those strange hours between darkness and light. I vowed that if He would heal my body and lead me to my soulmate, I would dedicate my life to Love. After all, God is Love, isn't He?

Suddenly, I sensed light shining through my window. It took all of my remaining focus to lift my heavy eyelids. A pale bluish stream of moonlight illuminated my bed, casting my entire room in an otherworldly glow.

The lines defining reality blurred. The back of my neck prickled with that same odd sensation you get when you know someone is staring at you. It seemed like I was no longer alone in my room. Maybe I was dreaming, or maybe I was losing my mind.

Strangely unafraid of whatever evil or other spirit lurked in the shadows, I looked around. There was no one else. Just me and the moonlight, and yet there was still something. A calming presence like this celestial beam brought more than light into my room.

My breath caught in my throat, and I knew He had heard me, and then, mercifully, I fell into a deep healing repose.

August 1992
Holt, Michigan

KATHY

*E*ventually, I awoke from that month of hell and was healthy enough to skate again. That first day back at the rink, I stepped onto the ice and inhaled the cool moist air, deeply grateful to be where I felt most at home. One push from my left foot and I was gliding across the smooth surface. I let my momentum carry me across the ice on one foot, relishing the chilled breeze as it rippled through my long hair. Like a bird with a newly mended wing, I wanted nothing more than to leap into the air and soar.

That was when I noticed him. The super cute guy with jet black hair who had caught my eye several months ago with his fast, effortless skating now appeared to be a rink employee and was cleaning the hockey glass. I had seen him several times at the rink and walking around campus. Either he had a class in the same building as me, or I always just "happened" to see him after Calculus. I didn't even know his name, but for some reason, every time I caught a glimpse of him, my cheeks flushed with heat, and I giggled like a five-year-old. Despite almost daily encounters, we never exchanged more than shy smiles, though I always hoped he would say something to me.

Never in my life had I even thought about approaching a guy, but that day, something made me skate over to him. My face felt red hot, as if I had been staring into a fire, when I said, "Hi."

Now that I'd broken the ice between us, he had the courage to tell me his name.

"Hi, I'm Jesse."

He had a great smile.

"I'm Kathy." I skated little circles near him.

"Yeah, I know." Now it was his turn to blush.

"So you finally got a job here?" As soon as I said it, I thought it was the most stupid thing I could have said, but the words were already hanging there in the air between us. "It's good. Now I'll get to see you every day," I added, trying to make it less awkward, but my over-active brain was imagining all the worst scenarios. Maybe I was misreading things, and he didn't really want to see me every day. Maybe he just needed a job.

But he smiled sweetly. "Great! I applied here because I saw you talking to all the employees." He turned back to the glass cleaning and laughed nervously.

We exchanged some more flirty banter.

After what seemed like forever, he finally asked, "Do you wanna go see a movie with me this weekend?"

"Sure, I would love to," I said, feeling as if the ice might melt underneath me. I didn't care what movie. I simply wanted to spend time with him.

On August 26, 1992, we went on our first date to Burger King and a movie—Patriot Games starring Harrison Ford. I was instantly smitten with Jesse. He was devilishly handsome. He had a well-toned, muscular body and a smile that made my knees weak. Best of all, he made me laugh.

Over the next few weeks, we saw each other as much as possible. Sometimes, he borrowed a car and came to my house. Other times, we met on campus and walked to the house he rented with six other guys. To find privacy on nights when all his rowdy roommates were home, we would step out of his upstairs window and lay on the roof. We gazed up at the stars and sang along with CDs of *Miss Saigon*, *Les Miserables*, or *Phantom of the Opera*. I was impressed that not only did he appreciate Broadway musicals, he loved them. He was sophisticated and cultured, different from all of the other guys I'd met, and his laugh was a contagious rumble of joy emanating from his soul.

At first, my parents liked him too. He was invited to family dinners at our house a couple of times. He even played street hockey with my little brother, Dave.

Everything was perfect.

Then, it all changed. On September 26, exactly a month after we started dating, Jesse took me out to dinner at Bennigan's to celebrate. We ordered a dessert called Death by Chocolate—rich chocolate ice cream with almonds and marshmallows on an Oreo crust smothered in dripping hot fudge sauce. It was one of the best desserts I had ever had. I didn't get out much.

Afterward, in the car he had borrowed from his dad, he handed me a little velvet box. Surprised, I looked up at him.

"Open it," he said, smiling.

Before Jesse, I had only been out on a few single dates. Not that there was anything wrong with the guys. I was simply not interested in seeing any of them more than once. Even though I was only twenty, dating for me had one purpose—to find the man I was going to spend the rest of my life with. I could see that with Jesse. When we were together, hours went by in what seemed like minutes, but I wasn't certain he felt the same way.

So when I opened the little box and saw a little gold ring set with a green stone on top, it took my breath away.

"It's a promise ring."

My eyes started to fill up.

He took my hand in his. "I promise that someday I will ask you to marry me."

He slipped it on my finger. It was a little too big, but I didn't care.

"It's a peridot, the birthstone for August when we first started dating."

My throat tightened. It was beautiful. No one had ever given me such a present. In that moment, I knew it was God's design, the answer to my prayer that moonlit night. He had healed my body and given me someone to love.

The next day, as my mom drove me down I-496 toward East Lansing to drop me off at my French literature class, she noticed the ring on my finger. "What is that?" she asked.

"It's from Jesse. It's a promise ring," I said, looking down at it. A warmth enveloped me as I thought about him.

"He will not marry you!" she snorted in disgust. "How can you be so naive?"

Her outburst startled me and I didn't know what to say. Why was she so upset? To me, it seemed wonderful and perfectly normal. We were in love.

But all she could see was this boy who'd been dating her daughter for a month who had now promised to marry her. Somehow, she missed the irony that she and my dad got married after only dating for six months. We hadn't planned on actually getting married anytime soon. It was simply a declaration of our love.

Of course, in hindsight, as a mother of two college-aged daughters, I can see how it might have been unsettling to my mom, but I was young and blinded by love. Jesse didn't have any ill intentions. We were just two kids who had found soulmates in each other.

Mom turned off I-496 to the Trowbridge Road exit, and we sat at the light waiting to turn left. This beautiful woman beside me had taught me everything and was one of the most loving and kind people I knew. She had been both mother and best friend for twenty years, but now she glared at me and spit out the words, "He has you in a spell."

I didn't say anything, but I felt my blood begin to bubble in anger like the water in a teapot on the stove. Yes, I was under his spell, but it was his charm and the love I felt in him that had bewitched me.

She was quiet for a moment as if searching for more words. Then she blurted out, "It's against God." She paused to make sure I was listening.

The air in the car suddenly felt colder than the ice I skated on.

"The Bible says, 'Thou shalt not sow thy field with mingled seed: neither shall a garment mingled of linen and woolen come upon thee.' It doesn't matter how you feel. It's wrong."

Wait. What? I shook my head, angry and confused. Just last week, he had been invited to our house for dinner, but now that we were serious, it was against God because he was multi-racial? I didn't understand. How could God be the reason *not* to love someone? My mother had always taught me that God was love. Hadn't God brought him to me? It couldn't be wrong. How can any love be wrong?

Maybe my mom couldn't see that love. Maybe all she could see was her little girl, her best friend, leaving her too soon, but to me, it felt like she had just plunged a dagger into my heart.

Never had I rebelled against my parents. Up until that moment, I never had a reason to. That changed as soon as she uttered the words. I ignored her pleas to stop seeing Jesse because I couldn't stop.

In Plato's *Symposium*, Aristophanes tells the story that at one time, humankind was a whole being, not man and woman, but an entity that encompassed both/all. Zeus, fearing an uprising, split humankind into two beings. For the rest of time, these partial beings would be consumed by the search for their other halves. Where the original being was split determined whether man searched for man or woman or woman searched for woman or man to become complete. The Greeks believed this desperate search and then discovery of the soul who made you whole was love.[1]

In Jesse, I had found my complete being.

My parents didn't say much at first, not used to my resistance. Not-so-subtle passive aggressive comments were thrown in here and there to voice their displeasure with my disobedience and Jesse's "manipulative" schemes. I dismissed them as idle intimidations.

Then one crisp fall night, Jesse drove me home from a romantic evening exploring Greektown in Detroit. We laughed and sang show tunes at the top of our lungs the entire hour and a half drive back. It was late when we arrived at my house, a little bit after one in the morning, but I was a twenty-year-old college junior, and I'd never had a curfew. I wasn't paying attention to the time. As we pulled into the driveway, my parents were outside waiting for us, and they didn't look happy. We stepped out of the car, and then it was like a hurricane hit us and everything became a blurry mess.

There was shouting.

Crying.

Pleading.

"You are never to see each other again!" my father roared, getting right in Jesse's face. "Or there will be consequences!"

There was nothing else we could do or say. They wouldn't listen.

I broke into pieces. I'd discovered my soulmate. In his kind green eyes, I saw my future, but it didn't matter. They knew what was best for me.

Sick and disoriented, I felt like I'd fallen through the ice and couldn't find my way out of the frigid water back to the surface. Barely able to see through the tears, I watched Jesse climb back in the car and drive away.

I didn't have my own car, and there was no way to call him without the possibility of my mom listening in on the other end.

Out of fear, we stopped seeing each other for a while. My parents could keep us apart. They could not however, keep me from loving him, and after a few days without Jesse, I knew I didn't want to live in a world where God was used as a reason to put up walls between people. I refused to believe in that God.

The God I believed in brought people together.

Now I was forced to make a choice.

Either I would comply with my parents' wishes, like the good, obedient daughter I had always been, or I would choose my own path and risk losing my parents, my family, and maybe my salvation.

I prayed day and night for a sign, but none came. My heart already knew the answer that my brain was afraid to accept. I couldn't put it off any longer. I had to decide between my parents and my past or Jesse and my future.

December 18, 1994
Munn Ice Arena
Michigan State University
East Lansing, Michigan

*K*ATHY

I stood off the far end of the ice arena behind where the goalie would normally be in the tunnel that the Zamboni came out. As always, the air was chilly and carried that refreshing smell of the ice. Smoothing out my white silk shantung dress that my best friend Melody had made me for this day, I took a deep breath and then looked around at the stands.

All those people here for us. I wasn't nervous. I was excited. Well, maybe a little bit nervous, but this was exactly what I wanted. Finally, I was deciding the direction of my life.

It was almost time.

Bending down, I checked my skates and took off my guards, the hard rubber covering that protects skate blades.

I gazed out toward center ice, past the make-shift aisle created by bright red potted poinsettias. There was Jesse, standing in his tuxedo and hockey skates with his groomsmen beside him waiting for me.

The first notes of Pachelbel's Canon in D played on the arena speakers, and my dad took my arm. We stepped onto the ice. My dad, who had been a goalie all his life, skated perfectly in sync with me down the aisle. "I can't believe we're doing this," he said, gently squeezing my elbow.

"I know. I can't either," I smiled.

My dad, of course, was referring to the fact that Jesse and I were getting married on the ice.

It had been a joke at first, an off-hand comment made by Jesse's and my friend Kris Forester who also worked at the rink. "Why don't you guys just get married here on the ice? It's where you met after all," she said.

We laughed it off at the time, but when we realized we couldn't afford to pay for a church ceremony and our boss at the arena, Tom Campbell, graciously offered us an hour of open ice, we decided an on-ice ceremony would be a little crazy but also perfect.

So there we were, our entire wedding party dressed in tuxedos and velvet dresses with their skates on. Almost all of them were already either figure skaters or hockey players, including my mom, the flower girl, and even the judge who married us. The ring bearer and Jesse's parents were the only ones who weren't quite as comfortable with a quarter-inch thick blade strapped to their feet, but they happily, though carefully, glided down the ice anyway.

My dad and I easily made it to center ice where he gave me away to Jesse. A year ago, I had not believed this moment was possible. A year ago, it wasn't possible, but love and forgiveness are powerful. They can conquer fear if we allow them into our hearts.

Hand in hand, Jesse and I took one push together and glided to the judge. As we recited our vows, we gazed into each other's eyes. I had no idea where our journey would lead us, but I knew all that I wanted was to make the journey with him.

Skating back down the aisle, we were now Mr. and Mrs. Jesse and Kathryn McKendry. Then, with all of our wedding party trailing behind us, we took a victory lap around the rink. My straight-line dress with a slit was specially designed by Melody to be able to skate in, and she did it all for only the cost of the materials.

While our guests began to file out of the arena, we took the obligatory multitude of photos, which were kindly donated to us by Jesse's Uncle Gary, who took them all for free. Love surrounded us.

Pretty soon, it was time to ride the Zamboni the block and a half to our wedding reception, but unfortunately, the rink needed it for the hockey game that was about to start. Instead, we unlaced our skates, put our fancy reception shoes on, and walked over. Luckily, even though it was December in Michigan, it was a relatively warm day, probably around forty degrees, and there was hardly any snow on the ground.

The reception was like any other wedding reception, full of family, friends, music, and food. Many guests traveled long distances to attend, coming in from Wisconsin, South Carolina, Wyoming, and even Japan. I was grateful that so many people took their time to share in our special day.

Despite all that had occurred leading up to that day, I was

thankful my parents were there too. I loved them, and I always would. They made me who I was.

Growing up, my mom and I did everything together—cooking, singing, shopping, and skating. I was so shy as a kid that I told her I wouldn't take ice skating lessons unless she took them with me, so she did. She learned to jump and spin right beside me. I may have never been a skater without her supporting me that way.

We were best friends. Maybe that was part of the reason she had objected so much. She had felt like she was losing her best friend. I wish I had understood at the time. Then, I could have reassured her that the bond we had forged over the years could never be broken, but I was still too young to see that maybe the issue was more complex. Maybe it wasn't all just about me. I had never thought of how my leaving home would affect her life.

But for tonight, all of that was in the past, and everyone danced and celebrated our future together.

Jesse's aunts and uncles from Wisconsin, who played in a band, provided our musical entertainment for free, and his great Uncle Al led a very energetic polka, out-dancing me easily!

At some point in the evening, Gramps and Grams—the ones with whom I watched televised musicals—came over and wrapped their arms around me. Other than my younger brother, Dave, they had been the one constant well of support while Jesse and I dated.

"Tiger, I'm so glad you're happy," Gramps said, using the nickname he'd given me when I was four. "That's all that matters." He glanced at my grandma as if to prove his point. They had been together over fifty-five years, married as soon as they had graduated from high school. He continued, "We knew Jesse was a good egg, and we're so happy to have him in the family."

I hugged them tightly, grateful for their example of love which will live forever in our hearts.

The banquet hall was nearly empty by around twelve-thirty. Jesse and I walked down the corridor that led from the reception to the attached hotel where our honeymoon suite was. He opened the door and picked me up in his arms, and we crossed over to our new lives together.

6

"THE HUMAN HEART"

Summer 2017
Cleveland, Ohio

𝒥 ESSE

𝒶 t breakfast the morning after I arrived back home, I described every detail I remembered for Kathy, though my words seemed too small to portray the wholeness of the world that was *Once on This Island*. It was impossible to fully comprehend unless experienced. It was clear we had made the right decision to be a part of this production.

Though now after being there, the little voice in my head that kept telling me to leap head first into co-producing was impossible to ignore.

On my mental pros and cons list, the only real sane reason

for putting more money in would be that, as a co-producer, we would have a better chance to learn the business of producing. We would receive regular updates on sales and the financial results of the show and be able to sit in on certain types of meetings. It would mean having a deeper level of access than we would have as investors.

There was another way to do it without us having to put more of our own money in. Most co-producers don't put huge sums of their own money into shows. In fact, many regular co-producers won't put in any of their own money. Instead, they serve the critical task of providing funding for most Broadway shows, usually through a network of investors that they develop over the course of years. That method crossed our minds for about a second, but we quickly dismissed it. Being new to the business meant we had no network of wealthy investors to draw from. How could we ask family and friends to plunk down their hard-earned money for a Broadway musical? We didn't feel comfortable raising funds from others, especially on our first investment. If we were going to be co-producers on this show, the risk had to be all ours.

My mind went in circles trying to come up with a way to justify it. It just didn't make any sense as an investment, though, and I thought of myself as a sensible person. But I also was coming to the realization that we *had* to do it anyway.

Then, an idea hit me. What if this was a donation to theater instead of an investment? No return expected. Nothing more.

As a donation, it felt different. All that mattered was that our favorite musical was being resurrected on Broadway with our help.

Was it worth doing even if I knew that it would fail monetarily?

Would I rather be safe or take a chance and be part of something special?

No matter what I wanted, Kathy had to agree to it as well. It was critical that we were on the same page. We have always made the big decisions together as a team, talked things out, and shared our dreams, and this was one of our biggest or at least most expensive decisions.

As a young couple, we would often go on long road trips, talking the whole way and often writing down our shared goals and dreams. One time, we took a long drive somewhere in Michigan. I don't even remember where we were headed, but I do remember that for the entire trip, we wrote down all the things we wanted to do together by the time we were fifty.

Recently, Kathy found that piece of paper from over twenty-five years ago. There are one hundred and thirty-one items on our list. Adventure number four was drink red wine in Rome. Number thirteen was see a show in London. Some items are crossed off, about twenty of them, things like number twenty-eight—drive across the U.S., which we've actually done twice—number thirty-eight—go white water rafting, which was terrifying to Kathy but we did it anyway—and even number sixty-nine—see the Taj Mahal. Most of the numbers are adventures yet to be taken like books on a library shelf waiting to be read. Sadly, there is one that is now impossible to do—number twenty-four—see Luciano Pavarotti sing live.

So we have about one hundred and ten left and only a couple years before we're fifty, maybe if we live to one hundred, we can get them all in. Even if we never cross any more off, I will never forget sharing those dreams with each other. That day we wrote them all down, that was the important day when we planted the seed for shared adventures.

While being a co-producer on a Broadway show was not on the list—that wasn't something we even knew to dream—number thirty-two—see Broadway shows in NYC—can now be crossed off.

As Kathy and I cleared the table after breakfast to do the dishes, co-producing *Once on This Island* was all I could think about. Lost in thought, I tipped the plates just slightly, and a fork slid off and bounced onto the floor. I bent down to pick it up and looked at our yellow-tan-dirt colored seventies-style linoleum that no matter how much it was scrubbed always looked dingy. I'd promised Kathy twelve years ago, when we bought this house, that we'd get a total kitchen renovation. Every year, something got in the way, and we put the upgrade off. A new roof one year, Jessica's hospital bills the next, sports and music lessons for the kids, and then saving for a business. There was always something. In the meantime, our kitchen was breaking down more every year. Last year, one of our cabinet drawers broke, and it constantly pulled out crooked. Our method of fixing the drawer? Moving all the heavy silverware to a different drawer. We still get confused about where the forks are. If we decided to go through with co-producing, a new kitchen would be put off yet again.

Then, while my hands were in the warm soapy dishwater scrubbing the plates, I heard myself blurt out, "I think we should become co-producers on *Once on This Island.*"

I'm not sure why I said it. The words flowed out like a waterfall after a spring rain. I couldn't have stopped them if I wanted to, and now the foggy wisps of the idea remained suspended in the air between us. My heart had just betrayed my head.

Kathy looked at me, her softly rounded face glowing just like the first day I saw her skating at the MSU arena. I was prepared to argue my point, but she had been thinking the same thing.

"This is special to us, and it's not like we'll ever have this chance again." She smiled.

I put the plate back in the sink and looked at her. I wasn't sure how it was possible, but I loved her even more after all these years.

"Maybe this is the one place we can actually make a difference." She clasped her hands together in front of her under her chin like she does when she's nervous and excited.

"Okay. Let's do it!" As I said it, adrenaline rushed through my body, and even my forearms tingled with excitement.

Kathy jumped up and wrapped her arms around me. Her brown eyes glistened like a pond in the moonlight. She looked up at me. "I will be proud to help bring this beautiful story back into the world," she said, her voice rough with passion. We held each other tightly for a moment. Then she added jokingly, "And who knows? Maybe we'll even get to go to the Tony Awards."

The next day, my bones felt heavy with an anxious excitement. It had been a couple of weeks since I had told Ken that we couldn't make the co-producer idea work. I wasn't even sure there was still room for us. I was nervous about missing out now that we had decided. It reminded me of the day, almost twenty years ago, when Kathy and I had purchased our first home. As we had headed to our first closing, we looked at each other nervously, wondering if we were really doing the right thing or being foolish handing over that huge down payment check. It was scary to let go of that much money. This check for *Once on This Island* was going to be much bigger than any down payment we'd ever made on a house.

I looked down at the phone in my hand before dialing Ken's number. I took a deep breath and made the call.

November 16, 2017
Cleveland, Ohio

 ESSE

*A*fter dropping Ryan off at his guitar lesson, Kathy and I went to our little bank branch in Cleveland, Ohio, signed the paperwork, and wired the money to Ken's office in New York City.

In an instant, it was gone.

In that same moment, we became co-producers of the Broadway Revival of *Once on This Island.*

I expected a dark sense of remorse to settle in like a thick, ominous blanket of fog as soon as the money was sent, but it never came. Instead, there was a lightness in my spirit.

All my life, I'd been told to save for the future, which we did as soon as we got out of debt. Thankfully, our rice and gravy eating days to save for rent were in the past, but once we learned how to be frugal together, we never really stopped. We put every extra penny that had been going to our debt payments and put them directly into savings. We still shopped for sales and had lived without cable TV for years. I never stopped to think about when the future was supposed to arrive or what that money was going to buy. In buying a business, we would be putting our money to work, to make us more money to save for the future, to give us more freedom. So it was odd that when we wired the money, suddenly, I felt more free.

After twenty-three years of marriage, maybe "the future" was now. Our money had been, only a moment before, sitting lifeless in an account. Now, it would emerge from its cocoon-like vault as a beautiful work of art.

It would not break us with its absence. Sure, we would have to rein in our spending again for a while, but we knew how to do that. We both had good careers that we enjoyed, and we had enough retirement money locked away to live on later. No matter what happened, we wouldn't have to spend retirement crashing at our kids' houses.

Could we mentally let go of what we'd worked so hard to accumulate? The answer became clear immediately. We could, especially now that it was becoming something. We had set it free from its cold, dark box and had breathed life into it. We had planted a seed that would grow into the most beautiful tree, its branches breaking down all the barriers we had built in our minds about what our money was actually for.

7

"TI MOUNE"

January 1993
Michigan State University
East Lansing, Michigan

*J*ESSE

*A*fter Kathy's parents forbade us to see one another, we tried to stay apart for a while, but I was physically sick without her. Unable to focus on school, I was forced to withdraw from my classes for the remainder of that winter term and go back home to Detroit to recuperate. The doctor said I had mono, but I knew it was a broken heart.

When I finally returned to school for the next semester, I planned to tell Kathy we were done. I couldn't allow myself to believe we would be together only to lose her again. My heart couldn't survive that.

I should have known that seeing her again was a mistake, but I had to tell her in person, so we agreed to meet in one of the campus cafeterias. There she was, already sitting in a booth waiting for me. Her face glowed. Love radiated from her cheeks like the sun, warming every soul she looked upon.

How could I live without her?

My heart was in my throat as I hugged her for the first time in two months. Was this really going to be the last time I held her in my arms? My resolve was slipping. This meeting was a mistake. I wasn't strong enough.

"I've missed you," she said.

I couldn't get the words out. "Me too," was all I could manage.

"I've been doing a lot of thinking, and I don't care what my parents think. We will still see each other in secret until I can find an apartment."

I looked down at the table and anxiously rubbed my finger on a deep groove in the finish and half-heartedly protested, "I don't think I can keep doing this."

"Are you giving up?" she snapped.

"I can't… I can't make you choose between your parents and me." My throat tightened. "I can't lose you again."

I was afraid she wasn't strong enough. I was afraid *I* wasn't strong enough.

"I've already chosen you," she said.

Her eyes hardened with a steely determination, and her strength inspired me. I couldn't walk away. I agreed that we would see each other secretly.

Fall 2017

Cleveland, Ohio

ESSE

wenty-five years later, we were living another secret life but this time not because we had to. Honestly, this new adventure just seemed too weird to bring up in conversation with our friends and family back home in Cleveland and Michigan. Not many people walk around the Cleveland area talking about Broadway, so we never brought it up.

Most of our friends and family didn't go to the theater. Some of them saw *The Lion King* on tour when it first came out, but no one we knew had seen a musical on Broadway. For that matter, until recently, we hadn't seen more than *Phantom of the Opera* on Broadway, and that had been when the girls were little, so little we'd had to pretend Alyssa was five in order for her to get in. I think she was three, but she sat there in her fancy black taffeta dress, quiet as a sea anemone stuck on the ocean floor, bewitched by the scenes on stage.

If someone had asked us about Broadway, we would have gladly talked about it, but no one did. No one knew the significance *Once on This Island* played in our young lives, so we sort of subconsciously decided it was easier to not bring it up. Our kids were the only ones who knew, and even they didn't really understand us. The girls thought it was cool but maybe not worth that much money, and Ryan thought we were just plain crazy.

All of a sudden, we were now co-producers, but we still didn't know what that entailed. We could have put our money in and simply gone to Opening Night, but I was fascinated with learning everything I could about the business of Broadway.

Over the years, I've realized that I'm happiest when I'm learning something new, leaving my comfort zone behind, and, like Ti Moune, seeking out new adventures. I'm energized by actively working on a problem or activity that I've not encountered before, and I'm lucky that while Kathy may be more cautious and content than I am, she is also usually willing, if not always happy, to join me on most of my crazy undertakings.

One of the first things we learned about co-producing was that our name would be on the official billing posted outside the theater, but there are specific rules about whose names can appear. We weren't allowed to have our listing say, "Kathy and Jesse McKendry" unless we wanted to plunk down another huge sum of money. That was definitely not happening no matter what our hearts said. There could only be one name. We had to decide whose it would be. We could have come up with a combined name like JK McKendry or KJ McKendry.

"It should be your name," Kathy said. "You were the one who started this insane adventure by taking me to see it twenty-five years ago."

I made sure, however, that in the Playbill her name was next to mine in the few lines of description we were allocated. Normally, this is where people list their relevant musical theater or TV/movie credits, which, of course we had none. I sent in what I wanted ours to say. "**JESSE McKENDRY** (Producer) Jesse, Kathy and their three children live in Chagrin Falls, Ohio. They are all madly in love with this show." It was the perfect description for us, and it exactly fit the twenty-word allotment we received for our space.

Another perk of being a co-producer was that I would be kept in the loop on ticket sales and attendance and given daily show summaries, including technical issues and any injuries to the cast. It put me in a position to listen, learn, and ask a lot of questions. We were invited to things like the dress rehearsal as well as other informal gatherings with other people involved in the show. Of course we still lived in Cleveland and had no intention of moving, so we'd miss most of these events unless we happened to be in town at the same time.

Luckily, the dress rehearsal was scheduled for a day that I was already going to be in the city. That evening, I walked briskly to the theater, hardly able to contain my excitement of seeing *Once on This Island* again after twenty-five years. I handed over my ticket and went down the escalator to the lobby of the Circle in the Square Theater. The first person who caught my eye was Tyler Mount from the Tyler Mount Vlog on playbill.com. Kathy, Ryan, and I had become huge fans of his light-hearted, fun interviews with Broadway stars. My eyes widened, and I opened my mouth into a huge smile as soon as I saw him, another of my fangirl moments this show was giving me. That caught his attention, and he started walking my way.

"Hi, how are you?" he asked, opening his arms wide to embrace me. "It's so good to see you again!"

He must have interpreted my over-excitement as a sign that we already knew each other.

"I don't think we've met, but my wife and son and I are huge fans," I said. "I'm Jesse."

"Are you sure we haven't met before?" he asked. "You look so familiar."

"I'm pretty sure." I chuckled. I definitely would have remembered if we'd met.

We chatted for a few minutes about *Once on This Island*, and then the theater doors opened.

While this was my second time on the island, this was my first time seeing director Michael Arden's full vision on display. This new world had already evolved since I had been here for the tech rehearsal. The hurricane-ravaged island was littered with debris from the previous night's storm, and various pieces of clothing hung out to "dry" on lines encircling the theater.

I found my seat and waited eagerly for the show to start. I scanned the room to take in every detail. A little girl, dressed in a blue school uniform, sat on an overturned plastic milk crate in the center of the sandy island studying her school papers. Squares of metal roofing torn off by high winds laid haphazardly where they had landed. Coca-Cola cans and plastic refuse were scattered in the sand.

A real telephone pole, downed by the hurricane's high winds, rested where it had crashed on the beach, a half-crushed theater seat stuck beneath it, cracking the fourth wall between stage and audience. On this set, there were no dividing lines separating the audience from the stage. The moment I'd walked through the theater doors, I'd entered another world.

Because this was a dress rehearsal, the audience was limited to individuals connected with the show including investors and producers as well as guests of the cast and crew. In total, we filled less than half of the theater. I was seated in the third row of the two hundred section on the odd-numbered side of the theater, near where the telephone pole lay. While we waited for the remaining seats to fill, the action began on the island. It was a pre-show, a sort of mini-show before the show. An islander walked across the sand and greeted the little girl on the milk crate. Other islanders joined them and milled around the sand, hugging each other and saying prayers of thanks to the gods for having survived last night's tempest. Each one in turn went over to the fallen telephone pole and put their hand on the picture of a departed loved one affixed to it, paying homage to their ancestors. Then, they banded together to clean up the devastation, rebuild, and take care of one another.

As they milled around the island, picking up pieces of wreckage, one woman cradled a real live clucking chicken in her arms as if she was holding a baby. She walked around the sand letting a few lucky audience members in the front row pet it.

A cheer went up around me. I turned to see a live goat wearing a black diaper being led on to the island. Sparky and Peapod, the two goats who shared this role and probably made history as the first of their species to be part of a Broadway cast, were one of the many innovations on this set. Another was the assortment of trash "instruments" scattered around the island uniquely fashioned from repurposed materials that played consistent notes including a long piece of tubing and a metal bucket.

Lea Salonga, dressed as a humanitarian aid nurse, appeared directly in front of me, showing a mosquito net to the lady on my left. She explained how something as simple as a net can save lives. Here was another innovation, using this platform to spread awareness of the importance of mosquito nets. Child-Fund.org states every sixty seconds, a child dies of malaria. While not a complete solution, a wide distribution of insecticide-treated nets to sleep under has helped save millions of lives, according to endmalaria.org.

Several other islanders greeted people in the audience. We were no longer in New York City watching a musical. We were guests on their island.

The lights dimmed, and the wind whistled around us as two islanders picked up pieces of old plastic tubing that the storm had washed onto the beach. They whirled them overhead making a whooshing sound.

The petite woman who'd been holding the chicken stood on the overturned milk crate and raised her powerful voice to the wind. Her hands flew upward and then back down again, propelling her story on the wind to be carried across the Antilles.

Chills ran down the back of my neck. I looked around the sand to let every moment, every divine note sink in.

Even though it had been twenty-five years since Kathy and I had first seen it together, I remember as if it was yesterday. We had been just kids with our whole lives ahead of us. We didn't know how things would turn out, but we'd trusted each other and ventured out into the world together—driving to California, exploring the West Coast, having our first child... Those decades-old memories of us as young adults mixed with snapshots of our girls growing up, blurring the linear illusion of time.

I sat watching as the main character, Ti Moune, grew before my eyes from a little girl to a beautiful young woman searching for the purpose in her life. Old moments from our life came rushing back into my memory as the story unfolded on this new stage.

We had been parents for twenty-one years, and now I was experiencing this story I knew so well from a different perspective. We were the two old peasants.

My throat clenched tighter. I felt the warmth on my chest where, as infants, our children used to fall asleep to the rhythm of my beating heart. I couldn't have willed the tears away any more than I could have kept my kids from growing up. Just like Ti Moune, they transformed from children to young adults as swiftly as the sun sets. I closed my eyes and saw them as the tiny little bundles in my arms, their toes no bigger than the smallest grapes, so innocent and precious.

The day we brought Jessica home from the hospital, her tiny, fragile body was wrapped snugly in a blanket, and I tried to strap in her hand-me-down infant seat. I struggled to buckle the contraption in correctly. A momentary wave of panic rushed over me. I looked up at Kathy. "How can the hospital let us leave?"

How were we going to be good parents? We weren't prepared for this.

We were still kids ourselves trying to figure out our own path. How could we possibly be responsible for this new life?

"We don't know anything about parenting," I complained to Kathy as we climbed in and drove home with our new baby.

She smiled at me. "We'll figure it out."

My mind flashed forward to walking the hot summer streets when we lived in Philadelphia. Jessica was four and Alyssa was two as they strolled hand in hand, swinging their arms. There was nothing else in the world except for our little family in that moment. To keep their minds off the oppressive heat that felt like your head was melting, Kathy and I would make up stories for them as we walked to our fun destination for the day, the Please Touch Museum, the Franklin Institute, or historic old town Philly. We lived to see their smiles and hear their thunderous laughter.

The mental picture shifted one last time to Jessica as a teenager creating her own stories and spending months writing them down and Alyssa creating and directing Portlandia-type comedy skits then rolling on the floor with laughter.

Somehow, between then and now, they'd grown into beautifully talented adults with their own lives to live and their own paths to find. They were no longer our little girls, no longer hanging on my every word, no longer needing me.

With the birth of your child, especially your first, you know and at least attempt to prepare for the fact that your life is about to change. You even know the approximate date when it will happen. There is a clear demarcation between pre-fatherhood and fatherhood, but the difficult teenage years sneak up on you with the same silent swiftness as the wrinkles that creep across your face. You keep saying, "Oh, that's still years away. I don't have to prepare for that yet." So you are never ready when it happens.

In reality, the seeds of change begin to germinate years before it even crosses your mind. You're just too busy getting through each day to notice that your precious little bundle who once depended on you for everything has already begun the metamorphosis into an individual seeking their own independence, and there is nothing you can do to keep them small. Without even realizing what is happening, you change too and go from playing one role to playing another.

This was the exact same story I had seen twenty-five years ago, but I was no longer Ti Moune. I had grown up and become Tonton Julian, the old father. For some reason, this evening when I'd entered the theater, I had still thought of myself as Ti Moune setting off on new adventures. In some ways, Kathy and I were still playing that part, but somewhere along the road, we'd grown older. Our faces more wrinkled, our hair full of gray, we were no longer the lead in this story. In this revival, we had been cast as the old parents. I tried but failed to hold back a gasp as I was overcome with emotion at the realization.

Now, our girls had taken over the part of Ti Moune.

I worried, had I done enough as a dad?

I'd tried to give them guidance, to protect them from making the same mistakes I had, to prepare them for life, but I could only prepare them for what I knew, for the life that I had lived. How could I prepare them for the life they would discover? Had I taught them what they needed to know to make it in this harsh world, or had I unknowingly protected them from making mistakes they needed to make?

As new parents, we had felt like we were never quite doing enough. We were drowning in the sea of new baby chores, barely swimming fast enough to keep our heads above the water. Those tiny little humans trusted us completely, like we were the experts of life. They had no idea we were trying to figure it out on the fly, hoping we were doing it right while making plenty of mistakes along the way. Could we have done better if we had taken time out for deeper reflection during those days?

Probably.

But now it was too late. Time kept slipping away, and we had lost our window of influence. They were already grown women and had long since realized we didn't know everything after all.

Like generations of parents before us, we could see the many struggles on the horizon for all three of our kids, struggles they were oblivious to despite our warnings. If only they would listen, they could avoid the missteps. It was frustrating to watch them walk right into hardship when we'd shown them a path we knew was better because we had lived it ourselves. Yet, neither Jessica nor Alyssa wanted the guidance I felt they needed.

At twenty-two and twenty, our girls were not children any longer. They had grown into strong-willed young women, like Ti Moune, and they had found their own mountains to climb insisting on doing it their way even if it meant stumbling occasionally. It seemed they were destined to repeat some of our mistakes and make some new ones of their own.

Maybe our parents had harbored the same frustrations. A chill ran through me as I saw that by meddling too much, I was simply repeating the mistakes of our own parents.

We were Jessica's age when we had married. Though people tried, no one could lead me away from Kathy. I never "chose" to be in love with her. I *am* in love with her. It is a state of being integral to my soul, never a choice. My love for her didn't vanish when it was suddenly forbidden. Not even the gods could stop me from loving her.

Now as a father, it was time for me to let go, to let our kids forge their own path wherever that may lead. We would always be there for them when they asked, but we had become the supporting characters in their stories.

The theater went dark at the end of the final scene. I wiped my eyes and jumped to my feet, almost breathless. I had changed in that ninety minutes. Like an epiphany divined from deep meditation, I realized that my chapter as the main character had ended. Now, I understood that my role was to assist others in their journeys.

I wished I could stay in my seat and bathe in the island's beauty all over again. What else would I discover? My face still wet with tears, I stood stunned like I had twenty-five years ago, hardly believing what I'd just experienced. Maybe it was our connection with the story, an eerie similarity in the paths our lives followed. Whatever it was, this new production took my breath away. Opening night couldn't come soon enough.

8
"SOME GIRLS"

Fall 2017
Cleveland, Ohio

$\mathcal{K}$ATHY

$\mathcal{A}$lthough it was still several months away, we began planning for our big Opening Night on Broadway. Never had we been to this kind of fancy function before, complete with red carpet, celebrities, and an afterparty. It was exciting and a little overwhelming. I felt like Cinderella getting my chance to go to the ball, only I was bringing my prince with me. I just needed a fairy godmother to help me find a suitable dress.

Shopping is fun when I'm out spending the day with the kids —all three of whom love to shop—but for some reason, it's draining when I'm searching for my own clothes. Which is strange because I do enjoy dressing up when the occasion calls for it, but I'd rather re-wear a dress I already have than spend the time or money looking for a new one. The last time Jesse and I wore formal attire was at our wedding, and in that instance, my friend Melody designed and made my dress, so I didn't have to search for one or dish out a lot of money.

There was nothing in my closet formal enough for this occasion. My every-day wear consists of either jeans and sweaters or active-wear and ski pants to teach in, so I began to frantically hunt for something appropriate. Unfortunately, the department stores around me didn't have the right mix of understated yet classic elegance that I was looking for.

One evening, rather exasperated, I asked Jesse, "What do people wear to Opening Night?"

I should have known better than to ask him. He'd never been to an Opening Night before, and he knew even less about women's fashion than I did, which isn't much, but for some reason, I wanted the reassurance of his input as if he could magically make the perfect dress appear.

"Why don't you look it up on Google?" Jesse suggested, not really interested in the question.

For some reason, checking my phone or computer isn't my first instinct when looking for information. Jesse would say that is because of my age despite the fact that I'm only three months older than he is. Personally, I think it's that I like talking to people more than machines.

Realizing I wasn't going to get any useful information out of Jesse on the subject, I opened up my computer and typed, "What does one wear to an Opening Night on Broadway?" Google was about as helpful as Jesse. "Dress in formal attire."

No kidding.

I closed my computer with a little too much force.

Jesse looked up from whatever he was reading on his iPad. "What? You'll look great in anything."

"Thanks, but we're already outsiders," I complained. "I don't want to look like I just came in from the barn."

I was only sort of joking. Our three angelic children love to tease me about growing up in a small rural suburb of Lansing, Michigan, where much of the land surrounding our neighborhood when I had grown up was a vast array of corn or bean fields. You didn't have to drive too far to find cows either. After all, even Michigan State University, twenty minutes from my childhood home, had been founded in 1855 as the Agricultural College of the State of Michigan. Our kids, who had lived among other places in suburban Detroit, downtown Philadelphia, and suburban Cleveland, asked me things like, "Didn't you ride a tractor to school, Mom?" or "Was your prom in a barn?"

"No, of course not," I would say and laugh it off. Though, once I chose to add, "No barns but in elementary school, we did learn how to square dance."

That didn't help their perception of my hometown. They also knew the story of how we'd planned to ride the Zamboni to our wedding reception. As far as our kids were concerned, if we were happy to take a Zamboni to our reception, riding a tractor to prom seemed within the realm of possibility. I think they are still expecting to uncover a picture of me at my prom in a denim dress and straw hat sitting on a pile of hay.

"I don't want to be too fancy or too casual," I continued muttering to Jesse, though he had already gone back to reading and wasn't really listening anymore.

I'm not sure why I cared. I guess I wanted to fit in, but I was the only one making me feel like I didn't belong. I had this image in my mind of that rom-com-type scene where the kind of nerdy girl is told there's a costume party and then is the only one to dress up, and everyone else laughs as soon as she arrives.

"You worry too much." Jesse looked up. "No one actually

cares what anyone else is wearing. People are too wrapped up in their own worlds to pay any attention."

"Are you sure?"

"When was the last time you remembered what someone else had on?"

He was right. As long as I was wearing *something*, no one would care.

"Just find something you like."

Even that wasn't an easy task. This was a special occasion for us, and I wanted a special dress. There are far too many choices for women's formal wear. For Jesse and Ryan, formal options are relatively simple—pick a sport coat and tie. Their biggest decision was what color tie to wear, but for women, formal attire covers an endless range of possibilities—short dress, long dress, pant suit; bejeweled, pearled, or glittery... Even fabric type matters. Then, of course, there's the shoes and jewelry, and don't forget what hairstyle to wear. It's exhausting!

Unfortunately, no fairy godmother appeared to design the perfect gown, but eventually, after searching for several weeks online, I found what I was looking for—an elegant, floor-length silver dress and silver shoes to match. The best part was the whole ensemble came in just over two hundred dollars. I really am the Scrooge of the family.

Ryan and Jesse easily assembled their suit coats, dress shirt, and dress pants, and we were ready for our extravagant night out in New York City.

December 1-3, 2017
Opening Weekend
New York, New York

*J*ESSE

*W*e boarded our plane from Cleveland Hopkins International Airport to New York's LaGuardia Airport on Friday, December 1st. Upon arrival, we took an Uber to what was becoming our usual hotel, the Hilton Garden Inn on 8th Avenue. We loved this spot because even though it was only a block away from the crowds in Times Square, it was right in the middle of the theater district and close to all the great restaurants nearby in Hell's Kitchen.

The first thing we had to do after checking in at the hotel was to head over to the production company office a couple blocks away to pick up our Opening Night tickets for the performance and the afterparty. The three of us stood in the little office decorated with mementos from past Broadway shows and waited for the lady at the desk to go grab our tickets. She came out with the tickets as well as two gifts given to all the co-producers. One was a small candle with the *Once on This Island* logo printed on the glass. The other was a framed copy of the Playbill cover, the producer's credits page, and a picture of Ti Moune sitting on Asaka's lap on top of the overturned boat. Underneath those three items was a little brass plate with the date, "December 3, 2017—Opening Night" engraved on it.

There aren't many things in our house that we consider "prized possessions" other than old non-digital photographs of our wedding and our kids. This framed program commemorating Opening Day immediately made the list.

We returned to the hotel to stash the gifts safely away in our room and headed straight for the Circle in the Square Theater. Our tickets were for Sunday, but I wanted to show Kathy and

Ryan the theater which was quickly becoming my favorite spot in New York City. Before *Once on This Island*, we probably wouldn't have paid much attention to this theater, but now giant posters of the show hung on every spare surface outside the box office, and we carefully studied every one of them. Ryan ran up to the billing poster near the theater entrance to see if he could find my name.

"Dad, look! You're right there!" he said, pointing up. "Your name is on the theater!" He beamed.

It read: "Ken Davenport and Hunter Arnold and..." then five lines down, "Silva Theatrical Group/Jesse McKendry/Dr. Mojgan Fajiram"

In my wildest dreams, I couldn't have possibly imagined my name would be on a Broadway Theater, and yet somehow, the Gods had placed us here. We snapped a quick picture to remember the moment, but how would I ever forget it?

Of course I'd known it was going to be there, but standing in front of it that day, seeing *my name* on the front of a Broadway theater as a co-producer of my all-time favorite show was like nothing I'd ever experienced before. I don't really have the words to explain how I felt.

I thought back to a moment when I was five years old. I was standing in my Aunt Sharon's living room in Milwaukee, and we were all watching the Green Bay Packers on TV. I idolized the Packers. I had my favorite Packers helmet on and held a little toy football. I exclaimed to everyone within earshot, "Everybody can be somebody!" In that moment, my five-year-old self felt like I was a part of the team, part of something greater than myself.

Throughout school, I had done all the things I was told to do to be successful. I graduated from the right schools with the right degrees. I'd gotten good jobs and moved up the corporate ladder, but seeing my name on the theater was entirely different. It was my "Everybody can be somebody" moment. Now I really was part of something much greater than myself. My heart was full, and this new production hadn't even opened yet. All of this was because I had made that one seemingly insignificant decision to go to work at the Wharton Center on that cold November night twenty-five years earlier.

We had no idea that our story would ever weave back into the tapestry of *Once on This Island*.

Often blinded and discouraged by the detours in front of us, we could not see the bigger picture. At times, we felt like we were slipping backward, headed in the wrong direction away from what we thought were our goals. It never occurred to us that maybe the path was correct. It was the destination that needed to be changed.

Near the end of summer in 2011, frustrated with my work at the time, I left my job in Cleveland and was hired by another company in Seattle, Washington. It is an understatement to say that Kathy and the kids were not thrilled with the prospect of moving yet again. We had only been in Ohio for five years, which was a long time for us. Before that, we had moved six times to five different states in the span of six years because of graduate school and then my work. In Cleveland, we had finally found stability and put down roots, and now the kids and Kathy felt like they were being ripped out of the ground and transplanted yet again.

Of course Kathy and I made the decision together for me to take the new position, but I knew what she was sacrificing. She has always been the type of person who quickly forms close bonds with people. Her students, her co-workers, they all hold a special place in her heart. I knew she would have a hard time leaving them, and it wasn't only her work we would be leaving behind. Moving across the country would make it much more difficult to get together with her family and my parents who were only about four hours away in Michigan. It was a treasured family tradition to see them all at least twice a year, at

Thanksgiving and The Fourth of July, more often whenever possible.

"Are you sure you're good with this?" I asked before I formally accepted the offer.

"I'm not saying I want to move," she said. "When have I ever *wanted* to move? Yet every time we do, we meet all these amazing people who touch our lives, and our lives become more full. Now we have friends all over the country." She put her hand on mine and gazed into my eyes. "If you will be happy in Seattle, the kids and I will make it work. We can't be happy if you're not."

And so we put our house up for sale and prepared to move 2,500 miles from the place we had finally called home.

She tried to be stoic about it, but the day Kathy said her last goodbyes to her coaching partner and best friend, Lori, and all of her students, a little bit of her perpetual radiance vanished from her face. A little piece of her would always be in Cleveland.

We took a glorious two weeks to drive across the country, feeling a bit like the wagoneers of old heading West on the Oregon Trail and leaving the world we knew behind us. We explored places like Mount Rushmore, Yellowstone, and Devil's Tower. We saw the Corn Palace, which we decided was over-hyped and not worth the detour. Craters of the Moon, about three hours from Boise, Idaho, was worth a detour. As soon as we stepped out of the car and onto the massive black lava fields which had been formed thousands of years ago, it felt like we were on a different planet.

"This is so eerie. I wonder what the people on the wagon trains thought of this place," Kathy asked, gazing across the landscape dotted with dark columns of hardened earth and lava. Hundreds of thousands of pioneers in the 1800s had traveled for months along almost this same route, carrying all their belongings in a covered wagon, following their dreams of a new and prosperous life in the West.

While we weren't searching for gold or free land, we felt a kind of cross-generational connection to the souls who, one hundred and seventy years before us, had left everything behind for a new start on the Pacific coast. The lush beauty of the Pacific Northwest had always called to me, and I was eager to begin our new chapter in the shadow of Mt. Rainier. But on the way there, forces beyond my control were at play. By the time we reached Seattle, the job I'd been hired for didn't exist anymore. The company had decided to restructure and move me to a different position without informing me until I arrived. I never would have uprooted our family for this new position, though now that we were here, I had to make it work.

The stunning azure sky reflecting the blue of Puget Sound and majestic stands of pine forests surrounded us. Postcard-like views filled every moment, exactly how I had dreamed it would be. However, nothing else was.

After walking through several dozens of houses, the only one we actually liked, near a school for the kids, was over an hour from the nearest ice rink by car. By kayak, it was only fifteen to twenty minutes away. The thought of Kathy, who is terrified of bodies of water deeper than she is tall, having to commute by kayak over Puget Sound was kind of funny in a very dark sort of way but also totally unreasonable. My vision of living in Seattle was vanishing like a whale into the depths of the Pacific. I had only caught a glimpse of it.

It was one thing for Kathy to give up her students in Ohio and move out here, but to ask her to completely quit teaching skating or commute over two hours a day wasn't something I could do. To top it off, our house back in Cleveland still hadn't sold, and we were about to have to make payments on two places because our corporate temporary housing limit had been reached.

I had wanted so badly for this to work.

Oftentimes, dreams don't turn out the way you imagine, as many of the travelers along the Oregon Trail discovered as well. Over 20,000 people perished along the route, mostly from diseases like Cholera and dysentery but also from starvation/dehydration and the hazards of traveling in a covered wagon.[1]

At least for us, our survival didn't hang in the balance.

One night, gazing out of the big picture window of our corporate apartment to the gently swaying waters of Puget Sound, I knew what I had to do.

"I think I need to see if I can get my old job back in Cleveland."

"You would do that?" I could see a spark of that lost radiance rekindle in Kathy's eyes.

So I let go of my West Coast dreams, and we decided to pack everything up again and drive the 2,405 miles back across the country. We moved right back into our house which still hadn't sold, and I was rehired by my old company. Kathy and the kids were thrilled.

Seattle was not to be, at least not yet. The universe had other plans for us. I decided I would simply make the best of being back in Cleveland, and I was happy they were happy. After a few years, I was put in charge of my company's New York business, where on free nights, I reignited my love for Broadway.

I had been so disappointed when the Seattle job didn't work out, but if it had, I almost certainly wouldn't be standing here in front of Circle in the Square Theater now. The gods had put those roadblocks in front of us to lead us back to the island. I breathed in deeply, thankful for everything that had brought us here, all the good times and all the disappointments.

Kathy wrapped her arms around me. We stood outside the theater, soaking in the excitement as others passed by to peek at the posters and the theater. Kathy, Ryan, and I basked in the warm glow of gratitude.

But it was only Friday, and the opening wasn't until Sunday. How were we going to pass the time? I didn't want to wish two days in New York City away, and we had tickets to see other shows, but in that instant, there was no other show I wanted to see. Friday and Saturday became obstacles we had to make it through to get to Sunday.

Despite being December, the weather forecast called for sun and highs near fifty degrees for the weekend, so we decided to make the most of the two days by walking around Washington Square Park, spotting all of the cute dogs—one of Ryan's favorite activities—and finding great little restaurants and bookstores to check out.

Finally, Sunday dawned, and it was time to find the perfect breakfast. We took the subway down to 4th Street and walked down 6th Avenue. We passed the basketball courts and the little playground, which were empty at this time in the morning, and turned right onto Carmine Street. Only a few steps past Bleecker Street we could see the welcoming white and greenish striped awning of Jack's Wife Freda. In the summertime, the mostly glass doors are held open with flower pots, inviting guests to walk in. It was too chilly for that now.

This morning, we arrived early enough to beat the long line of the brunch crowd, so we opened the door and walked in. The soft glow emanating from the globe fixtures was the first thing I always noticed. It was warm and inviting. We were greeted with a cheery welcome and shown to the long family-style table in the middle of the dining room, which was our favorite place to sit. We were seated on long bench seats between a party of three having a "girls' morning out" and a romantic couple. The din of friendly conversation filled the air. It seemed like an old family reunion where you don't know everyone, but you feel a familial kinship toward them, all part of the big beautiful human family breaking bread together in this surrogate home.

We sat down and looked forward to the bottomless cups of coffee, which seemed to get magically refilled without us noticing. The attentive servers somehow knew we needed more before we did. Even the little packets of sugar on the table echoed the kind, caring atmosphere with little sayings printed on them like "HUG MORE," "BE PRESENT," and "HELLO MY SWEET."

The three of us scanned the paper menus on the table bearing the caricature of Freda, the grandmother of Dean Jankelowitz, co-owner with his wife Maya. During our many visits, we had tried most everything they offered, finding them all mouthwatering, but we had a habit of gravitating back to our favorites. Today for me, it was the eggs with green shakshuka; for Ryan, the grilled chicken kebabs and couscous; and for Kathy, the rose water waffles with honey syrup.

After we'd practically licked the plates clean and had our fill of coffee, we made our way past the bar stocked with bottles, glasses, little glass jars of fresh celery and lemons, and a cappuccino machine—all normal bar items but arranged with such care that they looked like a work of art.

As we reached the door to leave, the bartender called out to us, "Have a great day!"

We stepped out onto Carmine Street again and headed back toward Midtown. Indeed, we were ready to have a great day; it couldn't have started any better.

"C'mon, guys. Let's pick up the pace a bit," I said, wanting to get to the theater early.

"Isn't it a little weird that we're seeing same show twice in one day?" Ryan asked as we walked past the famous, Flatiron Building.

"Yeah, it's kinda weird," Kathy answered, "but weird is kinda normal for us."

We still had tickets to see the matinee performance of *Once on This Island* before the opening that night. Even I have to admit it was odd to see it twice in the same day. I had planned to sell the matinee seats once we'd made the decision to be co-producers and we had been given three tickets to the opening instead of only two. But some part of me whispered, *How many times will you be involved in a Broadway show? Enjoy every chance you get to see it.* So I never sold them.

Years earlier, before this revival was even a glimmer in our eyes, any time we heard about a nearby local production of *Once on This Island*, whether it was a performing arts group in San Francisco or a high school choir in York, Pennsylvania performing a concert of the songs, we had gone to see it. However, Ryan hadn't seen any of these performances. He had heard the original cast album because we played it now and then, but this was going to be his first time seeing the musical. He had no idea what to expect. He was about to find out.

9

"ONE SMALL GIRL"

December 3, 2017
Matinee Performance / Final Preview
Circle in the Square Theater
New York, New York

$\mathcal{K}$ ATHY

$\mathcal{A}$s we entered the lobby of the Circle in the Square Theater and took the escalator down to the theater level, I couldn't stop smiling. I was so excited to see the show again, and I felt my heart pounding in my chest like waves crash into the shore. I thought back to that November night so long ago when Jesse and I were just kids going on our first fancy date. It seemed like another life and yesterday all at the same time. Our lives had changed so much in twenty-five years. I had changed so much.

I didn't quite know what to expect seeing this beautiful story resurrected. The one thing I knew for certain was that I would be sobbing by the end. I cry at everything. It's not that I stand on an emotional precipice in my everyday life. Typically, I'm the rock other people come to when they're having a rough day, but when immersed in the emotions of movies or live shows that are the least bit sad, I cry. Every. Single. Time. I can't help it. I become too emotionally connected to the characters, and my empathy-mirroring response immediately kicks in even if I've seen it before. To this day, I lose all composure in *The Lion King* when Mufasa dies. With three kids, I've seen that one about a billion times, but it still gets to me.

I knew today the floodgates would open. I just had no idea when the rivers would start flowing.

As soon as we stepped into the oval theater, Ryan exclaimed, "Wow! So this is what you meant by it being a real island!"

I too was struck with a child-like amazement. We, the audience, surrounded the island on all sides like the ocean. Jesse had already described this to me when he'd seen the dress rehearsal, but words could not adequately relay the power of being there. I didn't expect it to feel so real, so authentic, so natural. We had entered another world.

The three of us took our seats in the front row, our feet sinking into the sand as if we were relaxing on the beach. We were on the island, physically connected to it, our feet planted in the sand like the roots of a newly sprouted mango tree. Jesse leaned over to me and said that he had picked out these particular seats because he wanted to be as close as we could get to being in the performance.

"This is cool!" Ryan said, looking all around the island. Maybe now he would understand why wanted to be a part of it.

An adorable little girl in a blue school uniform sat on a plastic milk crate in the middle of the sand, coloring. She was about the same age as many of my figure skating students. I smiled. My heart has a soft spot for all children. Maybe it's because I never really grew up, but in my eyes, they each have such special spirits. I'm incredibly lucky to be able to work with kids every day.

Destruction from last night's fierce storm surrounded this radiant little girl—plastic bags, sheets of tin roofing ripped from crude huts, pop cans, palm fronds, and a downed telephone pole that lay half in the sand, half in the seating area. It was as if the stage was already set with two competing forces, love and innocence and death and suffering.

Ryan and Jesse pointed things out to each other that they spotted in the sand—a steering wheel, a tire, Coke cans, a woman walking around holding a live chicken.

The sweet earthy aroma of frying onions wafted through the air. I turned to my right, wondering if my senses were playing tricks on me, but, no, there in the sand was a table with a hot electric skillet sizzling with onion ringlets. An assortment of candles and fruits were laid out surrounding the skillet. The whole display was set up as a shrine to Asaka, Mother of the Earth.

Farther to my right, in the corner of the theater, was the back-end of a real tractor trailer, looking like it had lost control during the storm and crashed through a building. This was the lair of Papa Ge, God of Death. His religious symbol, or vèvè, a Christian-like cross on a pedestal, was painted on the trailer's door. In Afro-Haitian Vodun, vèvè are often used to call the gods from the spirit realm.

In most theaters, the orchestra is situated in the "pit" below the stage, but here it wasn't possible to put them under the island. Instead, the musicians' deck was built above the tractor trailer bed that jutted out from the corner of the theater, made to look like construction scaffolding on the side of a building.

"Mom, look! A goat!"

Ryan pointed to the animal in a black diaper being led onto

the island by a stunningly beautiful woman who I assumed must be Merle Dandridge, cast as Papa Ge. Jesse had raved about her powerful new portrayal of the god of the underworld. I hadn't even heard her voice yet, but I could see why he was taken with her. She seemed to have a gravitational force that pulled my gaze in her direction. This was already unlike anything I'd ever seen, and nothing had even happened yet. This was the "pre-show" Jesse had told me about, though at the time, I didn't really know what he'd meant.

It was about fifteen minutes prior to the official show time, but as the audience continued to stream in and find their seats, villagers began to appear on the island, greeting the child and surveying the storm's toll. As with most natural disasters, there wasn't time to lose themselves in grief, so they gave thanks for those who were spared and began the task of cleaning up and rebuilding their island. Aid workers joined the locals on the beach and began picking up the scattered refuse and setting up a make-shift medical station. That's when I noticed Lea Salonga, dressed in a nurse's uniform, draping a mosquito net over a young audience member's head and explaining how nets save lives being lost from malaria.

A loud clanging of metal on metal made me jump in my seat. The rusty door of the tractor trailer bay had swung open and slammed against the side of the truck. I turned to see a strikingly handsome man sitting on the edge of the trailer bed and surveying the activity on the island with a sly smile. His well-defined biceps rippled visibly under his sleeveless New York Knicks jersey. He is one of those rare people who commands attention when he enters a room. There was an aura, an energy, an intensity around him, and I couldn't peel my eyes away. After a moment, he stood and made his way up a few steps to a piece of scaffolding leading to the musicians' deck, but instead of going all the way up, he grabbed onto a sturdy cross-bar and did a set of pull-ups.

Ryan put his hand on my shoulder. "Wow! Mom, did you see that? That guy just did a bunch of pull-ups like it was nothing!"

From the moment we walked in, *Once on This Island* was different from anything I'd ever seen, a whole new type of theatrical experience.

Some cast members greeted and welcomed the audience to their island. One of the villagers came up to Ryan and told him he liked his shiny, brown leather wingtip dress shoes. "Do you want to trade for my rubber sandals?" he asked, and Ryan laughed.

I'd never been to a musical where the cast interacted with the crowd. Here, I was a guest, not a spectator. The whole atmosphere of this theater was welcoming and close, like we were with old friends.

I had never felt that in a show before. There was always the physical barrier of the stage between cast and audience as well as the invisible wall that actors never breached. In most shows, if an actor looked at you, it seemed more like they were looking through you. Not here on the island. This was a one of a kind of show. In this theater, that wall had been cracked open from the beginning by the fallen "tree" connecting the real world with the realm of the island gods.

Another contrast was the way this company handled reminding the audience to turn off their cellphones. It is shocking how many times a phone will go off during a Broadway performance and disrupt the mood in the theater. In an attempt to combat this annoyance, most shows have a quick recorded announcement over the speakers just before it starts, kindly asking everyone to turn off or silence their cell-phones.

Here on the island, they had a more clever and persuasive approach. When most everyone was seated, a phone rang loudly. The cast looked around, annoyed that someone would have their phone on. They mockingly accused audience members, "Is that your phone?" Then they found the "culprit," an unsuspecting person sitting in the seat where a fake cell phone had been placed in a hidden pouch. They confiscated it, admonished the person playfully, and then tossed the fake phone around the island until finally, one of the villagers threw it to a fisherman perched above an actual pool of water at the far end of the stage to our left. He, of course, missed it, and the phone splashed in the water below him. The crowd gasped for a moment as the point became clear. Turn off your phone.

"Can you hear me now?" another villager shouted.

Then, the real show began.

Thunder rumbled in the distance, interrupting their fun, and all the villagers turned toward the sky. A loud crack ripped through the air, closer this time. The little girl screamed and ran to the arms of the woman who had been holding the chicken. This was Mama Euralie, played by Kenita R. Miller. In an effort to comfort and distract the child, she prepared to tell a story.

"Tee, Tee," she said, directing two of the villagers to pick up long plastic tubes from the beach that had been ripped from cars or buildings by the God of Water, Agwe, in his tempest the night before. The two men whirled the tubes overhead, producing a deep whistling sound as if the wind itself had blown into the theater.

Mama Euralie closed her eyes, only for a moment, as if saying a quick prayer to the gods. Then, she raised her powerful voice to the winds and began to tell the tale of Ti Moune.

She spoke only eight words, but those eight words carried the weight of Jesse's and my early history, and they crashed into me with the force of a tidal wave. I had to bite my lip in order to settle down. In that moment, I remembered everything that this story meant to us. Not that I had forgotten, but I had locked away the painful memories of that time, numbed them to where they didn't hurt as much. Now, they washed over me.

It was ridiculous, of course, to be on the verge of sobbing before the first song ended. This wasn't even a sad scene. It was happy, so happy that I was overcome. Everything in our lives had led us to this moment. My heart was full to the point of bursting, grateful even for the trying events that had brought us here.

The whole theater went dark, and thunder crashed again, this time all around us. A flash of lightning ripped through the night sky. The sound of wind whipped through trees. Islanders screamed.

A mother cried out frantically, trying to save her child from the hurricane's anger.

Agwe's rushing waters overpowered her.

Mother and child were torn from each other's arms.

She had sacrificed herself so that her daughter could live,

And she slipped into the surging seas.

We weren't even five minutes in, and another wave of emotion crashed into me, threatening to drown my last shred of composure.

How many times had that same scene played out less than three months before in the terrible chaos and devastation of Hurricane Maria? My mind flooded with thoughts of the thousands of people of Puerto Rico who had lost their lives.

This was only a representation of the real tragedy they had to endure.

Loved ones swept away in an instant.

Homes destroyed, everything lost.

An entire island *still* without power.

Flooding.

Total destruction.

I could only imagine their complete heartbreak.

Then somehow, they had to pick up the broken shards of their lives and fuse them back together, but like a puzzle with missing pieces, their lives could never be the same.

In this theater, we were, in some small way, paying homage to their loss through the telling of this story. I sat in my seat, the pain of mother and daughter losing one another sinking in as I thought of how we'd almost lost Jessica. My heart ached for this mother and all those mothers she represented. We had been lucky. Papa Ge had granted us more time.

But the gods are fickle and mischievous. How many more days will we be given? We have to live each day grateful for every new sunrise with each other and all of our children.

On the island, Agwe, played by Quentin Earl Darrington, commanded attention with his impressive physique, looking like he could hold up the heavens with one hand. His booming voice poured "Rain" down on us and then the "skies" above in the theater opened up, and as if by magic, real rain showered the island and soaked Daniel as he lay unconscious in the sand. It even smelled like a beach after an evening rain. All my senses were immersed in the island.

The villagers, hearing Ti Moune's cries for help, raced to the beach where Daniel had crashed his car on the slippery street. Some of them carried torches, illuminating the scene of the accident. We were so close that the heat from the fire warmed my face and I could hear the breath of the flames as they sucked in the surrounding oxygen. Like the fire, the actors seemed to feed off of the crowd's energy, creating a synergy that connected everyone in the room. It was as if for a moment, all of our hearts were beating as one. We had become a part of the story they were weaving. No longer divided between audience and performers, we had crossed over, transcended the boundaries of self, and merged into one being.

You can't get that from a TV or an iPhone screen.

Sitting in the front row, we were so close to the action that when the actors danced, grains of sand shot through the air and landed in my lap, so close that when Tonton Julian, played by

Phillip Boykin, shouted at Ti Moune, I jumped too. Phillip's deep voice rumbled through the theater like thunder. The normally jovial, soft-spoken Tonton wasn't raising his voice in anger but in fear. Fear has a way of changing people. Tonton, afraid of losing his precious little girl who had given his life new meaning, yelled at her.

My heart practically stopped. Jesse, sitting next to me, dropped his head and brushed a tear from his cheek. I knew he was thinking of Jessica and Alyssa. I was too. I reached over and held his hand in mine.

It's impossible to look at our amazing daughters, now young adults, and not see them as the chubby-cheeked little girls in yellow ballet tutus they used to be fifteen years ago. Where had the time gone? How is it already time to step back and let them make all of their important life decisions? I'm not ready to let go of these precious creations who are so much a part of me. I want to wrap my arms around them and keep them safe, to protect them from pain and heartbreak. When they suffer, I suffer too. Our hearts are forever bound together.

Sitting in my seat, I sobbed silently as Tonton realized he had already lost his little girl. She was now a woman who had to go and find her own way. He took a deep, ragged breath, knowing that if he didn't let her go, she would never want to return.

Mama Euralie clutched at her breast in despair, realizing her husband's wisdom. Despite their own heartbreak, they gave Ti Moune their blessing to go.

I had longed for my own parents to say those words.

Mama clung to Tonton, and both of them wept as they watched their little girl walk out of their lives forever.

We all know the day is coming when our children will leave us, though we're not at all prepared for when or how we'll feel at that moment. No one tells new parents, "This tiny helpless infant in front of you, whom you would give your life for, will soon outgrow you and will leave a hole in your heart where they used to be."

Of course, when *we* were kids, we didn't abandon our parents. We were simply learning to be independent, setting off on adventures, oblivious to their feelings. Then, our own children leave us tearing out a little piece of our hearts, and for the first time, we understand what our parents went through.

I remember when Jessica was first born, someone offered me the advice, "They grow up so fast. Cherish the moments you have." At the time, I thought that was a silly thing to say. I looked down at the tiny six pound bundle in my arms. A tuft of black hair covered her little head and I gazed into her dark brown eyes. Of course I will cherish her. I loved everything about her.

Then came the endless sleepless nights, inconsolable crying, piles of laundry and dishes, constant worrying, and late-night trips to the ER. Jessica was prone to croup, often needing breathing treatments in the wee morning hours. Sometimes, a thought crept in. *It will be so much better when she's older.* And that was the start of the end. As I looked forward to the day that each difficult stage passed, I stopped appreciating the moment I was in. Maybe those older, wiser parents were trying to tell me to cherish *all* the moments, not only the sweet snuggly ones but also the sicknesses, tantrums, and the talking back, the daily journey of being a parent, because making it to the finish line means they are gone.

Life is a series of separate occurrences swirling and flowing together like the rapids of a river. Embrace the ever-changing chaos. Understand that you didn't lose control. You never had it to begin with. Let the current take you where it will.

Sometimes, though, the current is too strong and threatens to drag your family under. Then, you have to assert what little control you have to hold back the waters. Many of us at some point are confronted with treacherous seas. We'd encountered ours when Jessica had been eighteen and just about to graduate from high school.

The doctor's words are forever etched in my mind. "Jessica is not on the path of survival."

My head spun. I didn't understand.

"She will not survive if you don't act immediately," the doctor continued.

I grabbed the door frame, fighting to keep my knees from buckling and crumbling to the floor.

I knew she was skinny. She'd always been stick thin. All of our kids were.

"Her weight is down to seventy-nine pounds." She said something else, but I could no longer focus on her words.

A month before that, Jessica and I had summited a fourteen thousand foot mountain in Colorado together, and now, the shadowy hand of death was closing its grip around her. How could that be? How had I not noticed that she was dying right before my eyes?

I didn't want to believe that my baby was sick, that she was somehow imperfect, or that somehow, I had been an imperfect mother. It was arrogant to think that I could hold death at bay, but I was her mother, it was my job to keep her safe.

Now, I had to accept what was before me.

We admitted her to an outpatient full-day treatment facility, and our long vigil began.

Several agonizing weeks went by. Both Jesse and I spent hours at her side, holding her hand as she choked down four thousand calories and then six thousand calories a day, which often made her so nauseated she had to sleep until the next meal. Our lives, Ryan's and Alyssa's too, were now consumed with getting enough food into Jessica.

She only gained a few pounds.

Months went by. Still only another few extra pounds stuck to her bony body. "Refeeding" alone wasn't working, but the doctors didn't know what else to do. The amount of calories she was taking in should have been enough. They suggested sending her to another facility in another state.

No, they can't send her away, I thought as I rushed out of the clinic to the elevator and hurried to my car. Sitting in the facility parking lot, waiting for her to be released for the day, I burst into tears feeling utterly helpless.

Oh, God...please hear me.

I prayed.

That was all I could do. I was her mom. I was supposed to provide for her needs, and I'd failed. Now, we might lose her forever.

The doctors decided to try one more course of action, a combination of hormone therapy and anxiety medication. The Gods must have heard my prayer because after a week, her constant nausea subsided, and she was able to eat and keep food down. She started gaining weight faster. After almost five months, she was discharged from daily treatment.

Papa Ge had loosened his sinister grip and granted us more time with her.

Pulled from the past back to my seat in the theater, I gazed across the island and watched Ti Moune walk out of her parents' life. I sucked in a ragged breath, trying to calm myself, grateful that my little girl, who was as perfectly imperfect as her mother or anyone else, had conquered death.

I looked around me. Mine wasn't the only face glistening with salty streaks. I was surrounded by a sea of people who'd weathered their own storms, had their own tales of heartbreak. We were all moved together like palm fronds being blown in the wind, connected by this thick trunk of suffering. At some point, even though the scars remain, we all have to pick ourselves up and move on from the pain when the storm ends.

Enter Asaka, played by the incomparable Alex Newell from

Glee, who sauntered across the sand in his bright yellow flower print, vinyl wrap skirt, and floral headdress.

He swayed his hips with the sass of a runway model, stepping up the stairs into the audience, singing "Mama Will Provide."

And he certainly did.

He stopped at seat number 237, right on the aisle, bent down toward the lucky guest sitting there, and belted "OHHHH" in their face.

"Mama Will Provide" had been our favorite song to crank up as we had raced around Maui on our honeymoon, twenty-three years ago. We'd serenaded the birds and trees all the way down the winding mountain road to Hana.

Alex roared the last, otherworldly note with all the power of the gods. It's not often that songs/scenes in the middle of a musical deserve a show-stopping standing ovation, but this was one of two in *Once on This Island*.

"The Ball" scene is the other. Camille A. Brown's choreography is brilliant throughout the musical, but "The Ball" is stunning. For most of the musical, the entire cast is on stage. That translates to ninety minutes of choreography for everyone, whether it's small naturalistic type movements or running and dancing, and it's all done in the shifting sand. A set change is even seamlessly choreographed right before our eyes, and to be honest, I'm still not exactly sure what happens. At one point, I think it is during "Some Say," the cast pulls back a tarp parting the sand which unearths a carpet. About two scenes later, the cast rolls the carpet up as they prepare for the party, revealing a hard dance floor underneath like a hidden treasure. Then, the dance begins, though it's much more than just a dance number.

In a way, the dance scene serves as a metaphor for the two different worlds that occupy the island. The aristocratic Grands Hommes, forgetting their own deep cultural heritage as they, too, were descendants of the dark-skinned peasants, left the past behind to adopt the European ways. Totally absorbed in their own lives of privilege, they danced a simple waltz, void of emotion, done, it seems, only as a demonstration of their higher station.

When Ti Moune stepped onto the dance floor in her bare feet, the mood changes. As she took off her sophisticated heeled shoes, she dispensed with the fake aristocratic world concerned only with image and the traditions of Europe and had the courage to bare her true passionate soul. She moved her body freely to the beat of the Afro-Caribbean drums with an innocence and abandon, almost as if she had been possessed by the ancient loas or spirits. It inspired the servants in the room to throw off their own chains of bondage, if only for a moment, and relish in the freedom to express their deep-rooted heritage, a heritage that, through the Code Noir of Louis XIV in 1685, was prohibited from being openly expressed in the French Antilles. Catholicism was the only lawful religion, which spurred the adoption of Christian likenesses to represent Haitian Vodun gods.

Even Daniel was swept up in the tide of the movement and rises against his father and his Euro-centric traditions for the first and only time in his life.

Sitting with my feet in the sand, I could literally *feel* the power and energy of their stamping to the drums. The vibrations traveled from the soles of my feet up my spine into my soul, carrying the weight of history. It left me breathless.

But as in real life, neither triumphs nor disappointments last. Everything is fleeting, and here, Ti Moune's momentary victory turned sour as she learned that despite his "love" for her, Daniel was not willing to break down the racial walls that had been built on the island. Instead, he was preparing to marry the aristocratic beauty, Andrea Deveraux.

Betrayed and alone, Ti Moune again called on the island gods, but only Papa Ge answered her. In a chilling scene complete with a cool fog rolling in over the island, Papa Ge gave Ti Moune a choice: kill Daniel and forget that she was ever in love or sacrifice herself in his place. The rest of the cast, sitting in the sand surrounding Ti Moune, eerily chanted "Kill him." They screamed and writhed, the demons of darkness now controlling their souls. It was as if all of the island's history and pain had come back to haunt this moment. Ti Moune, by plunging a dagger into Daniel, could punish the Grands Hommes for all their injustices. Possessed by the destructive spirits of fear and anger, she held Papa Ge's dagger, ready to draw his aristocratic blood.

But she cannot.

In her heart, she still loved him in spite of his betrayal. She could not bring pain upon him as he did to her. Darkness only breeds more darkness. The light of love is the only force that can bring a new dawn, and so she sacrificed herself for love and overcame the power of her fear and desire for revenge.

She let go and forgave him.

At the gates of Daniel's palace on the day of his wedding, Ti Moune lay dying in the sand of a broken heart.

A moment of silence descended on the theater.

Mama Euralie cried out, calling to her little girl, her voice raw and full of the anguish of losing her child. My heart broke with her.

All I could hear were the sniffles of audience members as well as my own. How close we'd come to losing Jessica. We'd made it through the darkness with her still beside us. Papa Ge had been merciful.

And then, the gods took pity on Ti Moune and transformed her into a tree. Her spirit of love and forgiveness were free to forever change the island's traditions, breaking down the wall separating the island's two distinct worlds. I thought of my parents and the courage they had to come to Jesse and genuinely apologize for what they'd said and done. I thought of

Jesse, forgiving them with all his heart because of his love for me.

Forgiveness.

I could scarcely imagine the strength that took.

Memories and emotions flooded me. I didn't want this moment to ever end. I wanted to drink in all this beautiful energy of love and forgiveness forever, but all too soon, the ninety minutes had passed, and the show was over. Jesse, Ryan, and I jumped to our feet in a standing ovation. I was crying and laughing and cheering all at the same time. I even saw Ryan wipe his eyes as Jesse and I held each other.

The ushers began to shoo everyone out of the theater. It was much easier to walk through the sand and up the stairs knowing that we would be back on this island in just a few hours.

10
"THE BALL"

December 3, 2017
Opening Night Performance and Party
Circle in the Square Theater
New York, New York

J ESSE

W e walked back to the hotel to collect ourselves. It was time to prepare for our big night. Ryan and I donned our suit jackets and dress pants, opting out of black-tie attire. Kathy positively sparkled in her elegant silvery floor-length gown. We were ready to attend our one-and-only Broadway Opening, complete with a red carpet and after-party.

First on the night's special agenda was a pre-opening toast at The Palm on 50th Street across the street from the theater.

Producers, co-producers, and special guests were invited to meet and mingle to celebrate the big night. We were led through the dining room past guests who feasted on lobsters and prime-aged steaks and directed to a private back room of the restaurant where several people had already gathered. The mood was as bubbly as the glasses of champagne being handed out.

"Happy Opening!" was the greeting of choice between guests.

The first person we ran into that I knew was Ryan Conway, the general manager, whom I'd met at the tech rehearsal. He introduced us to his boyfriend, Ryan, and I introduced them to Kathy and our son Ryan. We had more Ryans in the room than an Irish pub!

Being new on the scene, I only recognized a handful of other people. We made our way around the room so that Kathy and Ryan could meet the few guests I knew. Someone mentioned that Ken Davenport was about to make a toast. We quickly ordered two champagnes and a Coke, and we were ready.

Ken stood at the front of the room, beaming. He thanked everyone for believing in this production, and we all raised our glasses to the opening of *Once on This Island*.

I noticed Tyler Mount had come in with his partner, Chris, and this time, he *did* recognize me, so we headed over. We shared congratulatory hugs and chatted about the night's excitement, and then, I had a serious question for him. Ryan and I had been having an on-going debate about whether you needed to fully turn your phone off in a Broadway show or just put it on silent.

Ryan, being a tech-savvy teen, had said, "Dad, you can put it on silent, and it can't make any noise. That's sufficient."

I'd made my rebuttal, stating, "But Tyler said on his Broadway vlog, 'the number one thing you must do when at a Broadway show is to turn off your phone, not just silence it.'"

This was the perfect time to prove it to Ryan, to teach him

that maybe he doesn't know everything yet. Already knowing Tyler's answer, I asked with a bit too much confidence, "Okay Tyler, at the theater before a show, what do you do? Turn off or silence your phone?"

"Oh, I just silence mine," Tyler said without hesitation.

Ryan looked at me, grinning, his silent smile saying, *See?*

I stood there for a moment, stunned, and then laughed. Maybe I was the one who didn't know everything. How many times have I thought I was going to teach him a lesson thinking I knew better because I'm the older, wiser parent, only for it to backfire? I hope I have taught him *some* lessons that he's taken to heart, but honestly, he's taught me a thing or two as well.

We continued working the room, introducing ourselves and making small talk with other guests. Then, Kathy noticed someone walk into the room. She leaned over to Ryan. "Oh my gosh, Ryan. Is that Jordan Fisher?"

Our daughter, Alyssa, is a huge fan of his and had shown Kathy his music videos, but people often look so different in person she wasn't sure. Ryan thought it looked like him, though neither of them could be certain. Too bad Alyssa wasn't with us. She would have known instantly and probably freaked out a bit too. I had no idea. I'd only seen him once, when he played the roles of John Laurens/Philip Hamilton in *Hamilton* because Alyssa had wanted to see him specifically in the role.

Even if it was him, there was no time to find out. The main event of the night was just about to begin, and everyone started to leave the Palm to head over to the theater. We didn't want to risk being late to the Opening so we made our way out.

As we crossed the street, a small group of teen girls ahead of us bounded over and excitedly surrounded the Jordan Fisher doppelgänger. They screamed and giggled as they professed their undying love. It was definitely the real Jordan Fisher. He graciously greeted his young fans, took pictures, and thanked them for their support.

In the emails from Ken leading up to this special day, I had been told there would be a red carpet picture area, but we didn't know where to find it nor did we know the protocol. I spotted Jenna Ushkowitz from *Glee*, a fellow co-producer of *Once on This Island*, and some other TV and movie stars headed to a door leading into the theater. Surely that was the way to the red carpet. Were we supposed to go over there? We had no idea.

Instead, we happily joined the other line that seemed like it was for everyone else. We showed our tickets and went down the escalator to the theater's entrance. As we descended, we caught a glimpse of Jelani Alladin—who originated the role of Kristoff in Disney's *Frozen* on Broadway—and Phylicia Rashad on the other side of the upstairs lobby, giving interviews and posing for their pictures on the red carpet. We had chosen the correct door.

Excited people streamed off the escalator like a line of ants. We joined them and anxiously gathered in the lower lobby, waiting for the theater to open.

The energy in the theater was infectious. Most everyone in the room was somehow connected to the show, either as a producer, investor, part of the creative team, or an acquaintance of one of those. People all around us rushed to hug and congratulate each other. It was jubilant and hopeful, a celebration of the rebirth of this divinely human story. We stood there and happily took it all in.

Finally, the doors opened, and the usher showed us to our seats, which, coincidentally, were directly behind the seats we had sat in a couple of hours ago at the matinee. Despite having literally just seen the show, I couldn't wait to see it again. I felt like our beagle, who begs incessantly for another treat despite having already finished all his food for the day.

We sat down and waited for the pre-show to begin. Kathy discretely elbowed me and whispered, "Oh my gosh, isn't that

George Costanza from *Seinfeld* behind us? What's his real name?"

Slowly, trying not to look too conspicuous, I turned. "Yes, that's Jason Alexander."

He was sitting in the row right behind us, and I noticed Clay Aiken in the row behind him.

Ryan tapped me on the shoulder and said, "Look, Dad, Jordan Fisher is sitting right over there!" Ryan pointed him out sitting on the aisle over to our left. How strange and wondrous that we were here as well.

The show began. I looked over at Kathy and our eyes met. She took my hand in hers and squeezed three times, our special silent way of saying, "I love you." I squeezed back four times in reply. I'm not sure how I got so lucky to have this amazing woman beside me. I cherished every moment with her. Over our twenty-four years, we'd had plenty of momentous occasions together, but this one was so unexpected and different from anything we'd ever even dreamed about, and yet here we were.

I don't know how this opening performance tugged at my heart even more than a few hours earlier. Maybe it was my excitement, or maybe it was the heightened energy throughout the audience, but this one hit me harder. The incredibly talented cast fed off of the electricity surging through the theater and dialed up their performance to an intensity I did not think possible.

At the last note, the crowd sprang to its feet for an extended standing ovation. No one seemed to want to move from their spot. We all wanted to bathe in the love and light of this show all night.

But we had a party to get to. It was time to celebrate! Eventually, everyone filed out of the theater in triumph. This revival had been everything we hoped it to be and more. We hung out in the lobby, watching the euphoria all around us, soaking it in.

Jordan Fisher stood nearby. He wasn't engaged in a conversation at the moment, so I took the opportunity to walk over to him to tell him our daughters were huge fans and that they loved seeing him in *Hamilton*.

"Tell them 'hi' for me. I'm so grateful for their support," he said.

"I will! Do you have a minute to meet my wife and son?"

"Sure!" Jordan stepped over to where they were standing. He reached out to shake Ryan's hand and said, "Hi, I'm Jordan Fisher."

Ryan, too awestruck for a moment to speak, shook his hand back, and finally replied, "Yeah, I know," then added, "I'm Ryan."

We all chuckled.

"How did you like the show?" Jordan asked him.

"It was amazing," Ryan answered, still clearly dazed that he was *talking* to Jordan Fisher.

Then, a middle-aged gentleman dressed in a nice suit came up to all of us with a big smile on his face. He looked right at Ryan and said, "I sat directly across from where you guys were sitting and was watching your expression the entire night!" He shook Ryan's hand. "I'm Keith. It's so wonderful to see young people who are engaged in the theater!"

He mentioned that he runs a theater program in Birmingham, Alabama and that he got to know Jordan through his participation in his program.

"Keith's program started me on my path, and I will be forever grateful to him," Jordan explained to us.

At that point, Jordan could have graciously made his exit to go chat with someone else, but he stayed there and kept talking to us. He asked Ryan what he liked to do. Ryan explained that he had started his own band and loves most types of music.

"Really? What instrument do you play, and what kind of music?" Jordan asked.

"Guitar. I play in a rock band of kids all under fourteen," Ryan answered, clearly feeling more comfortable.

"That's awesome! I started out playing guitar," Jordan replied.

The lobby started clearing out as people headed off in their various ways. We said our goodbyes to Jordan and Keith and headed out to the party.

Now it was time for the last part of the evening. We walked three blocks over to the Copacabana Night Club on W. 47th street for our first ever after-party. The Copacabana is a famous nightclub that moved several times around New York City after opening in the forties. There is even a Barry Manilow song named after it. This newest incarnation was a multi-level nightclub with different areas to eat, mingle, drink, and dance. The main floor, at least tonight, was more like a nightclub with loud music, bluish mood lighting, and a large dance floor that was already full of people by the time we entered.

Off toward the back of the room was a buffet filled with food and a bar serving up any beverage you could want, including fun *Once on This Island*-themed drinks like Poison Mango Punch and my favorite, Tonton's Gin and Tonic.

We walked around a little bit starstruck, not quite knowing what to do. We had to pinch ourselves to believe we were at a party with the entire *Once on This Island* cast! We were getting a tiny peek at a different world.

The first thing to do was eat. Before the show, we had been too excited to get dinner. Now, all three of us were hungry. We looked for a place to sit. Like most night-club type places, the focus is on dancing as well as meeting and mingling with new people, so there weren't too many tables or chairs. Despite Kathy's grace on the ice, she's notoriously bad at the juggling act of holding a plate and a glass of wine without spilling or breaking something. Luckily, near the back of the room, we found a little table with a couple of cushy chairs and took turns at the buffet, filling our plates. Ryan and I went up to the bar to bring back drinks, a Coke for him, another Tonton Gin and

Tonic for me, and a glass of white wine for Kathy. The three of us ate, drank, talked, and soaked in the atmosphere. Of course, sitting in the back of the room didn't encourage others to come up to us and talk. If we wanted to meet people to make the most of this special evening, it was time to wander around the club.

Our first stop was the bar to refill our drinks.

"I'd better stick with this one," Kathy said, looking at her mostly-full wine glass. "I'll just finish it slowly." It was only Kathy's second glass of wine, but that's when she usually starts getting tipsy. "I'm clumsy enough without alcohol," she added.

Despite this being the fanciest function we had ever attended, it was like any other party with groups of people hanging out in different areas, some dancing, some eating, all enjoying being in one another's company for the celebration. Since we only knew a handful of people here, we decided that we would start by introducing ourselves to the cast and briefly thank each of them for their heartfelt retelling of our favorite musical and meet whomever else crossed our path.

As we wandered around casually looking for cast members, we met several people: producers, co-producers, and friends of cast members. I wish I remembered all their names. That's something I have to improve. At one point, we crossed paths with Michael Starobin, who did the musical orchestrations for the original *Once on This Island* and was co-orchestrator on this new revival. It was such a pleasure to have the chance to talk with him.

There weren't many people Ryan's age at the party. Actually, I don't think there was anyone else Ryan's age, so we stood out a little bit more than we would have had it just been Kathy and me. That caught the attention of Vaughn, the father of one of the girls who played young Ti Moune. He came up to us, and we talked with him for quite a while. We had both lived near San Francisco, so we talked about the Bay Area and its sports scene. He, of course, was a Golden State Warriors basketball fan, archrivals of our hometown Cleveland Cavaliers. He introduced us to both of the lovely young ladies who shared the part of young Ti Moune, Emerson and Mia.

Emerson's eyes lit up when she saw us. "Oh, yes, hi! I recognize you! I saw you in the second row!"

The talent agents of the two girls—a husband and wife team—stopped by to say hello, and Vaughn introduced us. We were all standing in sort of a close circle so we could hear one another over the loud music. Somehow, Kathy shifted positions and tipped her wine glass just enough that it spilled on the husband.

"Oh, no. I'm so sorry," she said, looking mortified.

Luckily, it was a small amount, and he reached behind him to the buffet table, grabbed a couple of napkins, and cleaned it up quickly. I could tell from Kathy's expression that her brain was running through all the ways our night would now unravel as she had just exposed us as uncultured outsiders who had just come in from the barn. A few minutes later, we politely exited the conversation and continued meandering around.

"I'm so embarrassed!" Kathy said. "I can't believe I spilled wine on him!"

"Are you drunk, Mom?" Ryan joked.

"No! Not from two. Three would do it, though." She laughed.

Shortly thereafter, we caught up with Valerie Novakoff from Ken Davenport's office.

"Jesse! Have you seen the *Times* review yet?" she asked.

I hadn't, but the huge smile on her face gave it away. It must be good news. For Broadway shows, all the major reviewers see each show in the week leading up to the opening, when the show is technically still in previews but is usually "frozen" to avoid additional major changes prior to the Opening. They write up their analysis and wait for Opening Night. After the Opening performance, they publish their official reviews. Producers, investors, and the cast anxiously await the results.

Valerie beamed. "They've just been released! You have to read it."

Of course, we realized that great reviews were important, but at the time, we didn't quite grasp the weight they carried. If a revered critic wrote something like, "This cliché-filled musical is not worthy of a high school stage in Cleveland," the show could fail in less than a month.

I took out my phone and quickly searched. The press gods were with us tonight, and the *New York Times* wrote, "Revived and Ravishing!" What a wonderful start to what we hoped would be a long run on Broadway.

As we stood reading the flattering review, a line of people formed just off the dance floor to our right. A big gold backdrop had been set up for party photos. We hadn't snapped any pictures of the night, so we went over to check it out. They provided a box of props to liven up the pictures. Kathy picked out a feather boa and wrapped it around her shoulders. I chose some sparkly star-shaped glasses, and Ryan chose a top hat and microphone. It was the only photo we took all night.

We wandered up to the second floor and, to our delight, found most of the cast hanging out there. I was as excited as Ryan would be walking into a room full of puppies. I wanted to meet every one of them and thank them for helping to make this evening possible. It might be my only chance to show my appreciation for the incredible performances they gave every day in that sand.

It must get tiring at some point to perform the same show eight times a week, especially a physically demanding show like this one where everyone is running around and dancing in the shifting sand. Does it ever lose its luster and become just a job, one gig in a long line of many? We've never been to a show where we felt the actors were just going through the motions. How do they keep it fresh? Somehow, they make it feel as if this one performance you're watching is the first and last performance they will ever give. What could the world accomplish if we all brought that much passion to our work?

Over the course of the night, we were able to meet many of the cast members, at least for a moment, including Phillip Boykin, whose deep voice is just as striking in speech as in song, and David Jennings, who played Daniel's father and was the one who offered to exchange shoes with Ryan in the preshow. We asked him if he thought his character was a little tough on his son for falling in love with the beautiful Ti Moune.

"Absolutely not! He should know better!" he replied, jumping right back into his character.

Hailey Kilgore and Isaac Powell had a large crowd around them so we talked to them for a split second and moved on.

Then, we spotted Kenita R. Miller, who plays Mama Euralie. Her entire spirit glowed with warmth and love, like a living embodiment of the heart and soul of *Once on This Island*. We had to go say, "Hi." She was talking to someone, and there were some other people milling around her, but there was no obvious line. We stepped closer, at which point another person who was just diagonally ahead, seeing our direction, quickly sashayed in front of us.

"Oh, I'm sorry! Are you in line for Kenita?" I asked.

"Oh, yes, that's okay." He laughed. "She's so popular, and I just have to congratulate her."

He looked a little familiar to me, but I had no idea from where.

"I'm Jesse, and this is my wife Kathy, and son Ryan." I said, hoping to find out where we knew him from.

Ryan leaned in to Kathy and whispered just loudly enough for me to catch it, "Don't spill on him too, Mom." He looked up at her with his mischievous grin.

All she could do was smile back at him.

"I'm Antoine Magic Raimone." We shook hands and engaged

in the normal get-to-know-you questions, and then he said, "I'm a cast member in *Hamilton*."

That was it!

"We actually saw you perform recently! What an amazing show. I have a question." I paused. I'd had a couple Tonton Gin and Tonics and wanted to make sure the words came out right. "Most of us have jobs that become a chore, and we kind of go through the motions. Does it ever get to be a chore to perform the same thing eight times a week?"

"Sure. Sometimes, if I'm not feeling good, it's harder to go in." He smiled. "But the bottom line is, I love every chance I get to be up on stage." He looked at Ryan. "Are you in musical theater?"

"No, but I love performing with my band."

"What kind of band?"

"Rock and roll. We play lots of different types like Black Sabbath, Muse, and Rage Against the Machine."

"Wow! That's awesome. Where do you guys play?"

"All around Cleveland. We're from Ohio," Ryan said proudly.

"Cleveland? Wow!" He clearly hadn't expected that.

Pretty much everyone we met was surprised to hear where we were from. They wondered how on earth we had gotten involved with *Once on This Island* if we were from Cleveland.

We've seen a few shows on Broadway that specifically make fun of Cleveland in the dialogue, such as *Groundhog Day* and *Aladdin*. The jokes always get lots of laughs from the whole audience, including us. We never thought of Cleveland as a great place to live either until we moved there twelve years ago. Cleveland may not be the most exciting city in the world, but it is a great place to live with wonderful restaurants, little trendy coffee shops, and a fabulous live music scene. After all, Cleveland is home to the Rock & Roll Hall of Fame and Playhouse Square, our local theater venue. Of all the cities we've lived in or visited, Ryan rates Cleveland first then New York then Paris. Maybe he's a bit biased, though.

It was finally our turn to talk to Kenita. She was just as wonderful to meet as her spirit suggested. She may be small in stature, but if her positive energy and love were measured in height, she might be the tallest human on the planet.

"Thank you so much for what you do!" I said when we approached. "This was our favorite musical twenty-five years ago, and we just want to thank you for helping give it life again."

"Oh, thank you." She smiled wide and put her hands to her heart. "That really means so much to me." She asked if she could give us a hug, and we happily obliged. There were other people still waiting to see her so we thanked her again and moved on.

Before we knew it, it was almost one in the morning. We sat down on a couch to rest for a bit.

"Guys, can we go back to the hotel now?" Ryan asked. "I'm tired." He slumped his head over onto my shoulder.

A small gesture that he didn't even think about, but to me, it was gift. Ryan hadn't done that in a long time, and I was grateful he wasn't totally grown up yet.

Both Kathy and I looked at him like he was crazy. Being the horribly irresponsible parents we were, Kathy said, "Are you kidding me?"

I added, "We are here at a party with *Lea Salonga* and *Alex Newell*... We are not leaving!"

We weren't ready to end our Cinderella night and turn back into pumpkins, but no matter how much we wanted this night to last forever, like everything in life, it was destined to end. We dragged Ryan off the couch and went to see if we might be able to meet Lea Salonga. We found Alex Newell and Ms. Salonga near each other, both surrounded by lots of friends and family. This was our one chance to say, "Hi." Kathy gave them each a quick congratulatory hug, and I got the chance to tell Ms.

Salonga that we'd been huge fans of hers since her Miss Saigon days. I know, I know, I'm sure she hasn't heard *that* before...

Then, we moved on so that Kathy could visit the dessert station for chocolate.

An hour had passed, and we were all exhausted. We told Ryan maybe it was time to head home. Giddy from both the free drinks and the experience, the three of us walked back to our hotel, and our night at the ball was over.

"SOME SAY"

December 4, 2017
New York, New York

JESSE

"*Once on This Island*, Revived and Ravishing![1]"

The next morning, we had a chance to read the full *New York Times* review by Jesse Green, who goes on to say, "... what a delight it is to enter the world of *Once on This Island...*" It was named a *New York Times* critic's pick. I felt like a proud parent, thrilled that others were recognizing it as a magical piece of theater transporting audiences to another world.

For me, this show seemed to have an odd gravitational pull. The closer I was to it, the closer I wanted to be. If I was not at *Once on This Island* while we were in New York, I was, by definition, missing out on *Once on This Island*. On this trip, we'd already seen it twice so we couldn't go again even though I wanted to. Instead, we bought tickets to *Wicked* and *Meteor Shower* with Amy Schumer and Keegan-Michael Key. They were both great shows. There is probably no better ending to an Act 1 on Broadway than that of *Wicked's* "Defying Gravity." *Meteor Shower*, written by Steve Martin, had us rolling in our seats with laughter. But sitting in the theater watching each of them, I had an urge to be back in the Circle in the Square experiencing *Once on This Island* again. Waiting the three weeks until Christmas break when we were bringing Jessica to the island for the first time seemed like forever.

On a side note, *Meteor Shower* was maybe our second bad parenting moment of the weekend. Amy Schumer probably isn't considered a kid-friendly comedian. Most comedians aren't, for that matter, and this show tipped the scale of appropriateness a few times. We did, however, know what we were getting into when we purchased the tickets. Honestly, we've never felt the need to shelter our kids from the rawness of life. Sometimes, seeing things that pushed the boundaries a bit are great ways to open discussions on difficult topics. Plus, Ryan wasn't even that young anymore. He was a teenager with two older sisters, though he hadn't hit his growth spurt yet, so he looked more like an average ten year-old. He pretty much knew all the stuff we would want to shelter him from anyway, but the looks we got were about as hilarious as the show.

The three of us sat in the front row. Amy Schumer came out and immediately looked directly at Kathy, Ryan, and me. Of course I don't know what she was actually thinking, but I swear I detected a split second cringe that seemed to say, *"Wow, these are the worst parents ever for bringing their kid to this show!"*

A different time, comedian Mike Birbiglia actually did say that in the middle of his show, *The New One*, at the Cherry Lane Theater in West Village. He paused in the middle of his monologue, looked right at Ryan, and said, "You know you have the worst parents ever for bringing you here, right?"

Ryan happily played along, and the crowd, including us, burst into laughter. We're used to it, and we don't really care. Every time we've taken Ryan to *The Book of Mormon*, we get disapproving stares. The first time had been on his tenth birthday. Granted, he probably looked more like eight, but he's always been mature for his age. He practically fell out of his seat laughing that night. He absolutely loved it. It is still one of his favorites. As we walked out of the theater that night, we heard at least two women commenting loudly enough to make sure we heard, "Oh, my, did you see that? That kid has to be like seven! Just terrible." They shook their heads in disgust, confident we were headed straight for Hell. For us, it only added to the humor of the night.

December 26, 2017
New York, New York

KATHY

We returned over Christmas Break, excited for Jessica to experience the show. Unfortunately, the second day we were in New York, she fell ill. We were actually in an Uber heading back to the hotel after seeing a magic show, and she turned to me with a look of panic and whispered, "Mom, I think I'm going to puke."

I looked around. There were no plastic bags or anything. We

asked the driver if he could roll the back window down. "Just try to breathe in the fresh air," I said, hoping that would ease her nausea.

But there was no holding it back. She stuck her head out the window and vomited. When you're traveling with kids, even if they're in their twenties, it's always an adventure. You never quite know what you're going to get. Luckily, we were only a couple blocks from the hotel, and we asked the driver to drop us off at the next corner. He was incredibly kind about the situation and handed me a water bottle and some tissues to give to her.

"I'm so sorry," Jessica said.

"Oh my god, don't even worry about it. I have kids too. At least it's all on the outside of the car!" he joked. "I'll take it to the car wash, and no problem. I just hope you feel better for the rest of your trip."

"Thank you so much," I said.

"So sorry," Jessica repeated as we got out of the car.

I wiped off the outside of the door as much as I could before he pulled back into traffic.

We hear so many instances about people not treating each other with empathy and compassion, but this warm-hearted driver simply did for us what he would have wanted someone to do for him, and I was grateful for his kindness.

We didn't have anything else scheduled that night so we hoped that with a good night's rest, she would be cured by morning.

Jessica woke up feeling a little better, but by the afternoon, her skin took on a pale-green pallor. Ken Davenport had invited us to an informal dinner at the Circle in the Square Theater with the company of *Once on This Island* in between the matinee and evening shows. Jessica didn't feel like going anywhere and especially not to eat. I hated to leave her sick in the hotel while we went out and had fun, but she insisted.

Maybe if she slept now, she could at least make it to the show later. Her heart was set on seeing Merle Dandridge as Papa Ge.

It was a two-show day for the cast, so for a late lunch, the staff had set up a simple little buffet in the theater lobby, and everyone grabbed a plate and sat on the floor in little groups. It wasn't really a party, more like an indoor picnic. I think we were the only people there who weren't part of the cast or crew, but it was nice to be included in this little family. Jesse, Ryan, and I found a spot on the floor far enough from the different pockets of cast members to allow them privacy but not too far to look like we were trying to be anti-social. It was fun to see them all laughing and interacting together, to have this little window into the life of a Broadway actor/actress, to see them off stage and not just as performers.

"Oh, there's Ken," Jesse said.

I looked up from my plate. The first thing I noticed was his smile, big and genuine. Ken, a dark-haired man who looked to be about our age, saw Jesse and started walking over.

"And see Ryan, he's wearing a sweater and looks really stylish in it," Jesse added.

Jesse had been trying to convince Ryan for several weeks to mix things up and wear nice sweaters to school instead of wearing band t-shirts and hoodies all the time. It was a great way to get girls' attention, Jesse had told him.

Ryan adamantly disagreed, saying that only old people wore sweaters.

Ken had heard Jesse's praising of his sweater, and as he sat down on the floor to eat with us, he said, "Why, thank you."

Ryan raised an eyebrow. "Exactly my point, Dad," he quipped. "It does look nice on *him*."

Jesse, of course, had to explain what had just occurred.

Ken laughed. "I'm so glad you guys could make it, today. What do you think of the show?" he asked Ryan.

"It's amazing," Ryan answered. "I love how close the audience is to the stage."

Ken smiled. "The odds are pretty good that we'll be nominated for a Tony Award."

"Really?" I asked, trying to unsuccessfully scoop a bite of salad into my mouth. It slipped off the plastic spork and clumsily tumbled back onto the plate except for one stray piece of lettuce which I watched fall in slow motion, bounce off the plate, and plop onto the floor beside me. My cheeks flushed with heat, and I quickly picked it up, hoping no one noticed.

"Wow, that would be incredible," Jesse added.

Ken leaned into the little circle the four of us made on the lobby's carpeted floor and explained that only two other revivals were slated to open for this Tony's season. Up to three could be nominated. "We even have a chance of winning."

My brain could not fully comprehend that statement. *Once on This Island*—Tony Award...winner? I was thrilled to think that this one-of-a-kind musical with its incredible cast and creators could win the top honors. It certainly deserved it as far as I was concerned. The notion that *we* would then be Tony Award winners didn't sink in. That was simply ridiculous.

We talked about who might win the original musical category.

"*The Band's Visit* will be a favorite," Ken predicted.

"Are you and your wife ready for your exciting new arrival?" Jesse asked.

Ken's face took on a new glow at the mention of the impending birth of his and his wife Tracy's first child.

"It's a girl." He beamed.

How strange that this part of our lives was coming to a close while others were just beginning this adventure.

"Uh, oh. Be careful," Jesse said. "She'll have you wrapped around her little finger in no time."

"Yes, I'm sure she will." Ken turned to Ryan. "How's your band going, Ryan?"

"It's been great! We've actually been asked to play at one of the biggest motorcycle rallies in the country. Thousands of bikers come to Sandusky, Ohio every year."

"That's wonderful! You know we're always looking for child musicians to audition for certain parts on Broadway. If you're interested, I could put you in touch with the casting director for the *School of Rock Musical*."

In addition to Davenport Theatricals, Ken was also the executive producer of the North American branch of Andrew Lloyd Webber's Really Useful Group, which produces the *School of Rock Musical*. He explained that the kids cast for that show have to be under a certain height to look the right age so the turnover is pretty high.

What an opportunity! I looked at Ryan trying to convey without words that he should say, "Oh, thank you. Yes! I would love to do that!" Not because I wanted him to be on Broadway but because I believed in him and his ability. I wanted him to take risks and go for things when they presented themselves even if he didn't make it, probably because there were a couple of things I wish I had tried.

Instead, Ryan smiled and graciously said, "Oh, wow. Thank you. I'll think about it."

Something in the way he stiffened ever so slightly, something only a mom would notice, made me guess that inside he was thinking, *oh, no. Mom and Dad will want me to do this.*

Ken turned to his left a bit to get the attention of a guy sitting nearby. He introduced us, "This is Hidayat Honari. He's the guitarist for *Once on This Island*."

Learning that there were many options to utilize his musical abilities was eye-opening. Ryan's first love is playing in his band, Fake ID, which he founded with the friends he met while at the actual School of Rock, the music school not the musical, but it was always good to know there were other avenues available.

After we finished dinner, we headed back to the hotel. On the way, Ryan said, "It would be really cool to play guitar on Broadway, but I can't sing or dance."

I hoped maybe he would change his mind and at least try out. That's always a good experience. But after being a parent for twenty-one years I also knew it had to be his decision.

Back in our hotel room, Jessica had tried to eat a few pretzels, but she couldn't keep them down. Despite how badly she wanted to see *Once on This Island*, she realized she couldn't go. She had to stay back and rest while we went to the show. The whole reason we'd planned this trip was so she could see it over her college break. We had no idea when we would be able to bring her back. I felt guilty going to see it without her, but there wasn't anything we could do.

"Mom, it's okay. You go. I'll just be sleeping anyway," she said, trying to make me feel better about leaving her. I hoped there would be another chance for her to see it.

Jesse, Ryan, and I made the quick walk back to the theater and sat down in the front row near where we had sat at the last preview, with our feet in the sand. Unfortunately, I had chosen to wear my boots instead of my heeled sandals. It would have been much better to feel the sand with my toes. I made a mental note to choose the sandals next time.

Scanning the island for things I may have missed before, I noticed a spoon and a little metal box protruding from the sand. They looked like items swept up in the storm's fury. It was brilliant! These pieces of "debris" were the same items that, during the show, Cassondra James picks up and uses as a percussion instrument while sitting in the sand directly in front of our feet. I searched for other hidden "instruments." The long piece of plastic tubing and an old metal bucket lay inconspicuously in the flotsam, waiting to add their sounds to the voice of the island.

Inside the tire that was partially buried in the sand near me was a hidden speaker or monitor—I didn't know which. Somewhere online, we had watched an interview with the cast and creators in which they mentioned how difficult it was to coordinate sounds in a round theater because some notes would get lost while others were too prominent. There were spots on the island that a cast member could be singing from and not be able to hear the other people they were singing with. How did they make it sound so good? Hidden monitors all over the theater helped. I looked for others, but I couldn't find more than that one, and I pointed it out to Ryan.

"Oh, yeah. Of course, Mom. I noticed that the first time."

Jesse, not wanting Jessica's empty seat to remain unused, turned around and talked to the lady sitting alone behind him. "Our daughter couldn't make it, and we would hate to have her seat go to waste. Would you like to use it?" he asked.

She happily accepted.

The pre-show began. David Jennings, who on Opening Night wanted to trade his sandals for Ryan's shoes, came over and said "Hey, I remember you! Welcome back to the island!"

We were starting to get a reputation.

Because this was our third time on the island, we noticed more and experienced even deeper levels of the production. We made sure to look for the pieces of garbage on the sand that later turned into parts of the gods' costumes—the Coke cans that become Papa Ge's spinal plates, the plastic bags that reappear as Agwe's beard, and the stethoscope that becomes Erzulie's belt. We spotted the old car doors and windshield that transform into Daniel's car, and we watched closely for when and how the switch of Daniel to Papa Ge takes place. I don't want to give all the magic away, but the rest of the cast creates a loud and chaotic distraction during the song "Pray," taking the audience's attention away from the swap.

"Mom, did you see it?" Ryan nudged my elbow and whispered, thrilled when he figured that part out.

When it was over, all I could think about was *when are we coming back?* It had a mystical hold on my heart. I had to see it again.

Almost every month for the next few months, we found reasons to head back to New York. Every time, we bought tickets to *Once on This Island,* usually the same seats if they were available. Yes, we bought tickets. As co-producers, we could have picked up "house seats," generally premium seats you can buy at standard prices, but because we wanted to sit in a specific location, we bought our tickets like everyone else.

The Circle in the Square Theater is an intimate venue with every seat in close proximity to the stage, but when sitting in the sand, there is a sort of divine connection between actor and audience. It is as if they are speaking only to you. You're so close you can see teardrops roll down their cheeks then drop and disappear into the sand.

We sat on the other side of the theater a few times, in the sand near the fallen telephone pole, but we liked our original side the best so we began calling it "our side."

We have a friend, Johnathan, who, like us, was drawn to the island like a gull to the sea. He wanted to experience it from as many different seats and angles as he could. What differences would stand out from another point of view? He saw it seven times in total. His friends started to wonder if he was okay. Luckily, our friends had no idea how many times we had seen it. In each new seat, Johnathan noticed both visual and auditory nuances that were hidden when viewed from a different perspective. When he was done, he concluded there was no "best" angle to see it from and wrote a blog post about his experience. He did, however, have a favorite area—section 102-146. In his post, Jonathan describes a lighting effect seen from this view during the "Sad Tale of the Beauxhommes" scene that creates a silhouette of the cast, highlighting the classicism and colorism of the island's history.

We went back so many times to the exact same seats I thought the cast might suspect we were some kind of weird Broadway stalkers. In a way, we kind of were, though I prefer "super-fans" to "stalkers."

David Jennings seemed to be the only one to recognize us, and he always gave us a hearty welcome to the Island.

We weren't totally crazy. Well, maybe we were, but being a little crazy is okay sometimes.

One trip back to the city, we brought my parents with us. My mom hadn't been to New York City in fifty years, and she was thrilled with the opportunity to dress up and be taken out on the town. We took her and my dad all over the city. We walked Central Park, saw Grand Central Station, shopped at Macy's, and took them to an opera at the Met and, of course, to see *Once on This Island*. I'm so thankful we brought them when we did. Because of my dad's advancing Parkinson's disease and dementia, this was the last big trip they took with us before becoming essentially home-bound.

My father, so full of life when I was growing up, who played hockey until he was seventy-five, who managed the State of Michigan's pension funds, who got his black belt in Shorin-Ryu style karate when he was fifty, could not remember how to tie his shoes. His days were filled with difficulty speaking, confusion, and hallucinations. He was constantly tripping and falling, walking at a snail's pace, and sitting in chairs that weren't underneath him. One day, he asked me to write on a note card the steps to using the toilet because he had forgotten. Yet all his doctors told us he was physically fine, and he could live another ten years. It was his brain that had lost its ability to process information and was getting signals crossed. It was heart-breaking to watch.

At the time we brought them, he was only beginning to exhibit some strange behavior, though I was a little concerned that he might get up in the middle of the performance and try to cross the sand. Thankfully, he sat quietly in his seat beside my mom, holding her hand, and watched the entire show. I don't know how much of it he understood, but when it was over, his only words were, "Too sad for me."

My mom wiped the tears from her face. "That was one of the most beautiful shows I've ever seen."

In the spring of 2018, Alyssa and her boyfriend, Shakib, traveled with us, which gave Jesse, Ryan, and me another excuse to see it without seeming insane. On that trip, we were also able to set up a special meet-and-greet through a program called Audience Rewards, a loyalty program for theater ticket buyers. Theater-goers earn points by seeing shows, and you can use those points for special experiences. Our favorite is the meet-and-greet where you can meet a cast member of the show you're about to see followed by a backstage tour. Of course we chose to meet someone from *Once on This Island*.

Alyssa and Shakib had already planned something else for before the show so Jesse, Ryan, and I met the Audience Rewards representative, Victoria Weinberg, at Sardi's. Open since 1927, Sardi's is a well-known restaurant in the theater district and is famous for its more than 1,300 caricatures of show business celebrities that hang on the walls.

This was our second time doing one of these meet-and-greets. We did our first one the previous summer before seeing *Natasha, Pierre and The Great Comet of 1912* starring Josh Groban in his Broadway debuting role. That night was his final performance in the show. *The Great Comet* was a musical adaptation of a section of Leo Tolstoy's *War and Peace*. The stage had been set like an opulent Russian tea room, complete with cabaret-style tables on stage for lucky audience members who don't mind being part of the action. That was the day we first met Victoria, who had introduced us to Nick Gaswirth, one of the ensemble's cast members.

Just like that first time, we met Victoria upstairs at Sardi's. As soon as she saw us, she exclaimed, "McKendrys! How are you?" She hugged each of us like we'd known each other for years, and yet it was only the second time we had ever seen her.

We sat down and caught up with her. After a few minutes, Cassondra James, one of the Storytellers from *Once on This Island,* walked in.

She sat down, and Victoria introduced us and helped get the conversation flowing. Victoria was present as a facilitator to make sure the meeting went smoothly, to ask questions if things got silent or awkward, and probably to make sure whomever signs up for the event was respectful to the actor/actress.

"What were you doing prior to working on this show?" Victoria asked.

Cassondra told us that before coming to *Once on This Island,* she had performed around the world with many different artists including Christina Aguilera, Alicia Keys, and Gladys Knight. I was thinking, *Oh my gosh, what?*

But Jesse calmly asked, "So how did you come to the Island?"

"One of my friends told me about the audition and encouraged me to try, so I went, and I got the part!"

She made it sound so simple to make your Broadway debut. Of course it helps if you're clearly overflowing with talent like Cassondra. In addition to being a *Once on This Island* cast member who also plays the flute in the show, she was attending graduate school, working toward her PhD in sociology. How on earth was she able to perform eight shows a week plus extra rehearsals and still manage to go to school for her doctorate degree? Some weeks, I feel like I hardly have time to think, and I only coach figure skating part-time.

Where does all my time go? What more could I do if I put my mind to it?

Ryan had been sitting quietly and mostly listening, commenting when he had something to add. At thirteen, he could have been paying more attention to his phone, but he wasn't. He was engaged in the conversation.

Cassondra turned to him and asked, "What do you like to do? Are you in theater or music?"

"I play guitar in a band." His eyes lit up as he said it.

"Really? Do you have an Instagram?" she asked.

"Yeah."

She and Victoria immediately followed his band's account.

We couldn't talk too long because Cassondra had to be at the theater to get ready for the show.

"We'll meet afterward in the theater for pictures," Cassondra said.

They both hugged us, and we all headed out. We walked back to the hotel to change and met up with Alyssa and Shakib.

Neither of them had any idea what to expect. We tried to explain that *Once on This Island* was staged with real sand and water, but it really was something you had to see in order to comprehend. Alyssa had heard the original cast album when she was a little girl but didn't remember the story, and Shakib didn't know anything about it. As soon as they stepped into the theater, they gasped.

"Oh my gosh, it actually looks like an island!" Alyssa said.

I smiled.

Jesse and I headed to our usual seats, and Alyssa and Shakib went with Ryan to sit almost directly across from us. Ryan loved hanging out with them, and he wanted to be able to point out things he thought they might miss.

That was our sixth or seventh time seeing it. We were starting to lose track. Each time we saw it, we found a nuance that we'd missed before. It took us several times before Ryan and I figured out when Little Ti Moune changed from her school-girl uniform to her red dress during the storm scene. Jesse never ended up seeing it. We would tell him to watch at a certain time, but his attention was always focused elsewhere until it was too late.

"I missed it again!" he would say after every show.

Normally, we don't rewatch the same movies or TV shows over and over again, but every moment in this theater was just as special as the first time, and it would always be a part of us.

It had only been a month since we'd last seen it, but we already missed it, and on that night, we were eager to watch Alyssa's and Shakib's expressions as they experienced the show. That was another unique aspect of this production. Because it was staged in the round, you could clearly see the reactions of the people seated across from you or in any of the front-row seats around the stage. Their laughs and tears were visible to everyone else in the theater. It could either add to the energy or sometimes take away from it, like the night I spotted a guy falling asleep in the front row. I couldn't imagine how anyone could be sleeping, but maybe he'd had a rough day. Who knows?

During the pre-show, Cassondra came out and immediately acknowledged Ryan. She pointed him out to David and another cast member. "I know him. He's a rock star."

David answered, "Oh, yes, he's been here before many times!" He was a little confused though and asked, "Did you come alone?"

Ryan pointed across the sand to where we sat, and David waved.

The theater darkened, and this show that we had seen multiple times began yet again. It was like we were visiting old friends. I looked at Jesse and squeezed his hand.

On the Island, Tonton and Mama pleaded with Ti Moune to stay, but now, all that my eyes could see were Alyssa, Shakib, and Ryan.

The three of them reminded me of Jesse, me, and my little brother Dave years ago. Where had the time gone? Now, both of my brothers had families of their own, and though we maintained an emotional closeness, we all lived in different states, and we were lucky if we saw them twice a year. As a little kid, I couldn't imagine *ever* not being near them and had envisioned a future where we all lived on a giant plot of land with four houses on each corner, one for me and my future family and the other three for my parents and my two brothers' families. In reality, my closest brother lived five hours away. I missed them dearly and hoped my kids in the future would be able to stay close to one another in proximity and emotionally.

As the show continued in front of us, I watched as Ryan pointed out important details during key scenes for Alyssa and Shakib to pay attention to. Their stunned reactions were priceless.

After the show, the three of them walked over to join us.

"That was amazing!" Alyssa exclaimed, tears still staining her cheeks.

Shakib echoed her sentiment. "I've never seen anything like that," he said, smiling.

The five of us sat back down in our seats and waited for Cassondra to come out.

There was a group of people waiting in the theater behind us as well, and then a couple of the cast members walked back out into the sand and sat down on chairs they had brought out.

Out of the blue, the strikingly muscular cast member who slams the trailer door open and does pull-ups in the pre-show looked at Jesse and asked, "Who *are* you guys? I've seen you here a lot, haven't I?"

"Oh, we're just really big fans of the show," Jesse said quickly so he didn't hold up the talk-back that was just about to start. A talk-back is a question and answer session for any of the audience members who want to stay after the show and ask questions of the cast. This particular talk-back, we learned later, had been set up privately for a group from Alabama.

Victoria walked down the theater steps and sat behind us. Cassondra joined us, and we introduced her to Alyssa and her boyfriend. She said she wouldn't be able to take us on the backstage tour tonight, but she wanted to get a picture with us, and since we would miss the tour, we could come back in and stay for the rest of the talk-back if we wanted to. Of course we wanted to! We never got tired of watching or hearing about the show.

We followed Victoria and Cassondra out of the theater into the lower lobby and took some pictures in front of the *Once on This Island* backdrop. We thanked both of them again and said our goodbyes. Then, we headed back in to listen to the talk-back and quietly slipped into some seats in one of the middle rows.

After it was over, we hung around in the theater for a few minutes, talking and waiting for the other group to leave.

The actor in the New York Knicks jersey who'd spoken to Jesse earlier bounded up the stairs toward us. He was perfectly chiseled like an African God from the darkest brown onyx, his bulging biceps popping out of his sleeveless shirt. Even more stunning than his physical presence was that he positively glowed with a lightness of spirit, and he had this huge ear to ear smile on his face.

"I have to shake your hand. I'm Rodrick Covington." He reached out to Jesse.

"I'm Jesse," he answered, shaking his hand.

"How many times have you seen the show?"

"Six for us," Ryan said, gesturing to me and himself, "and seven for him." He pointed to Jesse.

"Wow! Where do you guys live?" he asked.

"Ohio!" Ryan said.

"Whaaaaat?" he asked in a high-pitched, almost scream.

"Thank you!" He put his hands over his heart. "Thank you so much for supporting us. Every time you come, I watch this guy's face." He gestured to Ryan. "He's into it every time! It's incredible." He shook all of our hands then added, "You have such a beautiful family. When are you coming next?"

"We'll be back in May," I said.

"Thank you. Thank you. See you in May then," he said gratefully. "Thank you for coming." He put his hands to his heart again.

How had he noticed us? Sure, we sat in almost the same seats every time, but the cast sees over five thousand people every week in the audience, not to mention the millions of faces he must encounter every day on the streets of New York. He was actually *seeing* people. The audience wasn't just a faceless blob of humanity somewhere in the background.

Meeting Cassondra and Rodrick made our night, but we still had one more show to go to. Jesse told me he had arranged a surprise, but he hadn't told anyone what we were seeing, not even me.

He always had a habit of surprising us. Sometimes, it was as simple as telling the kids to go grab all the blankets and pillows in the house so we could make a fort in the living room. Or it could be a big surprise, like when we had traveled with Jesse to Chicago for business, and then afterward, we told the girls we were driving home to Michigan, where we lived at the time, but instead, we drove all the way to meet my parents at Disney World in Florida. Of course, I knew about that surprise. We told them it was our "magic Jeep" that did it. They were thrilled, but for years, they wondered why our "magic Jeep" didn't surprise them again.

This time, though, I had no idea where we were going. Even though we've been to New York several times now, I still get turned around. I'm not one of those people who has a map inside my head, I could easily get lost in Cleveland, and we've lived there for twelve years now. So as Jesse led us to our next destination, I remained clueless. Alyssa and Shakib were getting tired. They mentioned that maybe they would just go back to the hotel for the night.

"You have to eat dinner anyway. Just come with us," I said, hoping I could convince them. Grudgingly, they decided to come along.

Soon, we arrived at Feinstein's 54 Below, a swanky supper club on W. 54th Street just a short walk away, and were seated in one of the bigger booths in the back so all five of us could fit. I recognized Keith Cromwell, whom we had met at the opening, almost immediately. His theater program, Red Mountain Theater Company in Birmingham, Alabama was performing tonight. He saw Jesse and came over to our table to say, "Hi."

Then, it hit me. I looked at Jesse. I think my mouth was hanging open in surprise. "Oh my God, is Jordan Fisher performing here tonight?"

"Wait, what?" Alyssa heard me and almost shrieked, "Jordan Fisher is here?"

Jesse nodded.

She almost jumped out of the booth. "EEEEEEEE!" she let out a quiet squeal. She was about to see Jordan Fisher perform live, up close and personal.

Shakib wasn't quite as thrilled. Not that he didn't like Jordan Fisher. He did. He was excited to see him, but he wasn't thrilled at how much Alyssa liked him! Ah, young love.

Ryan was about as excited to see him again as Alyssa was. It had meant a lot to Ryan that Jordan had taken so much time to talk and get to know him on Opening Night.

This supper club show was a wonderful opportunity for the students from Red Mountain to show off the skills they'd acquired to a New York audience. They also had the good fortune to perform on stage with stars like Jenn Colella from *Come from Away* and Jordan Fisher, two of the celebrity guest performers that evening. They sang songs from *Hamilton, Rent,* and a number of other musicals. It was a wonderful night of musical theater.

After the show, we had a chance to talk to Jordan again briefly. He remembered Ryan right away, which of course totally made his night, and Alyssa was over the moon that she got a picture with him.

Once on This Island kept connecting us with the Broadway community in unexpected and wonderful ways.

"GOSSIP"

April 2018
Cleveland, Ohio

*J*ESSE

A few weeks later, around the beginning of April, we were back home in Cleveland when Kathy got a phone call. It was Alyssa calling from college.

"Mom, you're never going to believe this." Her words came quickly. "I dreamed that *Once on This Island* won the Tony Award!"

Kathy laughed. "That would be amazing!"

"What if it really does win? Would Dad be a Tony Award winner?" Alyssa asked.

"Well, yes, if that actually happened, he would be."

It was possible, but the Tony nominations hadn't even come out yet. As a revival production, it would be competing only against the two other revivals for the Best Musical Revival category, not the full array of brand new musicals. Ken had mentioned that the Tony committee can choose three revivals for nomination. For this Tony season, the revivals were *My Fair Lady, Carousel,* and *Once on This Island.* It would most likely get nominated for Best Musical Revival. Winning was much more difficult, so we put it in the back of our minds.

There was plenty of fun and excitement traveling back and forth to New York, and other opportunities came up that we needed to consider. Ken proposed a couple new projects that our original investment opened up that he felt we might be interested in. As an investor or co-producer, you have the right to participate in other forms of the show, like national tours, cast albums, and movies, which can generate additional returns. Revivals, however, are more limited than original productions because the producers and investors of the original version still own the rights and get first right of refusal, meaning if they decide not to participate, it allows other people down the line an opportunity. Ken offered us the chance to help fund the production of the *Once on This Island* cast album, which, of course, meant putting in more money.

Again, Kathy and I talked over the pros and cons. We hadn't received much money back from *Once on This Island* yet, but at least so far, tickets seemed to be selling pretty well.

We decided to invest in the cast album. In our hearts, we wanted to do everything we could to spread the love and joy of *Once on This Island* as far as we could, and it seemed like this would be the go-to album for the next twenty years or so until someone else decided to do another revival.

May, 2018
Cleveland, Ohio

*J*ESSE
We were getting ready to head back to New York in the beginning of May when the Tony Award nominations came out. *Once on This Island* was nominated for eight Tony Awards!

*B*est Revival of a Musical
Best Lead Actress: Hailey Kilgore
Best Direction: Michael Arden
Best Costume Design: Clint Ramos
Scenic Design: Dane Laffrey
Orchestrations: AnneMarie Milazzo and Michael Starobin
Lighting Design: Jules Fisher and Peggy Eisenhauer
Sound Design: Peter Hylenski

*A*s soon as we heard the news, we jumped up off the couch and did a mini-celebration dance. Since we have absolutely no dance training, it probably looked more like some strange exotic bird courtship-dance than anything humans should do.

Then, Kathy asked, "Wait, it wasn't nominated for Best Choreography?"

"No, it wasn't."

"Why not?" she asked. "The choreography is amazing!"

Of course, neither of us knew anything about how "Best Choreography" is chosen, but she was slightly outraged that Camille A. Brown wasn't one of those nominated.

That evening, I received an email from Ken congratulating *me* on being a Tony-nominated producer.

The two other revivals, *Carousel,* which opened April twelfth, and *My Fair Lady,* which opened April nineteenth, were also nominated. The early talk around town was that *Once on This Island* had a good chance, but these classic musicals might resonate with the older Tony voters, which included members of the Broadway League, certain theatrical union members, and others intimately involved in theater. Some of the websites with early predictions had *Once on This Island* on top; some said *Carousel;* some said *My Fair Lady.* I put it out of my mind and relished the fact that our show had been nominated for eight Tony Awards.

All of these nominations brought up an interesting question. Would we go to the Tony Awards in June? Could we? Was that a silly idea?

"How does that even work?" Kathy asked. "Do they give us tickets, or do we pay for them? And if so, how much are they? And, oh my gosh," she added excitedly, "what on earth does one wear to the TONY AWARDS?"

"I have no idea, but I'm sure we're going to find out!" I said.

Pretty soon, I heard from Ken's office. Yes, we could go to the Tony Awards at Radio City Music Hall on June tenth, 2018. Yes, we would have to pay for the tickets. As I expected, the tickets were not cheap, but being in June, Ryan would be out of school, so the timing would work.

I was at work when I got the email. I called Kathy right away. "So what do you want to do about the Tony Awards?"

"Can we get three tickets? Or are we only allowed a certain number?"

"Yeah, we can get three," I replied.

"Well, I think it would be fun," she said. "If we don't go for *Once on This Island,* we would never have another reason to go." She paused. "And what if we win?"

I could hear the joy in her voice.

"But I'm fine either way," she added.

I thought for a moment. "You're right. It would never mean as much as it does now. Okay," I said, already excited about going. "I don't think we can pass this up, and in the off chance that we actually win, I would regret missing it."

We hung up, and I looked at the available seats. There were three areas of seating reserved for the producers of *Once on This Island,* all with different price points. We could either choose the cheaper seats higher up in the balcony, or we could be on the main floor, which was considerably more expensive.

Then, there was the after-party at the Plaza Hotel. On a previous trip to NYC, we had gone into the Plaza on a cold wintry day after walking around Central Park with all three kids. We thought we might stop in to have a hot cup of tea or hot chocolate in the lobby restaurant. The hostess quickly assessed the five of us, scrunched up her nose, and asked if we'd like to see the menu before we were seated. Hmmm, that was a little odd. I took the menu and scanned it. Seventy dollars for a cup of tea and some light snacks per person...well, maybe not. I guess she'd judged us correctly after all.

But now, we had a chance to be at the Plaza Hotel for a private party. I called Kathy again. She answered the phone while she was outside gardening, the birds chirping in the background around her.

"Do you want to go to the after-party at the Plaza Hotel?" I asked.

"The Plaza? Does it cost more?" Kathy asked.

"Yes, quite a bit more," I answered.

I heard her sigh dreamily. "But when will we ever go to the Plaza again?" she asked.

I knew she wanted to go. I could picture her standing in the garden with her ripped jeans and a t-shirt on, planting flowers and getting dirt all over herself, dreaming of going to a party at

The Plaza. This would be our second chance in a year to be Cinderella at the ball.

"Okay, we'll splurge and go."

It began to dawn on me that just like buying a house, the upfront cost of a Broadway investment is only the beginning. Then, there's the cost of being in NYC, buying show tickets, and if, in the very slim chance your show gets nominated for a Tony, you can't pass that up or the lavish after-party. All the downstream expenses that pile on seem to never end, like the constant expenses of keeping up a home. Of course, spending money on show tickets and seats at the Tonys is a lot more fun than getting your moss-covered roof replaced.

There was one more question. "We still have to decide where we're sitting at the Tonys."

"Oh, okay. We probably don't want to be too far, just in case…" she said.

I'm not normally the one to let my imagination take over, but as soon as she said that, an unpleasant scenario popped into my head of us saving money and sitting way up in the balcony. The Best Musical Revival Award is about to be announced. They open the envelope and call out the winner: *Once on This Island*. I jump up and start to run for the stage, but everyone else is on the main floor and almost there. I call out in a weak despondent voice, "Hey, wait for me," but no one hears, and by the time I get to the stage, they have all been sent off, and the next category is being announced. I miss the whole thing.

Nope. If we're going to do this, we might as well go all the way.

"We'll sit on the main floor then and go to the Plaza for the after-party," I said. We couldn't go to the Tonys and the after-party and not sit on the main floor.

"EEEEEE! Oh my gosh, I'm so excited!" she squealed.

Hopefully, we would never be nominated for another Tony Award because we couldn't afford it.

J ESSE

*I*t seemed like it had been forever since we had been to Circle in the Square, though it had been only about a month. Especially after the nomination announcements, we could hardly wait to finally be heading back to the Island. Even if we hadn't been investors or co-producers, it would have been our favorite show on Broadway. On days we didn't have tickets, we often found ourselves walking past the theater to watch the lottery and join in on the cheering for those who won cheap tickets. Sometimes, we walked by just to be near it. Occasionally, we would "happen" to walk past when the cast was coming out for autographs after the show. We stood in the back of the crowd with ear-to-ear grins and added our applause to the general celebration for the cast as they appeared.

More than a couple times, Ryan said, "Dad, I love the show, too, but can't we go get dinner now? I'm hungry."

Each time, I found it difficult to tear myself away. It was like we were proud parents. We glowed with the joy of seeing our child do amazing things. Eventually, we would listen to our actual child and go find Ryan some dinner.

On days that we went to the show, we stood outside afterward and waited until the entire cast had left. As each cast member came out of the stage door, we screamed and hollered.

We didn't need autographs or pictures. We just wanted to stand there, to be a part of the incredible energy, and to show our love and appreciation for our favorite cast on Broadway.

Every once in a while, David, Kenita, or Cassondra, would exit from a different door, see us standing there, come over, and chat with us for a few minutes. The two little Ti Mounes usually waved to us shyly as they were whisked away from the crowds.

One time, I was standing out there by myself because I was in New York for business, and Kathy and Ryan had stayed home. The little Ti Mounes came out, saw me, waved, and said, "Hi."

The lady whose job it was to care for the girls while at the theater looked at me suspiciously and quickly ushered them away. In the distance, I heard one of them say, "Oh, we know him. He's okay. We met him on Opening Night."

One of my favorite things to do after a show was to listen to people as they exited the theater, raving about what they'd just experienced.

"That was the best production I've ever seen! I'd never even heard about this show!" one older man exclaimed.

One woman left the theater saying, "Why have I not heard more about this? That was incredible!"

A teenage girl came out exclaiming, "That was amazing! Everyone needs to see this!"

I never heard anyone leaving the theater who didn't love it. Maybe that one guy Kathy caught sleeping in the front row didn't like it, but from what we saw, he was an exception.

This performance tonight would be the last time we could see it before the Tony Awards. We sat in our usual seats. While we waited for the pre-show to begin, a man with salt-and-pepper hair caught our eye across the Island from us. He was one of those people that you notice when they enter a room. He was dressed in a trendy, expensive-looking suit. I knew I'd seen him before, maybe at the Opening or the dress rehearsal, I couldn't quite remember. Tonight, it looked like he had brought a large group of people to see this performance. I suspected he was a producer as well, but we hadn't had the chance to meet. If we happened to see him in the lobby afterward, I would introduce myself, but now it was time for the show.

The whole cast was energized by the recent Tony nominations, and they were extra interactive. Cassondra, usually one of the first to come out, saw us. Never breaking character, she said in her island accent, "Hello, my friends!"

Rodrick did his usual set of pull-ups on the scaffolding bar that attached to the tractor trailer and then walked out into the sand. As soon as he saw Ryan, he squealed at Kenita. "Ahhh, this kid is my favorite!" He came over and literally jumped into Ryan's lap! Ryan burst out laughing.

Then, David came over and said, "Welcome back. I'm so happy to see you!"

Kenita brought her chicken over for Ryan to pet. I think the whole cast was giddy with the hopes of what was to come.

Even the crowd was more lively than usual. It's funny. Sometimes when we went, the audience was subdued, and other days, the audience was energetic and engaged, at times jumping up and giving Alex a mini standing ovation after "Mama Will Provide." I'm not sure what made the difference. I never tracked whether it depended on the day of the week and if it was a matinee or late show so I have no idea if those variables made any difference or if it was simply the personalities and energy of the people in the audience. This evening, I could feel the excitement in the air. Every song ended with a roar of applause.

We didn't want to leave New York the next day. We wanted to stay in the city and wrap ourselves in the love everyone was feeling for *Once on This Island*, but our time was up. By the following afternoon, we were back in Cleveland again.

It was always a little strange to come home after being in New York. Cleveland was home and had been for eleven years.

We had our friends, our work, and our normal lives back in Cleveland. Now all of a sudden, we were leading this second secret life in New York City that no one at home knew about. It was exciting and a bit bizarre.

It was also beginning to get more complicated. We had so much to arrange and do before going to the Tony Awards. First, Ryan and I had to find and get measured for our tuxedos.

We found a tuxedo rental place not too far from our home and went to check it out. An older lady behind the counter came over and measured us. She asked what we were getting them for.

"We're going to the Tony Awards!" I replied.

"How exciting! Are there any celebrities you would like to meet there?" she asked, her eyes gleaming with excitement as if she was coming too.

"I would love to meet Lin-Manuel Miranda," I answered without hesitation.

"Hmmm," was all she said. The sparkle faded from her eyes, and she finished measuring us in silence. I guess the name of *Hamilton's* creator didn't ring a bell.

Meanwhile, Kathy was busy searching for her own formal fashions and worrying about what to do with her hair.

"Just find a salon in New York." I said, "There are plenty around."

"Won't it cost a fortune?"

"We're going to the Tonys. It's okay," I said.

Eventually, she found one near the hotel that she hoped would be good and made an appointment for the big day.

The closer it got to June, the more excited we were, especially after a large envelope from the Drama Desk Awards arrived in the mail. Inside, I found a certificate proclaiming:

"DRAMA DESK NOMINATION

Jesse McKendry
Has Been Nominated In The Category Of Outstanding Revival
Of A Musical For
Once on This Island"

$\mathcal{I}$ reread it and couldn't quite believe that all this was actually happening.

Tonys talk was buzzing by this time. At one point, the *New York Times* made an early prediction that *Once on This Island* would win. All of a sudden, I was very interested in all of the predictions. I hadn't thought too much about it before this. Now, I wanted to study every piece of available data. It seemed like we had an early lead, but as soon as *Carousel* and *My Fair Lady* opened, it was impossible not to notice that *Once on This Island* was talked about less and less. A couple of days later, another site predicted *Carousel* would win the prize, and yet another one concluded the top honor would go to *My Fair Lady*. It seemed like all three revivals were in the conversation. It just depended on whose column you were reading.

There were several other award ceremonies that took place before the Tonys, though, and voting for these awards is seen as an early indicator of how a show would fare on Tonys night. The Outer Critics Circle Awards came first. *Once on This Island* had been nominated for six awards, one of which included Outstanding Choreography. Kathy was happy with that one. The winners were announced on May seventh. To our dismay, *Once on This Island* walked away empty-handed. *My Fair Lady* took Outstanding Revival, Outstanding Actress, and Best Costume Design. It also tied with *SpongeBob* for Outstanding Director. *Carousel* went home with the awards for Outstanding Orchestrations and Outstanding Choreography, all categories for which *Once on This Island* had been nominated.

Next came the Drama League Awards on May eighteenth. *Once on This Island* was nominated in two categories—Best Musical Revival and Distinguished Performance from both Hailey Kilgore and Alex Newell. Again, *Once on This Island* came home with nothing while *My Fair Lady* won Best Musical Revival, and Glenda Jackson from *Three Tall Women* won Distinguished Performance.

The Chita Rivera Awards were coming right up on May twentieth, and I felt certain *Once on This Island* would take at least one of the prestigious dance/choreography awards. The movement throughout the musical deepens the meaning of the story itself. The dancing isn't sugary fluff. It carries the weight of history and cultural oppression.

We had three nominations—Best Female Dancer, Best Choreography, and Best Broadway Ensemble. Somehow, the voters weren't seeing the genius behind what Camille A. Brown and the cast had done, and once again, the other musicals walked away with all the top prizes. Best Female Dancer and Best Choreography both went to the *Donna Summer Musical*. Best Broadway Ensemble went to *Carousel* and *Mean Girls* in a tie.

There was still one more awards ceremony before the Tonys. The Drama Desk Awards were taking place on June third. Maybe we could rebuild some momentum if we took home the big prize of Best Musical Revival here, but it was not to be. At the end of the night, *My Fair Lady* had won Best Musical Revival and Best Costume Design. *Carousel* took Best Choreography, Best Featured Actress, and Best Orchestrations. *SpongeBob* won Best Set Design. All were categories for which *Once on This Island* had been in the running. We did come away with one win that night for Best Lighting Design, which went to Jules Fisher and Peggy Eisenhauer.

Among the revivals, *My Fair Lady* and *Carousel* had swept nearly every award. Just like that, there was no more talk of a

possible Tony win for *Once on This Island*. Our show had
dropped off the radar. All of the critics and Tony prognostica-
tors were writing that the *Band's Visit* would take most of the
categories, and the Best Revival of a Musical category would be
going to *My Fair Lady* or *Carousel*. As far as everyone was
concerned, *Once on This Island* had totally dropped out of
contention.

For me personally, it was a bit of an emotional rollercoaster.
I enjoyed hearing the early talk about the show as it entered the
awards season, and I have to admit that I got caught up in the
excitement of thinking we might win. Reading a blog predicting
our win was like watching the Cleveland Cavaliers score. Then,
I'd read a blog forecasting *My Fair Lady*'s win, and it was like we
were down by two. As the other awards were announced and
the expectation of *Once on This Island* winning a Tony Award
began to fade away, I realized I had started to think of it almost
like winning the NBA Finals. We would either be Tony winners
or losers, but in reality, part of what makes theater special is
that there are no winners and losers. It's not like a basketball
game. Half of the audience at a Broadway show doesn't go home
a loser. With great theater, everyone wins. Everyone can be
moved by a Broadway musical. I could go see *Carousel* and *Once
on This Island* on the same day and fall in love with both of them.
It's much harder to be a fan of the Cleveland Cavaliers and the
Golden State Warriors at the same time.

I'm assuming that this rationale came to my mind as a self-
defense mechanism once it became clear we were not going to
win, but I started to understand that winning or losing a Tony
Award wouldn't change what *Once on This Island* was or what it
meant to us.

The more I pondered why I loved theater in general and
Once on This Island specifically, the more I was okay with the
idea of just being a part of the Tony Awards this year. Actually,
more than okay. I was ecstatic! When we first decided to

support *Once on This Island,* the Tony Awards hadn't even crossed our minds. We just wanted to be a part of our favorite musical. Now, we were going to the Tony Awards to celebrate the beauty of it. No matter what happened, it would be a night to remember.

13

"AND THE GODS HEARD HER PRAYER"

June 10, 2018, Tony Awards Day
New York, New York

KATHY

 opened my eyes and looked at the clock. 8:45 a.m. I turned over. Jesse was already awake reading on his iPad. I put my hand on his arm.

"Good morning, love," I murmured, the wisps of dreams still fogging my brain.

"Good morning." He kissed my forehead.

Outside the window, it was a gray, gloomy day, and rain loomed in the clouds overhead. I tried in vain to close my eyes and go back to sleep, knowing tonight would be a late night. Usually, I don't have a problem hitting my internal snooze button, but today, I was too excited.

Jumping out of bed, I went over and checked on Ryan, who was still sound asleep. Even when they are teenagers, there is nothing quite like watching your child sleep peacefully. They take on an otherworldly angelic quality, which, some days, they shed immediately upon waking. Luckily for us, Ryan had pretty much always been a good-natured kid.

"Let him sleep," Jesse said, "or he'll be exhausted at the after-party."

"Okay," I said, suppressing my urge to wake him.

My brain demanded coffee so I made a cup of the in-room brew for Jesse and myself. It's not quite good coffee, but it's good enough. Reaching in the mini-fridge, I grabbed a yogurt we'd bought at the grocery store the night before. Unlike Jesse, I've never been able to skip breakfast. He's like a snake. He can eat a huge meal and then not eat for a day. I'm more like a hummingbird. I need a little bit of food every couple of hours, and I'm always on the lookout for dark chocolate.

Glancing at the clock, I realized barely twenty minutes had passed. I handed Jesse his coffee. "It's only just after nine!"

"I know." He grimaced as he mindlessly scrolled through sports news stories.

There was nothing to do before my hair appointment, which meant we had a lot of time to kill. At home, I hardly ever sat still. I could read or write for a little bit, but then I had to get up and do something more active. It was especially difficult today. I kept getting up to look out the window or checking to make sure our clothes for the evening were out and ready. It reminded me of waiting for our wedding day. Adrenaline had rushed through my veins, and I hadn't been quite sure what the future would hold.

Jesse opened up the heavy blue envelope with the Tonys tickets, which we had picked up the day before. Inside was a black folder with an "Antoinette Perry Tony Nomination" certificate with Jesse's name on it, three black and silver tickets to the Tony Awards, three silver tickets to the Gala at the Plaza, and a small black and silver magnetic pin, which read, "Tony Nominee 2018."

"Oh my gosh!" My heart fluttered at the reality of it. We were really going to the Tonys today!

Finally, Ryan woke up around eleven-thirty, and it was time to head out. Ryan and Jesse walked me to David Ryan Salon, just a couple of blocks away. It was closer than I anticipated so we got there a little bit early. My stylist hadn't arrived yet, so the person at the counter directed me to a little bench by the window, where I waited. The boys headed out to find a place for a quick breakfast while I was being pampered.

I have to admit I was a little nervous about the appointment. My hair is very long, straight, and boring. It doesn't do much of anything I want it to. A quick, no-fuss tight bun is my go-to style. Other than the fact that I needed an updo, I had no idea what to tell the stylist. The rest could be totally up to him or her. Hopefully, they could work some magic on it.

After about ten minutes, a pretty, petite woman hurried through the front door. The manager at the desk introduced her to me as Soni. We completed all the normal pleasantries that you go through when meeting someone new, and she led me to her chair.

"So what are we doing today?"

"We're going to the Tonys tonight so I need a fancy updo," I explained.

"Do you have a picture of the dress so I can see the neckline?" she asked matter-of-factly.

Luckily, I had thought of that in advance, so the picture was handy. I showed her and without further chit chat, she got right to work.

Back home, I hardly ever get my hair done. If I'm just going to wear it in a bun every day, why spend the money? The one time a year I do go to get a cut, I always go to the same person.

We've known each other for several years. I even taught her daughter figure skating when she was little, so we always have a lot of catching up to do. We chat about our kids and anything new in our lives.

Soni, however, was very quiet. She wasn't being rude or anything, just quiet. At first, I thought maybe it was me because I am more on the shy side when I first meet people. I've always been a much better listener than a talker. But as I watched her work, I sensed she was upset about something. I felt bad. Here I was in my own world, excited about my upcoming evening and oblivious to the world around me, and she was suffering. I didn't know why, maybe it was as simple as a bad day, but something was amiss.

It's funny how when things are going my way, I feel like the world is bright and full of promise, and when I'm having a bad day, the world is blanketed in darkness. The world doesn't actually care what kind of day I'm having. Lots of people have great days and horrible days at the same time, and the day I'm having only makes a difference to me. It's so easy to get consumed by our own story and block out the thousands of stories happening around us all the time.

Not knowing Soni, I didn't want to pry, and maybe I was misreading the situation. Maybe my own shy, awkwardness projected onto her to make me feel less self-conscious. I decided that it couldn't hurt to try to cheer her up somehow. I wracked my brain for how I could get her to smile. Asking questions was always a good start.

"How did you get into being a stylist?" I asked, figuring it was better to keep her talking about her life. At the moment, she didn't need to hear about me.

Gradually, she opened up. She told me how she started out young because she loved talking to people and helping them, and designing hairstyles was kind of like making an artwork.

After about an hour, we were laughing together. She handed

me the mirror and spun me around. I couldn't believe what I saw. She had created a masterpiece. My naturally pin-straight locks had soft and elegant curls resembling a bouquet of flowers tumbling down my neck. It was the best my hair ever looked.

"Thank you so much!" I hugged her.

When Jesse and Ryan came back, I couldn't wait to show them.

"Eeee, look!" I turned around so they could see. "I feel like a princess!"

Ryan wrapped his arms around me and said, "Mom, you're so cute."

My heart melted.

As soon as we left the salon, it started to sprinkle outside. Thank goodness Jesse had remembered an umbrella or the "feeling like a princess" would have been drowned out by a soggy mess.

Hoping to let the rain pass us by, we stepped into a little Greek restaurant around the corner from the salon for a quick lunch. Sitting in the hotel waiting wasn't our ideal way to spend the day, and it was too early to get ready for the night, but none of us wanted to meander in the rain. Maybe if we stopped for food, the sun would appear, and we could wander the streets later until it was time to get ready.

The food was excellent, but my stomach was too jumpy to eat much of the swordfish I ordered. Jesse and Ryan must have felt the same because none of us did more than pick at our plates. We got the rest boxed up to go.

The weather only worsened. Even with an umbrella, it wasn't a day for walking around, so we headed back to the hotel.

Unfortunately, in the room there was nothing to do but sit and wait. Sometimes when we go on trips, I remember to pack UNO cards to play on rainy days. Even Ryan thinks it is still a fun way to pass the time. Passing idle time, however, had not crossed my mind when packing for our Tonys weekend.

Instead we talked about what the night might hold, but that only made us more excited. We tried reading the books we'd brought, but none of us could concentrate. Every five minutes, I got up to look out the window. Still raining. Then, I'd look at my phone only to see that less than a minute had passed. Why does time crawl like a turtle on the beach when you're looking forward to something special?

We had to find something to do. Finally, Ryan asked Jesse if they could play mobile Fortnight together. They sat, huddled close, staring at the game on the iPad. I smiled. There aren't too many moments in life that are better than watching Jesse and Ryan spend quality time with one another, knowing full well that every year, those moments would happen less and less.

By four o'clock, even Ryan couldn't take it any longer and said, "Dad, can't we start getting ready now?"

Jesse got up and checked the Tonys tickets to confirm the time it started. He had already checked the time once, but you couldn't be too careful. He had been known to misread tickets before. One time, we were early, which wasn't a problem, but on another occasion, Jesse thought a show started at eight when it had started at seven-thirty. We could not afford a mistake like that tonight.

"'Doors open at five-forty-five p.m., close at seven p.m. Late-comers will not be admitted,'" he read out loud. "Okay, it's time."

Ryan jumped up and eagerly unpacked his tuxedo from the travel bag. I took my dress from the closet and headed to change in the bathroom. After a few minutes, the boys gave me the "all-clear" to come out.

I took one look at them and beamed. "Oh my gosh, you boys are so handsome! We have to take lots of pictures tonight!"

Neither Ryan nor Jesse are especially fond of pictures, but

they assured me, "Oh, sure. We'll take a bunch once we're at Radio City Music Hall."

"And remember being co-producers of a nominated show means we can enter on the red carpet. Those are professional shots. They'll be the best ones of the night," Jesse said, implying there was no reason to take any in the room.

I acquiesced. I figured I'd just take pictures without them knowing.

Instinctively, I looked down to put my phone in my pocket, only to realize ball gowns don't traditionally have pockets. I hadn't packed a clutch. Actually, I never bought one because I couldn't imagine having to gracefully handle a clutch plus all the other things you hold at a party, like wine glasses, hors d'oeuvres, and napkins. I didn't want to spill anything on this night. Now, there was no place for my phone. Maybe Jesse could put it in his jacket, but he already had both sets of tickets, his phone, and my lipstick in his small tuxedo pockets.

"There's no point in having three phones, I guess." I set my phone down on the room table. "You guys will take lots of pictures, right?"

They looked at each other and then at me. "Sure!"

I forced them to snap one quick picture in the hotel just to make certain we at least had one photo from the evening.

It was almost five now, and we were ready.

Jesse took a long look at me and pulled me into his arms. "You look gorgeous," he whispered in my ear.

I blushed.

Even after twenty-four years, he had the same effect on me. Maybe this was the first ball he was taking me to, but he would always be my Prince Charming.

The rain was coming down harder now. Radio City Music Hall was only about three blocks away, but given the weather, Jesse asked, "Do you want to get a car?"

Even though I was wearing four-inch heels, I thought it was

silly to take an Uber for three blocks. Plus we had been warned that some roads around Radio City were blocked off, so a car might have difficulty getting us close anyway.

"As long as we have an umbrella, and you hold onto me, we can walk," I said.

Especially in New York City, Jesse has a habit of walking at the speed of a cheetah and changing directions as if his dinner depended on it. There have been plenty of times in big crowded airports or cities like New York, where I was bringing up the rear with one of our lagging kids. Then, I would look up and with immense irritation realize that Jesse had practically disappeared. I love him to the ends of the Earth and back, but I have no natural sense of direction, and I swear, he wouldn't even know we'd gotten lost until twenty minutes after he arrived at our destination. Though I could walk fast in heels, tonight, I didn't want my hair to lose its magic or me to be a sweaty hot mess by the time we arrived at the red carpet. If Jesse was holding onto me, he would have to slow down to my speed.

As we headed toward Radio City Music Hall, I was surprised to see lots of other people wearing tuxedos and gowns filling the streets.

"Glad we aren't the only ones who decided to walk," I mused. Despite the rain, it seemed like everyone had decided to do the same.

The information that came with our tickets directed us to head to a specific entrance so we could get to the red carpet. When we arrived, though, there were police barricading that area. Jesse politely went up to an officer telling him we were instructed to enter there. He barely acknowledged Jesse and wouldn't budge. Instead, he instructed us to walk around to the other side, which we did, but the officers at that entrance told us to head back to where we just had been.

Other people were being told the same thing, and no one was being let through. It felt like a sitcom scene. Here were all these people dressed in ball gowns, carrying umbrellas, being sent back and forth in the rain and no one being allowed in.

One guy sporting a chic tuxedo, his exasperated date in a very short dress on his arm, raised his voice at the policeman. "We have *VIP tickets*. We're supposed to be in *there* on the red carpet." He pointed to what looked like the fancy picture spot on the red carpet, the one with the flower backdrop that says, TONY AWARDS. All of us could see it, but no one could get there.

The officer stood stone-faced, blocking the entrance, seeming to almost enjoy the guy's suffering. He was not going to let people through. He didn't care what kind of tickets anyone had. Nobody was getting through his checkpoint. It looked like the only people being allowed on the red carpet were those climbing out of limos.

We headed back around to where we'd started and saw Ryan Conway, the general manager for *Once on This Island*, who was walking with his mom. Even he was having the same problem getting to the red carpet. We figured if anyone knew how to get in, he would know, so we asked if we could join them.

We walked with them around to the side of the building and finally found a line where they were letting people in, just not on the red carpet. It was still raining but not as hard as before, so Jesse took a quick picture of me and Ryan outside of Radio City Music Hall before going in. I admit I was caught up in the idea of getting a professional picture on the red carpet, so it was disappointing when we had to settle for a quick picture in the rain on the backside of the building, especially since we hadn't taken any nice ones in the hotel. I knew we didn't need fancy pictures to remember this night, but I wanted them. The one time that we would ever have a legitimate reason to be on a red carpet, and we simply couldn't get there. There was nothing we could do about it. For a second, I thought maybe when we entered the theater, we could search for a different way to it.

Quickly, I realized that I didn't want us frantically looking around, searching for something we might not find. Why did I want that picture so badly anyway? A photo is only one moment in time, a false, staged representation of life. This night was not about us feeling special. This night wasn't about us at all. It was about the beauty of theater and the people who make it. The important thing was that we were here joining in the celebration, so I let it go.

It's been a long process, but I'm getting better at letting go of frustrations, which has benefitted Jesse a great deal over our marriage and maybe even saved his life once. Several years ago, Jesse and I traveled to India for a friend's wedding, and Jesse tricked me into going white water rafting down the Ganges River. I have always had an irrational fear of large bodies of deep water. It's not the water itself. It's what lives inside it— sharks, crocodiles, snakes, etc.

"Don't worry," he said. "We'll only be going over small rapids, and we'll have professional guides."

In other words, it was perfectly safe. Against my better judgment, I agreed to go. I should have known not to trust him. Jesse had a habit of engaging in semi-safe sports such as skydiving.

The first thing the Nepalese guides did was to explain all the things that could go wrong on the river and how to survive it, like, "If your boat tips over and you are trapped underneath..."

I didn't even hear the rest of the instructions. My stomach suddenly felt queasy. I wanted to back out, but I didn't want to sit on some beach in the jungle all alone while Jesse went down the river without me. There weren't any good options.

Then, the guides said, "Okay, everyone, you got that? Do exactly what we say, and you'll all be fine! We haven't lost too many people so far. Climb aboard!" They chuckled.

I didn't find it humorous at all. Climbing into the little blue rubber raft, I prayed that we would survive this expedition that meandered through the Himalayan valley and make it back home alive to see our children.

The headwaters of the sacred Ganges River were less than two hundred miles from where we stepped into the boat. At first, the water was calm, and we were surrounded by high mountain vistas and dense jungles. Jesse pointed out a flock of bright green parrot-like birds that suddenly rose from the canopy.

"Listen to the birds sing!" Jesse said.

It was beautiful, different from anything I had seen before. Unlike the rugged mountains of Colorado, which are covered in stately pines and aspen trees, these rainforest mountains were dotted with flowering species. Blossoms in bright reds and yellows painted the landscape. Monkeys swung through the branches along the banks as if they were following us. If only I hadn't been so focused on survival, I might have enjoyed it more.

Then, as we glided down the murky river, I heard distant thunder. Great, we were going to get caught in rain as well. After a minute, it dawned on me that we seemed to be getting closer to the thunder.

I froze with terror. It wasn't thunder.

Directly in front of us was a crest of water that had to be at least eight feet high, and our guides were heading straight for it. The angry waters frothed like a rabid wolf preparing to consume us. My life played out before me, and I knew I would never see our kids again. I could barely breathe. We were surely either going to flip or be sucked to the bottom and die in the middle of nowhere. As we approached the treacherous swirling rapids, I shot Jesse a look that said, *If we get out of this alive, I'm killing you!*

When our guide shouted, "Now!" I dug my paddle in and pulled hard, repeating it again and again against the gurgling water, literally paddling as if it meant the difference between our children becoming orphaned or not.

Somehow, our flimsy little rubber raft pushed up and over that wave, and we whooshed down the backside of it like the fall of a roller coaster. We had arrived safely to the calm on the other side.

Back on shore, everyone else was laughing and celebrating. I was still not quite over the *oh my God I'm about to die* feeling. Jesse felt a slight pang of guilt for stretching the truth when he saw how terrified I was. He had known all along what kind of rapids we would face.

"I knew it would be an unforgettable experience for us."

That it definitely was.

He apologized with a puppy-dog-like smile and added, "I didn't think you'd be that scared. You should have seen your face!"

Deep down, I was furious with him, but we had survived, and I didn't want the rest of the trip ruined. Despite his chicanery, I figured it was better to keep him alive, at least for a while. I didn't know how to navigate India on my own, so I let it go.

Now, I can laugh about it.

After being married for almost a quarter-century, I've learned that letting go is a very important skill. Most of the things that frustrate or even infuriate me aren't all that important in the grand scheme of things. What is important to me is that I share my life with my soulmate.

This evening at the Tonys, it wasn't even that difficult. There were no life-threatening waves, only pictures. We would get other great pictures.

Finally, we entered Radio City Music Hall. Built by John D. Rockefeller in 1932, it was the epitome of old-world elegance and grandeur with grand sweeping staircases, high ceilings, and vast arches. Huge vases filled with freshly cut flowers adorned the grand foyer. We tried to take a picture in front of the flowers, but swarms of other people had the same idea, and there wasn't any room to squeeze us in unless we wanted a bunch of photo bombers in the background.

It was still early evening, there was over an hour before the show began, but there didn't seem to be any point in milling around the lobby so we decided to find our seats. As soon as we walked through the theater doors, we were enveloped in a warm orange glow. The three of us let out a collective gasp. Gazing down the aisle, past all the soon-to-be-filled velvet seats, my eyes fixed on the brilliant blue words illuminating the stage, "Tony Awards." This was the calm before the storm of excitement.

Radio City Music Hall
New York, New York

*J*ESSE

*T*he usher led us to a row about one-third of the way down to the stage on the main floor. We weren't anywhere near the front, but we were here! We sat and talked excitedly about what the night might hold. The theater was still mostly empty. Many of the guests were mingling in the lobby or presumably getting their pictures taken on the red carpet.

I sat in the aisle seat with Ryan to my right and Kathy next to him. She decided that *if* we won, she would stay back and watch.

"I don't want to run in this gown and heels to the stage," she said. "I can just see myself tripping and crashing to the floor." She didn't want to be the viral comedic sensation of the night.

"Are you sure?" I asked.

"I want this to be your moment. You and Ryan go. I'll be back here cheering for you," she said.

We weren't exactly sure if Ryan would be allowed to go up on stage, but it was fun to imagine.

I supposed it was better to have a plan, and it was nice to spend a moment in anticipation when the future was still unknown, and we could live in the possibilities.

The audience started taking their seats. We began recognizing people around us and realized we were sitting in a section with all of the other *Once on This Island* producers. We had purchased the tickets through Ken's office so it makes sense that they would seat us all together.

Keith Cromwell from Red Mountain Theater Company was seated right in front of us. We talked to him for a little bit, and he told Ryan, "If we win, you're getting up on that stage too!"

Ryan smiled. He didn't need to be told twice.

Tyler Mount sat a couple of rows in front of us, and Ryan Conway and his mom were directly behind us. Then, I noticed the guy with the salt-and-pepper hair and beard who we'd seen several times at *Once on This Island* but never had the chance to meet. He walked in and sat two rows in front of us. He was the one who always dressed in super expensive-looking suits, and tonight was no exception. This was finally the perfect opportunity to go over and introduce myself.

"Nice to meet you, Jesse. I'm Diego Kolankowsky," he said with a hint of a Spanish accent.

As we had suspected, Diego was a producer of *Once on This Island*, as well as other Broadway productions such as *Spring*

Awakening and *Gettin' the Band Back Together*. We found out later he is also an international film producer from Argentina.

"Would you like me to take a picture of you in front of the stage?" I asked.

He happily handed me his phone, and I snapped a picture of him. He returned the favor for us. Finally, we had a picture. It wasn't on the red carpet, but it was pretty cool to have a photo of us in front of the Tony Awards stage.

We sat back down in our seats, but I had to get up again. I couldn't sit still. I felt like a kid on a Halloween candy sugar high. I had too much nervous energy, and there was still an hour before things were going to get started.

I looked around. There was nowhere else to go, so I stood in the aisle. I started a conversation with the two ushers standing near us. They asked where we were from.

"We're from Cleveland, Ohio," I said.

"Cleveland? I'm a huge fan of the Cleveland Cavaliers. I just love LeBron!" one of them replied.

We must have talked for almost ten minutes trying to deduce whether or not LeBron would stay in Cleveland.

More people started coming in, and she had to get back to work.

The theater was filling up quickly. We scanned the new faces coming in, watching for people we might know or celebrities. We hoped fate might bring us face to face with Lin-Manuel Miranda. Maybe we would bump into him, or he would walk past us. We didn't even know if he was attending. Most of the big name stars and nominees were sitting at the front of the theater anyway, but that didn't stop us from dreaming.

The show was finally about to start, and I sat back down in my seat. Ryan, Kathy, and I put our fists together in our family fist bump hoping this would bring some good luck our way. The three of us fidgeted in our seats, unable to contain our excitement. Giant robotic camera booms swept over the crowd preparing to film the night's events.

"Dad, look!" Ryan whispered and pointed up to it.

Other than a couple professional sporting events, we'd never been to anything that was filmed live for TV. I took a deep breath, subconsciously trying to hold onto this moment.

Someone came out on stage and informed us the show was starting soon and explained how the night was going to play out. The show would be broken up into two parts, the live-aired portion and the taped sections. There were around thirty awards that were to be given out that night. Not all of them would fit into the prescribed TV time slot, so the categories that drew fewer viewers were taped and edited. During the live portions, no one was allowed to leave their seats, so if you had to use the restroom, you could only go during the taped sections, and then you had to hurry back before the live recording began. It didn't matter if you were a superstar. If you had to go, you had to literally run in your gown to get back in time. If you didn't make it before the cameras started rolling, the producers of the Tony Awards had someone else sit in your seat for the sake of the television viewers. They didn't want anyone to think there were empty seats. We didn't plan on leaving our seats. There was no way we were going to miss a minute of this night.

14

"MAMA WILL PROVIDE"

June 10, 2018, 8:00 p.m.
Orchestra Seats Aisle D Row J 311-313
Radio City Music Hall
New York, New York

*J*ESSE

*A*nnouncements over the theater speakers told us that we would be live in sixty seconds, forty-five seconds, thirty seconds...

And then we were live. The atmosphere was electric. The lights went down, and when they came back on, two glistening, black grand pianos appeared on stage facing each other. Josh Groban and Sara Bareilles walked out. The crowd went wild with applause. Kathy and I looked at each other in amazement. Were we really here?

Josh and Sara sat facing each other from across their enormous grand pianos and began playing and singing.

"So it begins. This is the Tonys..."

It was a song they'd written especially for tonight.

"We're your hosts, and we're perfectly suited to be because did you know neither one of us has ever won anything?"

They paused.

"That can't be right, Sara, no. You? No Grammys for you? Really nothing?" Josh asked.

"No, no, nothing, nothing." She shook her head. "Yeah, I know, and I'm shocked for you."

"Yeah, well, you know. It is what it is..." Josh answered, looking down at the piano dejected.

"Anyway," they harmonized and went right back to their song, *"So this is for the people who lose! This one's for the loser inside of you."*

The audience roared with laughter. Then, ensemble members from every nominated show joined them on stage and helped them finish the song. They made it clear in the next verse that while everyone wanted to win, that wasn't the most important thing by saying, don't worry about losing because then you might be a host like us. The whole crowd jumped to its feet.

Their main message and Kathy's favorite part of the song was that if you create works of art, you are part of the cure for this sometimes scary and difficult world. That was the real point of this night, celebrating all the hard-working, talented people who make Broadway what it is. Theater has the power to move people, to compel them to see life from a different perspective or more clearly from their own. It can be a catalyst for difficult conversations. It can be the seeds for change. This was what we were there to celebrate.

There was a break for a commercial, and people jumped up to dash for the restrooms. The action on stage never stopped. As soon as the live cameras were off, various other Broadway or TV stars, acting as co-hosts, came on stage to present the smaller awards, which presumably don't have the same television viewership as the main events of the night. For each commercial break, there was time for about one award to be presented and allow the winner to get to the stage and make a very brief speech. Speeches had to be completed before the live cameras came back on. The live-televised award winners seemed to have even less time to make their "thank you" speeches, about ninety seconds. There were several winners who had more to say, but CBS cut their microphones mid-sentence, played music over them, and ushered them off stage.

It happened to a number of people. Here they were, on stage at the Tonys, being presented with an award for something they had poured their heart and soul into, a once-in-a lifetime achievement, and they had to sum up all their thoughts and thanks to everyone in a minute and a half! It was barely time to process that they'd even won. One winner, I don't remember who, was right in the middle of his speech, and he was basically shooed off the stage. We all understood that it was live TV, so it had to be this way, but Kathy looked at me, cupping her face in her hands and said, "Oh that's so sad!"

There were countless memorable moments that night. Both Andrew Lloyd Webber and Chita Rivera won the Lifetime Achievement Award in Theatre. John Leguizamo won a Special Tony Award to recognize his commitment to theater and to bringing diverse stories and audiences to theater. One winner wished his boyfriend a happy birthday and asked the crowd to join him in singing. We all raised our voices together and sang Happy Birthday.

Then, in one of the most emotional moments of the night, members of the Marjory Stoneman Douglas High School

Drama Department appeared on stage. The students were illuminated by several individual bluish spotlights. I don't know if each light represented one of their classmates who perished just four months earlier in the deadliest school shooting in America's history, but that was how I took it, that their friends were still with them, shining down on them this night.

A piano played the first few measures of *"Seasons of Love"* from *Rent*, and these students from Parkland, Florida joined in, raised their voices, and sang out to celebrate the lives of their friends.

Fourteen students and three teachers were gone, gunned down in six minutes by an AR-15 on Valentine's Day 2018. In a story that never seems to end in America, a former student had come to the school and ended seventeen lives.

The students here tonight sang with all the poise of a Broadway cast's ensemble, filling Radio City Music Hall with their love and memories of those lost.

We, in the audience, erupted in a standing ovation. There was hardly a dry eye in the theater.

Their drama teacher, Melody Herzfeld, had sheltered sixty-five students in her office for two hours on that day of violence and chaos, protecting them until they could be led out safely.[1] A week later, she directed her students performing an original song called *"Shine"* for a CNN Town Hall on gun violence. Written by two students, the song expressed their pain and call to action.

Tonight, Ms. Herzfeld was awarded the Tony Award for Excellence in Theatre Education.

When all the special awards had been given out, it was time for the presentation of the Tonys for all the season's "Best" categories, like "Best Musical" or "Best Revival of a Musical." Every nominated show had its own sections in the theater where its producers sat so each time a nominee was announced, an entire section of people would stand and cheer. For each of the eight awards that *Once on This Island* was in the running for, our section jumped up and cheered wildly. It was as rowdy as a professional basketball game, only we were in tuxedos and no one spilled beer on us.

Because of the earlier results of the Drama Desk Awards and all the other Award ceremonies, I knew we didn't have a chance at winning any of them tonight, but it was still exciting to cheer for our nominees. I had told Kathy about all the predictions and how the tide had shifted over time, but I was slowly realizing I hadn't made it clear that *Once on This Island* would be going home empty-handed tonight. She and Ryan, forever optimistic, were certain it would win *something*. Each time we were up for a category, they would clasp hands and look at each other with this hopeful excited smile. Then, as soon as a different show's name was announced as the winner, they were deflated like a leaky balloon. It was adorable and heartbreaking at the same time.

The moment it really hit me was when the award for Best Actress in a Musical was announced. Ryan and Kathy collectively held their breath. Still holding hands, they attempted to send positive waves of energy to the envelope which they hoped held Hailey Kilgore's name for Best Actress. They were certain it did.

It reminded me of the time Ryan and I watched *Turner and Hooch* together when he was about nine. He quickly fell in love with the movie because of the dog, Hooch. Ryan rolled on the floor laughing at the pooch's antics. I loved seeing him full of joy. Of course I also knew the end of the movie and suddenly realized he was going to be devastated. Why had I picked that movie? Sure enough, by the end, he was sobbing and declared it the "worst movie" he had ever seen. I hoped tonight wouldn't turn into the "worst night ever."

The Tony Award for Best Actress in a Musical went to Katrina Lenk from *The Band's Visit*.

"I thought we would at least win a couple." Ryan hung his head in frustration, and I knew it was only going to get worse.

As the other awards were announced, *The Band's Visit*, *Angels in America*, and *Harry Potter* were running away with most of them. A couple other musicals and plays won one or two. Tony Shalhoub and Ari'el Stachel, both from *The Band's Visit*, won Best Performance by an Actor in a Leading Role in a Musical and Best Performance by an Actor in a Featured Role in a Musical respectively. Both of their speeches were emotional reflections on being Muslim Americans in this time of anti-immigrant and especially anti-Arab/Muslim fervor, particularly with the nationalistic and xenophobic policies of number 45's administration. I thought Kathy was going to jump out of her seat cheering in support before they finished talking.

In between awards, the casts of each of the nominated musicals took to the stage in full costume to perform a scene or mash-up of scenes complete with their show's unique back-drops. As soon as the announcer stated it was time for the cast of *Once on This Island* to perform, our seating section went wild.

The curtain lifted, and there on the Tonys stage was a miniature island.

It was beautiful. They had replicated the set of the Circle in the Square. Sand had actually been brought in, as well as the overturned boat and a goat. They even brought in the rain. To fully complete the replica, 360 degree on-stage seating had been set up around the sand. It was like a mini theater within the theater.

In those stage seats sat brave members from three different disaster relief aid agencies— All Hands and Hearts-Smart Response, Americares, and UNIDOS Disaster Relief and Recovery Program. All three organizations had assisted in the Hurricane Maria Puerto Rico rebuilding efforts.

Because the stage seating partially blocked the view of the larger Radio City audience, cameras had been put in place to video the action in the sand and livestream it to the large screens in the theater.

The moment Mama Euralie raised her arms to the heavens, I was once again under its spell, possessed by the gods of the island.

Thunder, lightning, and rain.
Mystical chanting, singing
And dancing.
Dancing to the gods, dancing for their freedom
The drum beat of life
To the tune of joy and sorrow.
A song shared by all humanity
But oft forgotten; walls built up around us
Divided from our cosmic oneness
Until Ti Moune weaves love back into the fabric of time[2].

*J*wondered how the cast must have felt up there, performing the show they had been doing eight times a week for six months in front of this enormous audience. If they were nervous, it didn't show.

Ti Moune, her hibiscus-red dress swishing in unison with the sensual motion of her instinctively swaying hips, belted out her defiant dream of loving Daniel to the gods. Daniel, by her side, was equally seductive in his unbuttoned shirt, displaying his impressive six pack abs.

As Asaka in his floral headdress and banana-yellow skirt prepared for his end run in *"Mama Will Provide,"* the cameras cut first to Papa Ge dancing with one of the goats. The big screen switched to a shot of Tyler Hardwick, an understudy for Daniel, who led the other goat up the aisle through the orchestra seating and crouched right next to Nathan Lane. Tyler, dancing to the drum beat, offered Mr. Lane a piece of lettuce to feed Sparky, or maybe it was Peapod, but Mr. Lane very quickly declined.

And then Alex provided us with the exhilaration of his powerhouse voice filling the hall.

My huge cheesy grin was that same one I had twenty-six years ago when I first saw *Once on This Island*. It was pure joy to watch them perform in this room filled with theater lovers.

The room exploded into cheers. It was the loudest standing ovation of the night. At least it sounded that way from where we were seated, and it wasn't just our section erupting in applause. It seemed the entire theater was on its feet. It was like we had already won.

Happy tears filled my eyes. I turned to Ryan and patted him on the back. "That was our Tony Award right there," I said, hoping to soften the blow later. My cheeks hurt, but the smile wasn't leaving my face anytime soon.

Ryan looked up at me with his big brown eyes and asked, "Dad, if we win, can we get a second puppy?" He smiled innocently and cradled his arms like he was squeezing a puppy. "It can be a girl for mom, and we'll name her Tony."

Ryan was growing up fast, but I treasured these moments where a tiny bit of the kid still left in him shone through. All three kids had been asking for a second dog. Kathy and I had held them off up until now.

I smiled back, wanting to keep his spirits lifted during this moment. "Sure. If we win, we can get a puppy."

Only after the words left my mouth did I realize that I had now sentenced him to another letdown at the end of the night.

Carousel and *My Fair Lady* also performed medley numbers from their shows, which were beautiful. Every performer that night was incredibly talented, and they all deserved their moments in the spotlight, but in our eyes, *Once on This Island* stole the night. In just a few minutes, we would find out what the Tony voters thought.

We had been waiting for it all night. In my head, I prepared for how I would handle it. I wasn't nervous. I knew Ryan would be upset. He wanted so badly for *Once on This Island* to win. He had been so disappointed just two nights ago, when the Cleveland Cavaliers had lost in the NBA Finals. He still wasn't quite over that.

I needed to set a good example for him. This could be a great lesson on how to respond in a positive way to disappointment. No matter which musical won, I would cheer and clap for the winner. My gratitude for being here and sharing in this beautiful night was more than enough. It was a once-in-a-lifetime experience for all three of us, and we had to enjoy every minute of it.

Ryan grabbed Kathy's hand. Then, he grabbed mine as Christine Baranski walked on stage. He squeezed tightly. Win or lose, the buildup to this moment was like the anticipation at the top of a roller coaster. My heart was racing.

Christine Baranski stood at the podium. "Once again, here are the nominees for the Best Revival of a Musical."

As she read each name, a short clip of each show's Tony performance was played across the stage screen. Our section erupted again in cheers as the clip of *Once on This Island* played.

Ryan continued squeezing our hands. I glanced at the two of them. It looked like they were both holding their breath. They so badly wanted a win. Up until this point, we had won zero out of seven categories. The night had gone exactly as predicted.

Ms. Baranski lifted the envelope up and began to open it.

Ryan and Kathy quietly chanted to each other, "Rally Spirit, Rally Spirit, Rally Spirit," over and over again. It was our family's good luck charm. They still held tight to each other's hands, believing in the impossible.

I was calm as Christine Baranski spoke again. "And the Tony

Award goes to…" It seemed like she paused forever as she fumbled with opening the envelope. "Oops, sorry."

I watched her on the big screen. She opened the envelope. Her eyes scanned the page. The tiny lines around her eyes turned up ever so slightly. Time stopped. She took a deep breath. I readied myself to hear *Carousel*, for her lips to press together to say *My Fair Lady*. In the back of my mind, I was still preparing for the appropriate "good loser" response as an example for Ryan.

Every detail was important. I watched as her lips began to part, opening wider and wider. I furrowed my brow in confusion. A surge of adrenaline rushed through my body. What was happening?

Her eyes gleamed. In slow motion, her lips moved wider, forming an "O."

My head tilted to the side. My brain couldn't process what it was seeing.

And then the sound waves of her voice hit my ear.

"*ONCE…*

Wait. What? I was frozen to my seat. The gears in my mind could not catch up to what was happening. My mouth dropped open, and I might have let out a scream. Our section—and it seemed the entire world—erupted in screams before she finished speaking.

…ON THIS ISLAND!"

People jumped up and down all around me. It was complete pandemonium. My head was spinning. I didn't know what was happening. *How?*

I stumbled out of my seat, looked incredulously at Kathy, who had tears streaming down her face. Ryan was jumping up and down, and for a moment, I just stood there looking at them. I didn't know what to do. My brain was incapable of processing what had just occurred.

Kathy looked at me and shouted, "What are you doing?" She pushed me and Ryan toward the aisle. "Go! Go!"

I regained consciousness for a moment. *Oh, God! I have to get to the stage before our ninety seconds are up!*

Our whole section ran like a stampede of wild buffalo. I don't know what happened next. It's all a blur. All I know is Ryan and I ran down the aisle following them. My feet moved clumsily and momentarily got caught in the TV camera's cables snaking down the aisle. Regaining my footing, I hurried to catch up. It was dizzying, like I was running through the fog of a dream. I heard screaming. Was I screaming? Or was it the crowd around me? Or someone running behind me? I'm not sure. I had no idea where Ryan was. He had come into the aisle with me, but where was he now? Had I left him? Was he behind me or in front of me? I didn't know.

It all happened so fast. I only remember little clips, snapshots of the night. Andy Mientus jumped up and down at his seat ahead of me on the right as I made my way toward the stage. At one point, I stepped on the back of Hailey Kilgore's dress, and she turned around. At least I think it was me, but maybe it was Ryan, or maybe it was someone else. I don't know. Someone stepped on her dress. I was having an out-of-body experience. It was like being in shock. Parts of my brain turned off or crossed signals, and I couldn't distinguish what was happening to me versus what I was witnessing. It all mixed together into one blob of events.

I was almost to the stage when I turned the corner around the front row of seats. Sitting there, right on the aisle, was Tina Fey. We locked eyes for a moment. I recall vividly the bemused look on her face. She smiled at me, as if to say that she was happy to see the underdog win one.

Somehow, both Ryan and I made it to the stage together in time, and we climbed the stairs and filed in behind everyone else over to the right side of the group. My breathing was ragged, and I realized I was crying. Ken Davenport was already in the middle of his speech, though I didn't hear a word he said.

I looked out at the crowd from the stage, bursting with gratitude. Like *It's a Wonderful Life* when George gets the gift of seeing the importance of each of his past moments, I thought back to times when I'd been frustrated by what seemed like dead-ends or giant, gaping potholes in our journey down the road of life. Like everyone else, I'd had moments of disappointment, being passed over for promotions or career changes that didn't work out the way I'd planned, things I regretted. I was always distracted by each setback, never able to see the bigger picture. In that one moment, I saw that every failure had led to something even better. All of those past disappointments, woven through the fabric of our lives, had brought us to this place. Though I had been discouraged in those moments, if anything had been different, if any one of those past defeats had been a victory instead, I might not have been on this stage. I never would have been traveling to New York for work, and I wouldn't have seen the broadway.com article about *Once on This Island* being revived. Everything in our lives for the last twenty-six years had led us to this moment. Everything.

Standing on stage, I was absolved of any regret. In an instant, my perspective shifted. I'm not implying that winning a Tony Award made my life complete. I would like to say it didn't change me at all because I wasn't up there to celebrate myself. This award was for the incredibly genuine and open-hearted cast and the show that I was proud of, that I loved. That moment we were living on stage at Radio City Music Hall with Ryan at my side and Kathy in the audience was such an unexpected gift. Nothing else we would ever do could compare to how we arrived there. The perceived importance of climbing the corporate ladder vanished. In that ninety seconds, my focus changed, and I knew that now I wanted to direct my energy wherever my heart led.

A wonderful lady in a red dress, another producer, looked back and noticed Ryan behind her. She motioned for him to step in front of her, no one between him and the audience of the Tony Awards. We looked out over the sea of people. I pointed out about where Kathy was sitting, and we waved to her.

Then, our ninety seconds were up. They started to usher us off stage left. I paused and hugged Ryan. We stood there for another heartbeat, mesmerized, and took in the incredible scene before us.

"Ryan, don't forget this moment."

We walked off to the backstage area with the rest of the *Once on This Island* group.

"You didn't expect this to happen, did you?" Tyler Mount asked as we joined the group.

"No, not in a million years," I replied, tears still streaming down my face. I gave him a bear hug. I wanted to wrap my arms around everyone in sight.

Another huge eruption of cheering came from the crowd, but we didn't know why. We were all still too immersed in our own joy—hugging, crying, and laughing together—to pay attention to anything on stage.

Lynn Ahrens stood in the middle of everyone. I'll never forget the look she had on her face, like a proud mama watching her baby do something incredible. She glowed with an ear-to-ear smile. Michael Arden was right near me. I hadn't had the chance to meet him yet so I introduced myself. I gave both Lynn and Michael a congratulatory hug.

A cast member from *The Band's Visit* was backstage watching our little celebration with delight. Everyone seemed happy for us until the stage manager, slightly annoyed, said, "Shh, you have to be quiet."

I hadn't realized we were being loud. In our dazed, deliriously happy state, we assumed the world had stopped for everyone else like it had for us, but no, we had our moment, and the world moved on. The Tony Awards were still going.

We were ushered farther backstage then led through a maze of tunnels somewhere underneath the audience and over to a tiny hallway alcove off stage right where we squeezed together for a picture. I guess we were still being too loud with our celebrations because someone said, "Shh, please be quiet. Bruce Springsteen is playing out there."

We settled down for the photo. Ryan and I kneeled down in the front of the group because we were the last ones to come in. The photographer was just about to snap the picture when Robert De Niro, who had just come off the stage, started to walk across the alcove. Then, he stopped so he wouldn't get in the way of our photo. The photographer, recognizing who it was, waved him past, and he walked right in front of us. Ryan and I instinctively stuck our hands out as he passed to high-five him. He walked by us and then realized what we were trying to do. He actually came back to triumphantly slap our hands. By sticking our hands out though, we ruined the picture so they had to take another one. Oh, well, it was worth it. WE HIGH-FIVED ROBERT FREAKING DE NIRO!

At the next commercial break, they led us back out to our seats. I couldn't wait to get back to see Kathy. She jumped up and wrapped us both in her arms. Then, she told us what had happened from her view.

"As soon as I pushed you into the aisle, you guys ran like madmen to the stage with the rest of the producers. I wanted to video you running up there, but that's when I remembered I didn't have my phone. You still had them in your pockets." She laughed.

Neither Ryan nor I had thought to give her one because we never imagined we'd win! It all happened too fast. We should have been filming as Ms. Baranski was announcing it just in case. If we had, we would have had video of that magical moment when the crowd exploded with joy as we won. Maybe then we could solve the mystery of what actually happened to Hailey's dress, but we hadn't thought of any of that. There had been no way to record the moment except to simply live it.

"I watched you up on stage, both of you hugging. I could hardly believe it was real."

"Did you see us wave to you?" Ryan asked.

"Of course I did, and I waved back. At least you took some pictures backstage right?"

Ryan and I looked at each other.

"Uh, nope, we forgot," Ryan said, grinning up at her innocently.

"Oh, you guys!" She shook her head at both of us.

Our whole section had returned to their seats, and we all sat down. We had missed out on seeing Bruce Springsteen's performance, whom Robert De Niro had just introduced. Kathy said the roaring applause we had heard as we exited the stage area was because of Mr. De Niro's rousing speech. The crowd gave him two standing ovations for his words. This must have been just before he high-fived us.

We made it back just in time to see the final award of the night, Best Musical. Four musicals vied for the coveted trophy: *The Band's Visit, Frozen, Mean Girls,* and *SpongeBob SquarePants: The Musical.* I don't think anyone in the room was surprised that the well-deserving *Band's Visit* came home the winner.

The 72nd Annual Tony Awards Ceremony was now done, and we were leaving the theater Tony Award winners.

Ryan looked up at me and smiled a devilish smile. "So, when are we getting our new puppy?"

15

"TI MOUNE'S DANCE"

June 10, 2018, ~11:00 p.m.
Tonys After-Party
Plaza Hotel
New York, New York

J ESSE

D iego, the producer from Argentina, came up the aisle as we were about to head out. He was still in shock too. "You're good luck!" he said, grabbing my shoulder and hugging me. He'd been a Tony nominee a couple of times already, but tonight was his first win.

"Are you going to the Plaza?" I asked them.

"Yes, of course. It's not far. Do you want to join me?"

We happily accepted. The rain had mostly stopped now, and

the city glistened in the darkness. We walked down 6th Avenue to the Plaza, talking the whole way like we were old friends, mostly reminiscing about the incredible evening we had just shared.

Diego turned to Ryan and asked, "Are you in theater, Ryan?" Ryan explained about his band.

"You play the guitar? I do too!" Diego added excitedly. "I would love to visit the Rock & Roll Hall of Fame in Cleveland someday."

"I've played on stage there a couple times! I would love to show you around the museum," Ryan offered.

Then Diego spotted a hot dog vendor on the corner and got an idea. He wanted to buy a New York hot dog, stand on the corner, and eat it in his tuxedo. He handed Ryan his phone and asked, "Will you take a picture?"

"Of course!" Ryan was more than happy to assist, took a few steps back, and then snapped the picture. Later, Diego posted that photo on Instagram. Ryan was proud to have taken it.

We made it to the Plaza in no time and were glad to have walked. Diego had to wait outside for another guest to arrive, so we parted ways.

"Thank you so much for walking with us," I said. "It was such a pleasure to meet you finally."

We headed up the steps of the grand entrance facing 5th Avenue to the party. Tonight, in order to get into the Plaza, you had to have a ticket, which they collected at the door.

"Do I have to give up my ticket?" I asked the big-bouncer-like guy manning the metal detector and collecting tickets.

"Yes," he said flatly.

"Can't we keep them as souvenirs?" I asked.

He looked at me like I had a mango for a head. "No," he answered, chuckling quietly.

I looked down at the fancy black and silver tickets and reluctantly handed them over.

As I mentioned earlier, we had been in the lobby before, but the spectacularly posh Plaza Hotel was even more dazzling tonight. The crystal chandeliers glistened with a golden glow. Everywhere we looked, flowers burst with color from grand vases, and guests were already crowded around an elegantly set buffet. There were so many people we couldn't really see what was being served, but we were ready to eat. Most of the small tables and seating areas were occupied with people enjoying selections from the buffet. We wandered around, hoping to find some of the cast members to congratulate, and crossed the dance floor, which was starting to fill up with people mingling and moving to the beat.

"Are you looking for a table?" An observant staff-person came up to us. "Go up to the second floor. There's hardly anyone up there yet."

"Oh, thank you!"

He leaned in as if he had a secret to divulge. "Get a seat by the stage up there. I've been told someone special will be performing, and then there won't be a seat left." He winked conspicuously on the word "special."

Who was he hinting at? We had no clue, but we didn't have anywhere else to go so we took his advice and headed up the staircase.

He had been right there were plenty of places to sit. We quickly found an empty table not too far from the small stage. There was another buffet set up nearby as well, and this one had almost no line. We filled our plates with food, ordered a Coke for Ryan and some wine for us at the bar, and sat down to enjoy a late dinner. It was almost midnight, and we hadn't had anything since our light lunch. We were looking forward to a delicious meal.

Dinner was good but not great, which was a little disappointing. Maybe the late hour was the reason they weren't serving a sumptuous spread. There was plenty of food, but given the price of the tickets to this party, we had imagined feasting on trays upon trays of freshly cooked lobster tails and fresh sushi wrapped in gold seaweed, divine dark chocolate fountains spewing liquid deliciousness and desserts fashioned for the gods. Instead, we dined on a very good poached salmon in dill sauce, pasta, and some type of chicken dish. Much to Kathy's chagrin, we weren't able to find any chocolate or desserts.

Several different Broadway performers took the small stage in front of us and began singing show tunes.

"Isn't that Josh Groban sitting over there?" Ryan said, directing our attention about two tables to our left. Yes, it was! He was doing the same thing we were, sitting and eating with his family, enjoying the evening. We would have *loved* to meet him. We'd seen him perform in his Broadway debut role in *Natasha, Pierre & the Great Comet of 1812* the previous year. To this day, Kathy gushes about him singing, "Dust and Ashes" literally right in front of her. He was so close she could have reached out and touched him. Tonight was his night to celebrate as well, so we simply delighted in the fact that he was two tables away.

Another *Once on This Island* producer, Jeff Wise and his wife, came over to our table to say, "Hi."

"We're heading over to the cast party," Jeff said. "We don't know anyone here."

We were still finishing up our food, so they gave us the address, and we said we'd be over in a while. When we were done eating, we looked around. We didn't know anyone here either. It didn't seem like there was going to be a special performer anytime soon, if one was coming at all. We also felt like we were missing out on celebrating with the *Once on This Island* family. We were glad we had come to the Plaza after-party to see what it was like, but as usual, we felt the pull of the

Island and wanted to celebrate this amazing night with a very special group of people.

On our way out of the Plaza, we saw a staged "red carpet" with a backdrop covered in red roses that said, "TONY Awards." Kathy's eyes lit up. We got in line. In a few minutes, it was our turn. I handed my phone to the lady who was the designated photographer for the night. She took a few shots and handed my phone back. We finally had our "official red carpet picture."

Fate never brought us face-to-face with Lin-Manuel Miranda. Maybe he wasn't even there, but we couldn't have asked for a more amazing evening. Meeting Lin would have to wait for another day.

Now, it was time to celebrate with the cast. The three of us headed for the grand foyer of the Plaza and walked out the door. While we waited on the street outside for an Uber to take us to Vida Verde on West 56th Street, Kathy and Ryan stood together on the sidewalk under an umbrella. I took a picture. It was one of my favorites of the night.

When we entered the cast party, it instantly felt more like home. It was crowded, and we had to squeeze around people to get in, but we knew or recognized many of these people. Festive music played over the speakers though the buzz of euphoric voices almost drowned it out. Alex Newell was right in front of us, so he was the first one I hugged and congratulated.

We made our way farther back into the narrow bar/restaurant and spotted Rodrick. His face lit up as soon as he saw us. He half-screamed and rushed over, embracing us in his huge biceps and incredible aura of light. He scooped Ryan up off the ground in his excitement. Like a celestial body, Rodrick radiated an energy, a glow, that warmed everyone around him. I've never met anyone quite like that before.

"Wait, are you guys involved in the show?" he asked.

"Yes, we're co-producers," I said. Our "secret" was out.

"Ahh!" he shrieked again. "I knew it!" He turned slightly and motioned for someone to join us. "This is my husband, Jay."

Jay had been a figure skater too. Kathy and Jay had an instant connection.

Rodrick mentioned he owned a fitness company in the city and that he had an early class to teach the next morning but asked, "When will I see you guys again?"

"We're coming tomorrow night!" I said.

"What?" he shrieked. "Will you meet me after the show? I'd love to talk to you guys more."

"Of course! We would love to," Kathy said.

We made our way around the party, meeting and congratulating different people. Someone, I can't remember who, maybe Ken, asked if I wanted to get a picture with the actual Tony Award, the one that had been handed to Ken on stage. Of course I did! He handed me the heavy award with its spinning silver medallion set on a black pedestal, and I handed him my phone to snap our picture. This night kept getting better.

After a while, people started to leave, so we wandered upstairs where we saw Kenita. "Ohh, hello, family!" she said, recognizing us right away.

We embraced, and she introduced us to her husband Justin.

"Can you believe tonight?" she asked.

"It's been amazing," Kathy said.

I shook my head in disbelief. "I didn't expect it at all, but this show and you guys dancing around in the sand, you deserve it. You make me cry every single time. Thank you."

She put her hands together. "Thank you. Will I see you again soon?"

"Tomorrow night!" Ryan said.

"Wonderful." Kenita laughed.

We said goodnight, and she and her husband headed home.

After an hour or two, there weren't many people left in the restaurant. Maybe it was time for us to head back as well. Our hotel was only a few blocks away, and the rain had finally stopped so we walked. Of course on our way, we walked through the covered alleyway past the Circle in the Square Theater. It was now around two-thirty in the morning, and no one else was on the streets. We stood in front of the *Once on This Island* sign and took several pictures. In my wildest dreams, I couldn't have conjured up this night, and yet, here we were. Adrenaline still pumped through my veins. I wasn't tired at all. I could have walked around the city all night, but there didn't seem to be any point in just wandering the streets. Our Cinderella night was over, and we headed back to the hotel.

Ryan and I changed out of our tuxes, and we helped Kathy remove about a thousand bobby pins from her hair, which took nearly a half hour.

None of us could stop talking about what had happened. Of course Ryan didn't hesitate to mention "Tony the puppy" several times either. Every time he brought "her" up, he pulled his arms in tightly like he was squeezing something tiny and adorable. I changed the subject quickly by going through the pictures we had taken, though there weren't many.

The three of us sat on one bed, huddled together, staring at my iPad as I searched online for any videos or photos that had been posted. All over the casts' Facebook and Instagram pages were little clips of the night.

Then, I found a video of the cast watching the result as it was being broadcast. They were on the bus heading back to the theater from their performance at Radio City and were gathered around someone who had it live-streaming on their phone. Like all of us in the theater, they waited anxiously as Christine Baranski opened the envelope. As soon as the "Once" sound came out of her mouth, the bus erupted with screams of joy, just like we had done back at Radio City. When they arrived in front of the Circle in the Square, they spilled out onto the street, stopping traffic as they celebrated their win. It was perfect. That was exactly how we had felt back at Radio City Music Hall. We watched that video over and over again, and every time, my heart pounded with that same elation. I couldn't get enough of it.

I continued searching for everything that was online. There had to be other videos. Then, I found the video clip of CBS's live broadcast at the Tonys, and there we were, Ryan and I on national TV. We were hard to locate if you didn't know exactly where to look, but I found us.

"Zoom in, Dad," Ryan said.

We zoomed in and watched me hug Ryan before leaving the stage, a moment in time I will cherish forever.

There was another moment I wanted to review. What exactly happened when I stepped on Hailey's dress? We studied the video, but when we watched it, Hailey gathered up her dress after it was stepped on much later than I thought, and Ryan and I were several people behind her. I clearly recalled stepping on her dress in the aisle. Was my memory wrong? Or maybe I saw what happened, and it merged into my own memories. So strange.

Exhaustion eventually overcame Kathy and Ryan, and they drifted off to sleep around three-thirty. Going to bed didn't even cross my mind. I had to find more videos, pictures, anything, everything. Falling asleep meant letting go of this incredible day. It meant it was over. I wanted to hold onto it as long as possible.

Around five, I finally sunk into sleep for a few hours.

By eight or nine the next morning, we crawled out of bed.

"Did that really happen last night? Or did I dream it?" Ryan asked, rubbing his eyes.

"I know it seems like a dream, doesn't it?" Kathy asked as she made us a cup of coffee.

Fatigue fogged our brains, but we were too excited to sleep any more. The coffee would help.

For breakfast in New York City, we usually made our way down to experience one of West Village's many intimate restaurants, but today, we decided to find food close by. From all the online reviews, the Blue Dog Cookhouse and Bar, about a block from our hotel, looked like a great new place to try. Kathy was hungry for French toast, and the menu had two different options. She couldn't decide between the crunchy French toast with caramelized bananas and the pumpkin-stuffed French toast.

"Get them both," I said.

"I'll never be able to eat all of that."

I knew that was true, but we were still celebrating, and I have the ability to eat far too much. It wouldn't go to waste.

"We'll all share a bunch of things," I said.

It took us about two and a half hours to eat everything, but we relished the time to sit and process the unbelievable turn of events. We laughed about Kathy having to push us into the aisle to start running and me stepping on Hailey's dress, though we still never found the evidence.

To everyone else in the restaurant, it was a normal Monday morning, nothing special. For us, the world was suddenly different. We were now Tony winners. The world keeps turning whether you've had the worst day of your life or the best. It was surreal. For the three of us, the memories of June tenth, 2018 would last a lifetime.

After stuffing ourselves, Kathy suggested, "Let's go get a *New York Times*. We can save the article about the Tonys as a keepsake."

I hadn't bought an actual paper newspaper in years.

Kathy assumed it would be easy to find one, but we searched several corner stores and always came up empty-handed. I was about ready to give up, when finally, we stepped into a little shop that still had some papers left. We flipped through the pages and were surprised that there wasn't much coverage on the Tonys. It did mention *The Band's Visit's* ten wins but had nothing to say of the surprise win for *Once on This Island*. We bought it anyway.

"What should we do now?" Kathy asked, ready to take on a day in the city.

"I think I have to go to sleep," I said, all of a sudden noticing that my eyelids were so heavy I could barely keep them open. Exhaustion had finally caught up with me.

Despite it being the middle of the day, we walked back to the hotel for me to take a nap. I had to have enough energy to make it to the evening performance of *Once on This Island*. I managed to get an hour or two of sleep before I woke, pumped to head out to the theater again.

Hoping last night's win would bring hordes of new ticket buyers out, we headed to Circle in the Square early. Prior to the Tony Awards, every time we went, the theater was becoming less crowded. It was disheartening. It should have been packed, sold out every night. It was one of the best shows I'd ever seen with an amazing cast, yet most of the people I talked to still had never even heard of *Once on This Island*. Why? Everyone who saw it raved about it and wanted to see it again and again. Why wasn't it getting the buzz it deserved? We hoped winning the Tony would generate renewed excitement. Maybe it would finally be "the show" to see on Broadway.

"Wow, Dad, look at the line!" Ryan said when we got there.

Tonight's show was sold out, and a large line of people anxiously waited in the cancellations line.

Inside, the theater buzzed with electricity, everyone intoxicated by the win. It had a similar feeling to Opening Night and the performance right after the nominations came out. The cast always performed with unmatched emotional intensity, but there were these few very special performances in which the impassioned audience combined with the fervor of the cast to create a fever pitch of excitement. We basked in the glow of that energy like a sea turtle soaking up the sun on a beach.

Tonight, this Tony Award-winning cast was fired up. Isaac Powell, playing Daniel, leaped onto the boat in front of Ti Moune with so much passion that he slipped a little. He fell on top of the boat instead of landing on his feet. People who'd never seen the show might have missed the slip up because he played it off so well, but we, of course, knew what was supposed to happen. Later, we found out through the show recap emails that the boat's surface had lost its grip and had become slippery. Luckily, Isaac wasn't seriously injured, though he did take a few shows off afterward to recover.

Every time we came to the show, we tried to start a standing ovation at the end of "Mama Will Provide." As soon as Alex began, the momentum started building for the show-stopping moment.

Over the course of seeing several shows, we realized that by putting in little energetic bursts of applause or hoots and hollers at key points in the song, like after Alex's first scream, it helped raise the energy level of the crowd. If there was enough electricity in the air, a well-timed raucous clap or shout of approval at key points in the song could add to the excitement, like forcing more helium into a balloon that was about to pop.

As he finished the final run of the song, no matter the crowd's energy, the three of us would always burst out of our seats. Occasionally, several people would stand as well. Being in the front row helped give people the "permission" to follow our lead. Many times, it seemed the audience didn't know they could stand in the middle of the performance, even if it was a "show-stopping" number. Sometimes, only a few people would jump up with us, but more often, we were the only three people standing. The next day, I would get the stage manager's email report, which read, "A couple of enthusiastic fans stood after

"Mama Will Provide." I always enjoyed making my way into the report.

Tonight, building on the Tony win, we had the right mix of energy, and Alex got the "show-stopping" ovation he deserved every night. Almost three-quarters of the house sprang to their feet.

After the show, we crossed the sand to the cast door and waited in the top of the stands for Rodrick, honored that he'd asked us to stay. The stage manager asked us who we were waiting to see. We told her, and she pushed on her headset and informed him he had guests. He opened the backstage door, and a smile lit up his entire face. Rodrick has this incredible aura about him, a radiance that brightens whatever room he is in.

"Jesse!" He hugged us tightly as if we were old friends. The four of us sat in the stands together. "Tell me more about your family."

We gave him a quick synopsis of our life in Ohio.

"You said you have a gym?" Kathy asked him. "We've been wanting to find a place to workout when we're in the city."

"Yes, it's called Core Rhythm Fitness on Mulberry Street." He gave us the information and how to contact him.

"We'll come try a class next time we're here," I said.

While we were all chatting, Phillip Boykin strolled over, and Rodrick introduced us. "This is Jesse, Kathy, and Ryan from Cleveland, Ohio."

In his smooth, deep voice, Phillip said, "Oh, I love Cleveland. Playhouse Square is a beautiful place to perform."

"It is a wonderful theater," Kathy replied, looking a little starstruck.

We talked until the theater's stage crew gave us a look hinting that they would appreciate our exiting the space in order to prepare the theater for the next show.

"We'd better head out. Thank you so much for meeting with us," I said.

"Thank you for supporting the show! When are you coming back?" Rodrick asked.

"We're coming back in July," Ryan said.

We walked back to the hotel in a euphoric daze, blown away by the weekend's experiences. Now, it was time to come back down to Earth and pack up our bags for the flight home in the morning.

"Honey, you might want to look at this," Kathy said as we folded up our tuxedos and placed them gently in the suitcase.

She handed me her phone and showed me our daughter, Alyssa's, Instagram story. She'd posted the picture of us in front of the "Tony Award" red carpet that we had taken at the Plaza Hotel. On it, she had written, "So proud of you Dad! Congrats on winning your first Tony last night," with two hearts.

Oh, boy. I'm only marginally active on social media, but I knew Alyssa had a lot of followers and that word gets around quickly in small towns like ours. We asked her to take it down, but she explained it would only be up for a couple more hours anyway, and all of her followers were kids her age, most of whom we didn't know. We hadn't told anyone except Kathy's mom that we were even going to the Tony Awards, let alone that we might potentially win one. Kathy's mom was the only one that even knew we were involved in *Once on This Island*. Things could get interesting when we got back home.

16

"TWO DIFFERENT WORLDS"

June 12, 2018
Cleveland, Ohio

KATHY

It was a bit weird to be back home, returning to our normal life as if nothing had happened. Except for Alyssa's Instagram story, we hadn't said anything to anyone. I posted some pictures outside of the Circle in the Square Theater in our formal wear, congratulating the show and its cast but never mentioned anything about us being a part of it. Only my mom knew, and she lived in Michigan. She'd been watching the coverage on CBS, hoping she would see us run up on stage, but the cameras panned over Jesse and Ryan too quickly for her to spot them. She did tell me that she jumped off the couch and screamed at my dad, "They won! They won!"

No one in our little world back in Cleveland, except Jessica and Alyssa and their boyfriends, knew what had happened.

We went to work, the grocery store, guitar lessons, all the things we had done before, except now, we'd had this incredible experience. Life had changed for us, but everyone else was exactly the same. Or were they?

Could it be that I wasn't looking hard enough? Was I too involved in my own life, work, and worries to "see" those around me? Everyone has a story to tell. I'm only the main character of my own tale, but there are approximately 7.8 billion other main characters on this Earth. So many lives intertwined like multi-colored silk threads weaving together to form the tapestry of humankind. What if I took a step back, relinquished my role as main character, and listened to the stories around me? What if I focused my attention on being the best supporting actress, to work harder to lift others up?

A long time ago, I made a commitment to live my life through love, but maybe that isn't enough. I'm seeing how lax I've been. Yes, I love my family and my friends, but that's as far as my waves of love radiate. What if I want to start a tidal wave of love, a tsunami of love that spreads across the land? I think it is possible, but I need to turn that love into action, to educate myself on the trials of all those other main characters, to speak out for those who cannot speak, and to amplify the voices of those who already have.

Now, Jesse, Ryan, and I were living in two different worlds, millions more stories all around us, and I had to listen and learn.

In one world, we were playing the role of an Ohio family of five plus one beagle. In the other, we were Broadway co-producers heading off to New York City to attend fancy red carpet events, and literally no one at home knew. It was fun and exciting to have our own little secret.

Our close friends and family knew we really enjoyed going

to New York a lot. They had no idea why, and they never asked us.

We didn't know how many people had seen Alyssa's Instagram story, so we didn't say anything until someone else brought it up. The first person to say something was my best friend and fellow figure skating coach, Lori. We've worked together almost every day for twelve years, and when we aren't on the ice together, we're often chatting, laughing on the phone, or grabbing a quick lunch. When our kids were younger, they used to play together. Jesse jokingly calls her my work husband.

Lori of course knew we had been in New York because I was missing work, and before we'd left, I'd asked her advice on what to do with my hair and what jewelry to wear to a "fancy party." I will readily admit I don't know much about fashion. My daily wear consists of leggings, ski pants, an Under Armour top, and about three jackets to stay warm on the ice. In twelve years, I think I've never worn my hair in a style other than in a neat bun. It's simply the most practical on the ice. Fashion questions were, to say the least, a bit out of the ordinary for me, and she must have known something was up, but she didn't ask.

On my first day back at work, however, Lori asked with a knowing smirk, "What were *you* up to over the weekend? Frankie and Gabby saw something on Alyssa's Instagram."

I chuckled.

Before I had time to answer, Lori went on, "The girls came up to me and asked, 'Hey, Mom, is a Tony Award something special? Because Mr. McKendry just won one.'" She looked right at me with her piercing blue eyes. "I thought maybe it was a joke or an acronym for something different, like a T.O.N.I. or something. Then, they showed me the picture. I blurted out, 'That little bitch! I knew she was up to something when she asked me for advice on her hair and fancy jewelry!'"

I burst out laughing and told her everything. I didn't want her to feel bad that I hadn't let her in on the secret, but I explained, "We only told my mom. Even my brothers hadn't known."

"Do I have to bow when you and Jesse enter the ice rink now? Or open doors for you?" Lori joked, bowing forward as if in the presence of royalty.

"Only for Jesse." I laughed.

The only other people who found out were Ryan's band-mates and their parents. We'd become close friends with all of the parents, especially since all the kids were too young to drive themselves to practice. The lead singer Norah also saw Alyssa's post. As soon as we all met for the next practice, they inquired about it. We had to explain everything.

"Oh, thank goodness. I thought maybe you were involved in some mafia organization always heading mysteriously to New York." One of the parent's laughed.

"That's amazing! You should wear the Tony on a chain around your neck everywhere!" another one teased. "I would if I won one!"

July 2018
Toni meets Tony
Cleveland, Ohio

𝒦 ATHY

𝒶 s soon as we got home from New York in June, Ryan asked, "So Dad, when are we getting little Toni?"

I knew Jesse was hoping I would step in and say absolutely

no more dogs, which, originally, I had said, but our handsome, floppy-eared beagle, Rory, was now five years old, and he was such a good boy. Even I thought it would be kind of nice to have a puppy in the house again, so he could have a friend to play with. If I was okay with getting a second dog, what could Jesse say? He had promised.

But it had to be a little dog and a girl. My girls were leaving me. I wanted one small girl that would stay small.

I authorized Alyssa to search for one under the assumption it would take a month or two or more to find the right one. I was still a little nervous about adding a new family member right away. Getting a new puppy is a lot like having a baby. It never is quite the right time. Only a few weeks later, she had found a toy Australian Shepherd who was just eight weeks old. The only catch? The little pup was five hours from our house.

I thought that was ridiculous. I certainly wasn't going to drive ten hours for a puppy, and I knew Jesse wouldn't.

"Mom, she is perfect! I know this is the one. She's the little girl for you," Alyssa insisted.

"I don't know. You found her so fast, and it's so far," I stalled, not really wanting to make the decision, knowing that despite how much Ryan said he would take care of a new pup most of the responsibility would fall to me.

"Shakib and I will drive to pick her up and bring her to you," she offered. "All you have to say is yes."

I looked at the picture of the little tri-color darling. "Eee! Okay, go get her!"

On Thursday, July nineteenth, 2018, little Toni came into our life. She instantly stole my heart with her bright black eyes and crooked pseudo-smile. The name Toni, though, didn't quite fit her personality. For some odd reason, from the first day we got her, she had a habit of crouching down low and then launching herself straight into the air like a kangaroo. That decided it. Her name was Roo. She is my perfect fluffy little princess, and unlike her human sisters, she will never leave us.

A little less than a month later, a heavy package arrived at our house. Ryan and Jesse tore the packing tape off like kids at Christmas. Inside was a black box with the silver word TONY Awards embossed on the top. Jesse opened it and pulled out the official Tony Award. There it was, a silver spinning medallion affixed to a black pedestal. The masks of comedy and tragedy adorn the front of the medallion with the words "Antoinette Perry Award" raised around the masks. On the back, it says:

The Broadway League and the American Theatre Wing,
Present the American Theatre Wing's Tony Award to
Jesse McKendry
Best Revival of a Musical
Once on This Island
Producer
2017-2018

*R*oo didn't seem to care at all about what was in the box, though she was interested in the packing tape. There was no way for her to understand that the shiny spinning thing on the table was the reason she was part of our family.

Late summer 2018
New York, New York

KATHY

I hated to leave our new little baby, but we had already planned to be back in New York the week after Roo joined our family. Jessica and her boyfriend, Noam, promised to take good care of her, so near the end of July, we flew back to the island of Manhattan. It was starting to feel like our second home when we arrived in Midtown. Circle in the Square was the first place we headed after putting our bags in our room. We already missed the Island. Since our last visit, they had installed a huge new graphic of the cast on one of the glass panes at the side of the theater. A red and white sign at the bottom proclaimed, "WINNER! TONY AWARD Best Musical Revival." Despite Jesse's general dislike of taking pictures, we had Ryan snap our photo in front of that.

A few hours later, we were back in our favorite seats in the sand. In honor of Rodrick's character, Ryan wore his New York Knicks jersey, but when we arrived, the cast board said he was out for that night. Ryan hung his head a little lower but decided to wear the shirt again Monday when we went to check out Core Rhythm Fitness, Rodrick's gym.

Before the pre-show began, it didn't seem like many people were coming in. I was hoping they were just hanging out in the lobby and would enter before it started, but the show began, and the theater wasn't close to being at full capacity. I tried to tell myself it was just an anomaly for this night. It had only been a little over a month since the Tony Awards. Ticket sales couldn't be dropping already, could they? The Tonys bump should last longer than that, shouldn't it? Lea Salonga had left the show on June twenty-fourth. Maybe that had affected ticket sales. Naive to the full impact a big name star had on bringing crowds in, I was disheartened. The entire cast overflowed with talent. One person leaving shouldn't make that much difference.

Darlesia Cearcy, who had been cast as the original Erzulie in the workshop before Lea Salonga came on board, took over the role again after Lea left. Darlesia's many prior performance credits include roles in *House of Cards, Law and Order SVU* as well as *The Color Purple, Ragtime,* and *The Book of Mormon.* Her version of the Goddess of Love was hauntingly beautiful. I wasn't the only one who thought that either. In an article in Broadwaybox.com[1], Jenny Anderson and Josh Ferri write that "Darlesia's performance as Erzulie, the Goddess of Love, feels nothing short of a revelation. Her 'Human Heart' is the musical equivalent of how first love actually feels—and her delivery makes you feel all those feelings all over again."

As usual, the ninety minutes of the show went by too fast. Afterward, in order to make the night last a bit longer, we hung out by the stage door to add our voices to the rowdy fans cheering as the cast came out. A large group of elated teens, determined to get autographs and selfies with the cast members, almost missed their tour bus. The bus honked a few times and then started moving. The kids had to rush away before it drove off without them.

Early the next morning, the three of us headed down to SoHo to Core Rhythm Fitness (CRF). As soon as we walked in the door, Rodrick turned around. "Ahh!" he cried out and ran over to scoop us into a bear hug. "Ryan, you even wore my jersey!" He put his hand on his heart.

"I had to!" Ryan beamed.

It was almost eight a.m., and several other people walked in. Rodrick greeted them with similar enthusiasm. Jesse and I sat on yoga mats next to each other and waited for class to start. Unfortunately, because Ryan was only fourteen, he couldn't join in the workout for liability purposes, so he sat on the built-in shelf right next to us and waited. He had his phone, so he didn't mind.

Rodrick started class. "Close your eyes, and think for a moment about what gratitude means to you. What are you grateful for today?"

Jesse and our kids were my easy answer. That's where "easy" ended. I thought I was in decent shape, skating almost every day, but about four minutes through the pilates warm-up, my stomach muscles were on fire. At this rate, I wasn't sure I would make it through the entire hour. Rodrick turned on the music and ran us through a set of ten different exercises that we did for a minute each. Sixty seconds doesn't seem that long until you're holding a squat with your arms above your head. Then, it seems like it will never end.

Rodrick seemed to sense whenever I was having difficulty, and he would call out, "I see you, Kathy! C'mon, hold it like you got love!"

And somehow, I looked at his smile, and I could hold it longer.

He did this for everyone. Sometimes, he would just let out a crazy scream and do a dance right in front of whomever was struggling to keep up. You couldn't help but laugh and keep going. Occasionally, he yelled out, "Don't give up, Jesse! Lordie G!"

I felt better knowing Jesse was having a hard time too. I've always been super competitive with Jesse, probably because I grew up with two brothers and felt like I had to compete with them.

I was dead by the end of the first round, and then Rodrick said, "We just have two more rounds! You get a sixty second break, and then we start. Easy peasy!"

Oh my god! Two more?

After what seemed like only thirty seconds, rest time was up, and round two began. I could swear that the sixty second timer he used for the break was different than the one he used to time the exercises. My legs felt like quivering jello already.

We stood up and did it all again. At one point, Rodrick called out, "Feel that core, Kathy. We gotta build the center of who you are!"

I pushed through the burn, sucking in breath when I thought I had nothing left because I couldn't stand to disappoint him. I had to do my best. Rodrick's contagious energy and his inspiring words fueled my body and spirit, and somehow, I made it through round two and three.

Then, he said, "Rest."

I melted into the mat, unable to move, feeling the vibrations of exertion coursing through my body.

While we were on our backs, he directed us through some stretches. Then, he asked, "What does it mean to have wholeness?" He walked around helping us press farther into the stretches. "How can you accept all the parts of who you are?" he asked.

In a pool of sweat, I lay there thinking.

All the parts of me.

Who am I?

Just a girl, nothing special...but I have love to give.

All the parts...

Quiet, nerdy, doesn't quite fit in.

Getting older—wrinkles, glasses

Dig deeper, darker.

An ever-present underlying thought made its way to the surface. I tried to keep it down, locked in the shadowy recesses of my mind, but it was time to face it.

Never quite good enough, never quite doing enough.

There it was, out in the open.

How do I embrace those parts of me? Getting old and feeling insignificant.

As if somehow hearing my inner question, Rodrick said,

"Even those things that you believe are weaknesses are part of what makes you you. The good cannot be there without them, so celebrate all of what makes you whole. You were born for this moment. You are exactly where you need to be. Live in this now."

I took a deep calming breath, letting the oxygen flow through my body. *Embrace my flaws. Age has brought me perspective and some wisdom. The feeling of not doing enough has made me strive to do better...but it is time to see the opportunities in each moment and do what each moment asks for, and that is enough. Live each moment in love.*

My body was tired, but I felt strong and spiritually uplifted, though I knew I would be sore as hell tomorrow.

17

"FOREVER YOURS (REPRISE)"

Fall 2018
New York, New York

KATHY

As a co-producer, Jesse received weekly email updates on how the show was doing financially. While seats were selling and the theater was about ninety percent full each day, the tickets were being discounted more and more just to reach this capacity. The show was bringing in just enough money to cover the operating expenses.

I didn't understand. Why weren't more people flocking to see it? There was nothing else like it on Broadway, nothing else like it anywhere. What were we missing?

Jesse stared at those numbers, not wanting to believe what they foretold. The end was coming unless something changed very soon. A cold tendril of a thought touched my brain, as if Papa Ge himself whispered it into my ear, "*Once on This Island* won't be around much longer." It was too soon. It hadn't even been running a full year yet. Barring a miraculous uptick in ticket sales, the show would be forced to close in the near future, and we were helpless to do anything about it.

Bearing that dark thought in mind, Jesse and I decided we would see it as many times as we could afford to before it again passed into the netherworld. Who knew if or when another revival would come along. It was here now. We had to take advantage of this year on Broadway. There may never be another chance, so we scheduled a number of trips back to New York for the rest of the summer and fall. Ryan, Jesse, and I were going to enjoy every minute of this adventure for as long as possible.

At the mere idea of it possibly closing, all I could think was *how?* The world needs this show.

"We need more love and forgiveness in this world," I kept telling Jesse.

But what could we do? We did our best to help spread the word by posting and sharing on Facebook and Instagram and buying tickets every month, but we're not influencers, and our social media accounts have an extremely limited reach. The best we could do was to continue buying tickets for ourselves and trying to share it with everyone we knew.

We had already brought my parents earlier in the year, and though my mom would have loved to join us again, it was getting harder and harder for her to take care of my dad even when they were at home. When they did go out, he would become confused and upset. He wasn't even that old, only seventy-nine, but the person I knew as my father was disappearing before my eyes. Sometimes, there were glimpses of him, a flicker of his old smile like he was trying to re-enter this dimension, and then it faded as quickly as it came. He used to have a hearty, full laugh and was always telling dad jokes.

I remember when I was in high school. We would sit together on our steps and talk about life late into the night. But Parkinson's took away his ability to form sentences, and he could no longer talk about much of anything. Though his physical presence was there, I was losing him piece by piece. He still remembered me, I think. It was hard to tell. But every time we went to Michigan to visit, I accepted that it could be my last time seeing him in this world. And each time I told him goodbye, I hugged him a little tighter and held on a little longer. I prayed that his spirit would soon be released from the prison of his disease, and yet I wasn't really prepared to let go.

Parkinson's disease can be hereditary. If this is my future as well, I want to live now with more intention, to spend my time with the people I love, to focus on what is important to me instead of wandering through life waiting for the future. Because in the future, mindless wandering might be all that I have left.

So before it was too late, we asked friends and family from all over to come and join us on the Island. Happily, many of them took us up on the offer.

One of Jesse's old college housemates, Ken, remembered hearing him play the original cast album on repeat twenty-six years ago, and he wanted to bring his family to see it with us. Our friend Jamie joined us another time. My younger brother, Dave, his wife, and kids came with us for one trip.

We loved bringing people to New York, especially people who were a little intimidated to vacation in the city on their own. When my brother Dave and his family joined us for a week, Jesse had the idea to make up challenges for them to complete, almost like a treasure hunt. Each challenge they completed helped them learn how to navigate their way around the city so they could feel confident coming back on their own.

For example, one of the easy ones was to find a good restaurant within a few blocks of our hotel. An advanced level challenge was to take the subway down to West Village. We awarded them points for each item completed. It worked like a charm. Now they're hooked, and our niece Isabella wants to live in NYC someday.

On this trip to New York, Jessica and her boyfriend, Noam, joined us. Luckily, she stayed healthy and was finally able to sit in the sand and experience *Once on This Island*.

As we sat in our usual seats waiting for the show to begin, I looked around the audience and realized something. The seats were filled with mostly older people. Where were all the teens and young women Jessica's age? Why weren't they going crazy about it on social media? It seemed that they simply didn't know anything about it.

Where was the viral buzz? Even Jordan Fisher, who has four and a half million followers on Instagram, posted about seeing it four or five times getting between thirty thousand and fifty thousand likes on each of those posts, but it never took off.

There were thirty other shows that opened in the 2017-2018 season on Broadway, not to mention several long-running shows, each one competing for the attention and money of theater attendees. How do you get your show to stand out from all the marketing noise? The word of mouth portion that stokes the viral take-off never happened. Maybe it had something to do with the fact that it was difficult, as a fan, to post an effective picture.

Because of all the pre-show action, as soon as you entered the theater for *Once on This Island*, all photos were prohibited. There was no way to get a picture of the actual Island, which was part of what made it so visually stunning and different from *any* other show. The only place photos were allowed was in the lobby in front of the *Once on This Island* backdrop—a simple white screen with the show's logo printed on it, which, unfortunately, didn't inspire a sense of "Oooh, I *have* to go see that."

Capturing the true beauty and uniqueness of the show was difficult if not impossible to share on personal social media, and the musical's important themes of challenging the racial and social hierarchies ingrained in the island's society were difficult to get across on a billboard. Seeing this show as a young woman had changed my life. I had hoped it would be around long enough to touch the hearts of thousands more.

I was grateful that it had now touched three generations of our family. We were never able to get Jesse's parents or my older brother Paul and his family to come out, but at least after tonight, all of our kids would know its beauty, bringing them a little closer to our past.

Before and during this evening's performance, Ryan pointed out important things for Jessica and Noam to notice, just like he'd done with Alyssa and Shakib. We couldn't see their expressions this time because they were beside us, but I could hear them trying to keep their emotions in check.

Jessica normally isn't a crier in movies or shows like I am, but tonight, even she could not hold back the tide. I wondered if she saw herself as the strong-willed, adventurous Ti Moune like I had at her age.

After the show, we exited the theater to cheer for the cast as they came out of the stage door like we always do. Jessica worked her way through to the front of the crowd to get every signature she could. After Merle Dandridge, who played Papa Ge, autographed her Playbill and took a picture with her, Jessica turned around to look at me, and happy tears filled her eyes. I was grateful that she'd been able to see Merle perform, let alone get a selfie with her.

$\mathcal{K}$ATHY

$\mathcal{R}$odrick was scheduled to play Papa Ge beginning at the end of October and running for a couple weeks. He had played the role several times over the course of the year, but we had never had the pleasure of being there any of those nights. There was no way we were going to miss it this time. As soon as we found out, we bought tickets for his first night in the role. Then about a week before we were scheduled to fly out to New York, he informed us he was leaving the show immediately after his Papa Ge run was over. The last time he would play his narrator role of Tee Tee was the night before he started as Papa Ge. We couldn't miss that either, so because we are insane, we bought tickets for the night before as well. We would have bought tickets for his *last* night as Papa Ge, too, but unfortunately, we couldn't make that work.

When we got to the theater and sat in our usual seats, it was bittersweet knowing this was the last time we would see Rodrick play the part of Tee Tee. Of course we were thrilled that he was getting the opportunity to be Papa Ge for an extended period of time, but very selfishly, we didn't want him to leave the Island. He was an incredible performer, and we loved watching him. It's hard to explain how it feels to see someone you care about doing what they love with so much passion on their stage. It is the sense that all is right in the world at least for that moment because this artist is putting their heart and soul, their entire being into the performance, giving themselves to anyone lucky enough to be watching. There is power in their vulnerability, which transcends physical boundaries and binds us on a deeper dimension.

Rodrick had no idea we were going to be there. We wanted it to be a surprise. Ryan wore his Knicks jersey again in his honor, hoping this time they could get a photo of them both wearing it. We practically held our breath until he made his appearance. The trailer door clanged open. Ryan's head swung around at the sound. Rodrick made his way up the steps to do his pull-ups, and then he sauntered into the sand. He caught a glimpse of Ryan in his jersey. There was that smile that lit up any room. "Ryan!" he quietly squealed, which was a muted response for him. Both Rodrick and David strolled over to greet us, never breaking character. Ryan eagerly played along and stuck out his hand to shake theirs as if it was their first time meeting.

If someone were to ask me what my favorite scene of the show was, I wouldn't be able to choose. There are so many that stand out, but during the "Discovering Daniel/Pray" and "Forever Yours" sequence there is one part that always gives me chills. Daniel's life hangs in the balance, and the spirit of Papa Ge is near. The tension rises as the villagers carry torches, dance, and chant as if possessed by the dark spirits.

Rodrick's character comes very near to where we sit. Tonight, he situated himself in the sand right next to my foot. He moved his hands toward me like the tendrils of death searching for their next victim, tugging at the depths of my soul. I shivered. I would miss his presence on the Island.

At the end of the show that evening, the actors lingered in the sand instead of heading off stage right away like they normally do. It was the beginning of the Broadway Cares/Equity Fights AIDS season. Broadway Cares/Equity Fights AIDS is a charitable, grant-making organization, which gives money to AIDS organizations as well as several others such as the Phyllis

Newman Women's Health Initiative and Hurricane Relief Grants. Each production on Broadway helps to raise money for this organization by holding little auctions after the show and having some of the cast members circulate in the lobby to collect donations.

The cast explained that, for one of the donation options, they were giving away a backstage tour led by Alex Newell. That sounded like fun. We had missed the backstage tour the night we met with Cassondra for the Audience Rewards event, and this was for a good cause. Why not? Plus, we wanted to wait for Rodrick.

After paying for the tour, the stage manager told us to wait in the sand for Alex. Figuring that Rodrick would come out, too, we just stood there, but of course he didn't know we were doing the tour and had gone into the lobby to look for Ryan. When he couldn't find him, he went back to the dressing room. If we had known, we would have sent Ryan out as well. Luckily, before he left for the night, Rodrick saw us standing with Alex in the sand and came down to see us. He had already changed out of his jersey, but he and Ryan took a picture together anyway.

We all got a selfie with Alex, too, and then we were off. I wanted to jump up and down with excitement. Not only was Alex Newell our guide, but we were about to see all the magic behind the scenes of my all-time favorite musical.

First, he led us inside the tractor trailer that was Papa Ge's lair, with parcels of foreign aid and skulls mounted to the wall.

I looked around in awe and thought back to twenty-year-old me, naive and unsure about almost everything in life, certain about only one thing—my love for Jesse. I was grateful for her courage to dream what is now my reality. What would she have thought of all this? Of her decisions that helped bring us here?

Hardened by time and experience, most of her has slipped away, hidden in the dark recesses of my memories. Only the light of her love lives on forever in me.

As Alex led us toward the semi-truck that is Papa Ge's lair, I slipped my hand into Jesse's just like I had twenty-six years ago and said a silent prayer of thanks to the young woman I had been.

Alex walked us around the one end of the theater where we got to see his costumes hanging on a rack in a tiny little hallway. I'm always surprised at how small backstage areas are. Not ever having been a performer myself, I picture it much more grandiose.

We also got to see where Peapod and Sparky, the goats, get to roam around during the show, a small room with hay covering the floor. For some reason, I never wondered where the goats went when they weren't on stage. Then, he took us around to the other side of the theater and showed us where the water flowed out to meet the shore.

It was wonderful to see this new side of the show.

The next day, Ryan decided to sleep in, but Jesse and I awoke early to catch a car to SoHo for another CRF class. Once again, Rodrick kicked our butts, which is, after all, why we kept going to his class.

After class was over, Jesse told him, "When we heard you were leaving the Island, we moped around the whole day."

"Jesseee." He stretched out his name. "Thank you."

Watching Rodrick perform was a special experience. Actually, just being around him was special. I've never met anyone quite like him. He exudes an energy, a lightness of spirit that illuminates the world and brings people together. I swear he's an angelic being sent to Earth to lift and inspire us with his radiating positivity. Anyone who meets him feels it within the first few minutes. No one else I know has that power.

Of course, it wasn't like we had to say goodbye. Even though we wouldn't see him on the Island, we would still work out with him at CRF when we came to the city. We were happy for whatever his next chapter in life was and were excited to see him in any new role he would take on, but the Island wouldn't quite be the same without him there.

"We can't wait to see you tonight as Papa Ge!" Jesse said.

"EEEH! Now I'm nervous!" he said with his whole body. He is always in motion. I'm not sure we've ever seen him perfectly still.

I laughed. I couldn't imagine him actually getting nervous.

"You'll be amazing!" I reassured him.

"I'd really like to go out to dinner with you guys next time you're here," he said before we headed out.

"We would love to," Jesse replied.

As Jesse and I walked out of the gym and up the stairs to street level, we marveled at the amazing turns our lives were taking. We had been given the opportunity to meet some of the most wonderful people because of *Once on This Island*. Somehow, it seemed to have a power that reached beyond the actual stage, a power to bring people together, which was more valuable than any return of cash on our investment. More than anything, it was the people around us who were making a difference in our lives. I could only hope we were doing the same for others.

That afternoon, Ryan, Jesse, and I had brunch with Victoria Weinberg, whom we'd first met through the Audience Rewards meet-and-greets. We wanted to get a chance to talk and get to know her, not just in a work setting.

Like many of the people we've met on this journey, Victoria is involved in several interesting projects. In addition to working with Audience Rewards, she produces and co-produces annual events like the PEN America Literary Awards and several one-time events. Victoria is also an associate producer for Glass Half Full, a production company based in London and has even started her own production company. All of that and she couldn't have been more than about seven years older than Jessica and Alyssa. Did New Yorkers ever actually sleep, or did they just keep working on amazing things twenty-four seven?

"Yay, McKendry family! How are you?" she asked as soon as we walked into the restaurant.

We all hugged, sat down at the table, and brought her up to date on what we had been doing. Then Jesse asked, "What have you been working on?"

"Right now, I'm working on a tour for *The Lightning Thief*, a musical about the Percy Jackson story."

"Oh, wow! Isn't that the one we saw, Dad?" Ryan asked.

"Yes, we saw it about a year ago when it was at the Lucille Lortel Theatre and loved it!" Jesse said.

Somehow, we got to talking about our dogs. Ryan probably brought them up. He is now totally dog crazy after adding Roo to our family. If it were up to him, I think he would just keep adding dogs to our house until the canines outnumbered the people. Of course he isn't really the one who takes care of them.

"Here, look." Ryan scrolled through his phone and showed Victoria pictures of our new little pup, and she returned the favor and produced photos of her adorable Chiweenie, Tobi.

"She's so cute!" Ryan said. "I want to meet her!"

"Well, she's right upstairs in the hotel above this restaurant." Victoria explained that her mom was visiting, and Tobi was in the room with her. "I'll bring Tobi down to meet you guys after brunch!"

"Yay!" Ryan exclaimed.

Jesse, knowing that Ryan could talk about dogs endlessly, changed the subject. "What other projects do you have that you're excited about?"

Victoria's stunning green eyes lit up, and she leaned in over the table. "There's this piece of work that is just incredible." Her words were quick and passionate. "It played at the Flea Theater, and it deserves a longer life. I'm talking to the writer to see if we can bring it back."

"What's it called?" I asked.

"*Syncing Ink.* It's a hip-hop musical."

We were immediately interested.

Even Ryan said, "Oooh, that sounds cool."

As a musician, he had an appreciation for most types of music, but in the last year or two, he had begun to really delve into hip-hop and rap.

We hadn't intended this brunch as anything more than to get to know Victoria better, but Jesse, Ryan, and I felt an instant connection with her. She reminded us a lot of our daughters. All of a sudden, we wanted to support her in any way we could. It was clear she was dedicated to taking on projects she believed in and ensuring the works remained authentic. Now, we believed in her.

We could have spent the whole afternoon chatting, but we were done with brunch, and Ryan wanted to meet Tobi.

Victoria went up in the elevators to bring her down. After a few minutes, she was back with her precious big, brown-eyed pup in her arms. This instantly elevated Victoria to honorary family member as far as Ryan was concerned.

"Oh, Tobi, you are so cute!" he said. He bent down and was instantly in his glory, giving hugs and pets to the beautiful little princess.

"Keep us posted on those new projects. We'd love to hear more," Jesse said.

There was another round of hugs for both Victoria and Tobi, and we headed out the door.

We had a few more hours to kill before Rodrick's big night as Papa Ge so we meandered around the city until Ryan led us into the Nike store, where he explained to us all the cool new features on each style and which ones were his favorites—like the newest Lebrons and a shoe that laced itself!

For dinner, we got a table at Jack's Wife Freda and ordered the Peri-Peri chicken and the chicken kebabs. We took our time savoring the flavors and talking. One of my favorite things about traveling was that we still all sat down, ate together, and had real discussions. At home, as the kids have gotten older, everyone is on their own schedules, coming and going from school and work, seeing friends, going to music lessons, and doing homework. It's hard to corral all of us into one room at the same time, but on trips, we had the time to slow down and enjoy meals together.

Even though I eat about as fast as a Galapagos tortoise, it was still early when we finished our food, and the show didn't start until eight. Normally, we would have gone back to the room in between dinner and the show, but this trip, we were staying at a different hotel that was quite a bit farther from the theater, and we had planned to head straight from the restaurant to the Circle in the Square. It looked like dessert and coffee were the answer to pass the time, which was fine with me. We ordered our favorite, malva pudding, which is similar to a sticky toffee pudding, and relished every bite. Jesse looked at his watch. Finally, it was time to head out.

In spite of the fact that this would most likely be our last time seeing Rodrick perform in *Once on This Island*, walking in the theater this evening was almost as exciting as Opening Night. On the surface, it was exactly like every other performance we had attended. The three of us sat in our favorite seats in the sand, like always, but tonight, our friend was transforming into the diabolical spirit of the underworld.

"Mom, look, there he is!" Ryan said, his eyes wide with admiration.

Both Jesse and I gasped as soon as Rodrick stepped onto the island leading the goat. His carefully sculpted body exuded celestial power. My heart stopped for just a moment.

Jesse leaned over to me and whispered, "Oh my gosh, he looks amazing as Papa Ge! But I'm kind of nervous for him all of a sudden!"

He couldn't come over to us. Papa Ge did not interact with the crowd in the pre-show, but he knew where we were. His intense, ink-black eyes, normally filled with love for everyone, took on a sinister cast and locked with mine for a split second. It was both stunning and scary. My stomach twisted with excitement and anxiety as I waited for the show to begin.

It is hard to explain how it felt watching Rodrick play Papa Ge. Only hours before, we had been with him, laughing and joking. Now, he had *become* the sly demon of death, possessed by the Iwa—spirit of Papa Ge. Goosebumps pricked my skin. It was hard to believe he could transform so convincingly into such a demonic role.

This was different from either Merle Dandridge's or Tamyra Gray's representation of the mischievous god, both of which were excellent. The depth and power of Rodrick's voice as well as his physically imposing body brought a darker, more ominous tone to his portrayal of Papa Ge.

The marvelous metamorphosis was complete. There was no trace of the Rodrick we knew, the one whose smile could melt the ice caps and lift the souls of those in need. There was only Papa Ge.

The only problem was that we found ourselves rooting for the malevolent god of the underworld even as a cool fog rolled in over the Island and he threatened Ti Moune's life, unsheathing his blade and pressing it to her neck.

The cast sat in the sand surrounding Ti Moune and Papa Ge. Possessed by his unearthly power, they writhed and chanted, echoing his entreaty for revenge.

Icy fingers of death tickled my neck. I shivered. Out of the corner of my eye, I noticed Jesse, totally entranced by the force of Rodrick's sinister spirit, with a big goofy grin on his face.

Why was Jesse smiling? A smile was completely inappropriate for what was happening in the sand in front of us. He must have realized it suddenly as well because he then attempted to contort his face to a more distressed look, but he could not contain his delight. The goofy grin remained.

His joy for our friend was more powerful than death.

Boise Holmes, playing the role of Tonton Julian in place of the injured Phillip Boykin, sat in the sand directly across from us. He glanced up right at Jesse, catching his ear-to-ear smile, and for a split second, I detected the slightest upward movement of Boise's lips, but he reined in his own delight and didn't break character.

For the first time, I distanced myself from Ti Moune's heartbreak. All I could focus on was Papa Ge, and he was glorious.

We had only really known Rodrick for five months, and yet he was one of those people who comes into your life and touches your heart so deeply you wonder how you ever got along before you knew them.

Rodrick transforming into Papa Ge made that night's performance one of the four most memorable nights we'd had on the Island to this point. The other three were Opening Night, the pre-Tonys show, and the performance the day after the Tonys win.

As soon as the final note was sung, we shot out of our seats for a standing ovation. The applause lasted for several minutes. The three of us waited until the ushers began to clear out the crowd. None of us wanted to move from our spot. I couldn't wait to congratulate him on his performance.

"We didn't officially arrange to meet him after the show," Jesse said, turning to me. "Maybe we should go up and catch him outside after he comes out of the stage door."

I was afraid we might not have the chance to talk to him, but I also didn't know the protocol. Maybe we did have to arrange meeting him in advance. Reluctantly, we headed out. As we walked toward the lobby, I turned my phone back on. I follow Tyler Mount's original advice, unlike Ryan. Instantly, I received a text from Rodrick. "Can I see you guys after in the theater?"

Jesse didn't think we would be allowed back in. I texted back that we were upstairs in the lobby.

"Come down. You're my guests!" he replied.

I wasted no time and spun around to head down the stairs. "Okay, let's go back down!"

Not knowing if the theater personnel would let us through or not, I led the way, acting like we were supposed to be there. Surprisingly, no one asked us what we were doing. I could tell Jesse felt a little awkward about going back into the theater, but I just pulled open the door and headed in. Ryan and Jesse followed.

Never having come in on this side of the theater, I was surprised to see a faux damaged ceiling covered in plastic with a rain barrel sitting under it to collect leaking water. Racks of foreign aid donated clothes, hats, and shoes hung from the walls displayed as if for sale in the street. I loved how every angle of the Island was a different experience.

Rodrick opened the door, his bright smile back. Papa Ge had drifted back into the netherworld. We rushed over to congratulate him.

"That was unbelievable!" Ryan said, hugging him.

His aura glowed with even more brilliance tonight.

"You were incredible!" Jesse said. "At the end, when you had your knife to Ti Moune's neck, I couldn't stop smiling! I was just so happy for you!" Jesse added.

"Thank you." Rodrick laughed. "Thank you so much for coming tonight. You don't know how much it means to me."

Other cast members came out and congratulated him. He introduced us to several of the newer cast members.

"Do you want to walk up with me?" he asked.

We talked all the way up to the main lobby, where Darlesia Cearcy came over to congratulate him. Darlesia's voice had a hauntingly beautiful, supernatural quality that made her a perfect fit for the role of the Goddess of Love.

"This is Jesse, Ryan, and Kathy," Rodrick introduced us to her.

She shook our hands.

"It's so wonderful to meet you," I said.

Turning to Rodrick, Jesse said, "Now, you need to go out that door and enjoy being a star and sign autographs." He pointed to the stage door exit where all the fans were waiting.

"Yes, I'm going." He chuckled. "Will you wait outside for me?"

"Of course," I answered.

Ryan, Jesse, and I headed out the door and watched as he and Darlesia made their way over to the stage-door exit. As soon as he walked out, we screamed and hollered along with the throng of other fans.

For the first time ever, Ryan took his Playbill and jumped into the fray. This was the one time he wanted an autograph. He handed Rodrick his Playbill. Rodrick looked up, laughed, and then signed his name. We waited until he made his way through the cheering fans and met him just outside the autograph area.

"Would you want to join me for dinner? The cast is headed across the street for sushi to celebrate Boise Holmes's last night in the show."

"Sushi?" Ryan's ears perked up. "I want sushi."

Rodrick laughed.

"We would love to," Jesse said.

When we first embarked on this journey to the Island, our only thought was how much this show meant to us and how much we wanted to be a part of its rebirth. Once we decided we could part with the money, we didn't expect anything in return, but *Once on This Island* kept giving back to us in countless other ways.

Rodrick led us to a table in the back corner of the restaurant. Other cast members wandered in and scattered themselves around various tables. David Jennings sat at a table nearby with two of his friends. He greeted us as we walked past.

A low and cheerful din of conversation filled the atmosphere as the cast prepared to send off part of their family. Boise had been playing the role of Tonton Julian for a number of weeks while Phillip Boykin recovered from a back injury, but now, he would be heading back to California. It must be great to have new cast members come in, connect with so many talented and amazing people, and add them to the family, but it must also be bittersweet when they leave. Because Jesse and I had moved around the country several times during our life together, we had become close to many wonderful people, and it was nice to know we had friends scattered all around the globe.

Darlesia walked in the restaurant and sat down with us. We had only just officially met her in the lobby not fifteen minutes ago. Rodrick ordered a large plate of sushi, and we all shared.

"How did you guys get involved in the show anyway?" Rodrick asked. Both he and Darlesia seemed curious about it.

I narrated a much abbreviated version of our tale. Now, they understood why we kept returning to the Island.

The sushi was excellent, and we McKendrys love our sushi, but the best part of dinner was having the opportunity to talk and get to know each other. It is in these little snippets of time, having conversations and learning about others, that wonderful relationships are built.

After we'd been there for a while, Rodrick declared, "We're family now. We have to keep in touch, and I want to come to Ryan's graduation!"

Ryan's eyes went wide. He was stunned and humbled by Rodrick's statement.

Ryan looked up to him. "As soon as I'm sixteen, I'm going to work out at Core Rhythm Fitness."

Now, it was Rodrick's face that lit up, and he patted Ryan on the back. "I can't wait."

In the past when Ryan has come with us to CRF, it's only because he wants to see Rodrick and tell him "hi." Then, he hangs out until we're done.

After dinner, Darlesia told us all goodnight and headed home.

Boise stopped over at our table to bid Rodrick farewell. He and Jesse had a quick laugh about Jesse's giant grin near the end of the show. We had actually met Boise previously on another night outside the theater when he and David had come out together and talked to us. This big amazing group of people really did seem like family.

It was getting late when Rodrick asked, "Which way are you guys headed? Do you want to share a car with me?"

Normally, our hotel was two blocks away, but this trip, we happened to be staying near where he and Jay lived.

"Sure," Jesse said.

The four of us hopped in a cab together and talked all the way to right in front of his building.

"When will you be back?" he asked before climbing out of the car.

"Just before Thanksgiving," I said.

"Thank you for a wonderful night! Text me when you're back!" he said, and he closed the door.

What a wonderful night, indeed. It was such a blessing to have his light in our lives.

18

"A PART OF US"

November 25, 2018
Cleveland, Ohio

JESSE

For the last twelve years, it has been our Thanksgiving tradition that everyone meets at our place and stays as long as they can. It's our favorite week of the year. We have eleven family members come in from Michigan and North Carolina: Kathy's two brothers and their families, her parents, and my parents.

Kathy loves cooking for everyone, and usually, we all help in the kitchen a little bit. My specialty is doing the dishes. One year, us boys all decided we could make dinner just as well without all the fuss and time spent. Kathy agreed to relinquish her command and let us try. We took the easy way out, and in the end, we decided to order a pre-made Thanksgiving dinner from Whole Foods. It was good, but Kathy took back control the next year.

We spend the week talking until late in the night, catching up with each other, watching movies together, and playing cards. The cousins run around the house and play games, have dance parties, and do karaoke. Then, all of the kids have a sleepover on "the boat," our sectional couch that we've pushed together to form one giant cushy spot that fills almost our entire family room.

Our house is filled with chaos and laughter the whole week. The only problem is that when they all leave, it's always a little too quiet and gloomy.

This year, the real melancholy began Sunday night, November twenty-fifth. Our families had just left our house, and I opened an email from Ken. My throat tightened as I read it. "*Once on This Island* will be closing January 6, 2019." This was like a punch in the stomach, even though I had a feeling it was coming. Officially, it would be announced on Tuesday, November twenty-seventh.

"Why?" Ryan asked.

Kathy had no words at all.

We weren't alone in our devastation. The *Once on This Island* Instagram account posted "FINAL WEEKS! MUST CLOSE JANUARY 6". There were over one thousand comments. Here's a small sample of what people commented on that day's post:

"NOOOOOO!"

"WHY????"

"thank you for telling the story"

"this show changed my life"

"best show on broadway"

"WTF"

"Why Gods"

"devastated"

christelle_floress wrote: "DAMN IT MOM GET ME TICKETS"

sharkbait_moo_haha wrote: "I saw this show front row and it was the best experience of my life. Thank you for that. (Two hearts)"

rjshayesteh wrote: "I'm so upset. I can say without a doubt that once on this island was the most beautiful piece of theatre I have ever seen. Thank you for telling the story."

michellephants wrote: "My 27th time on the island was a few weeks ago. I'll shoot for 28, 29, and 30 in the coming month, and I implore everyone to see it :("

suitcasefullofsummertime wrote: "I'm so not okay about this, don't even know what to say. Thank you so much for the last year, literally one of the most amazing shows I'll ever have the pleasure of seeing"

broadway.myway wrote: "This show has had changed my life it does not deserve this truly heartbroken"

herbertwhite_ wrote: "So I guess the world is ending. Oh okay. Just checking"

haalamama wrote: "Devastating. Thank you for such a beautiful piece of story telling. Feel privileged to have seen it. @michaelarden you are brilliance personified."

mei_cellino wrote: "agwe why you flood my eyes with tears"

maddiealgerr_ wrote: "this show left me shaking and bawling what the heck"

Several teachers wrote comments similar to manda-jean0857: "Nooooooo I was gonna take 50 of my drama students all the way from SC to see this in June (sad face)"

It went on and on. This show was affecting people. It was changing lives, and all of a sudden, it was going to be gone. Kathy, Ryan, and I all had similar reactions. It was too soon. This story was too important. We moped around feeling a deep sense of imminent loss.

This also meant that we would indeed lose most of the money we put in, but we had already come to terms with that before we even wired the funds over a year ago. What we were losing now was much more painful.

From the emails Ken's office had sent for the last couple months, it was clear this day was coming. Too many seats were left empty each week. People were simply not coming to the show in large enough numbers. If a show isn't bringing more money in that it is paying out, it has to close just like any other business. I was hoping against all hope that the inevitable could be put off, that something would change and all of a sudden attendance would surge. I was nowhere near ready for this journey to be over.

We hadn't planned on being back in NYC until January eighteenth, for a performance of *Syncing Ink* at Joe's Pub created by NSangou Njikam. This was the show Victoria had been working on and had been so thrilled to tell us about. Now, we had to plan another trip for the closing weekend as well. There was no way we could miss it. We bought tickets immediately and tried to put it out of our minds, pretending it wasn't real until we had to face the truth. There were other things to look forward to in the meantime: our twenty-fourth anniversary, Christmas break, and New Year's. We focused on those instead.

Kathy's younger brother, Dave, and his family came from Michigan to visit for a few days to celebrate New Year's. It was a wonderful way to forget what was coming, but when they left on January second, the closing loomed like a black storm cloud in front of us.

Normally, an upcoming trip to New York is an exciting escape from our day-to-day lives, but this time, it felt like we were heading to the funeral of a loved one. Our hearts were heavy as we headed to Cleveland Hopkins International Airport. We weren't ready to say goodbye. How do you say goodbye to something that has become a part of you? It had given us so much, much more than we had given.

Not only would we be saying goodbye to the show but also to the incredible people in the cast. Most of them we only saw at the show and in the theater where we got chances to talk with them and at *Once on This Island* get-togethers. The Island had brought us all together for a brief and shining moment and given us all this very special connection. Sometimes, when we stood outside the theater adding our voices to the crowd at the stage-door, David or Kenita or Cassondra would sneak out a side exit, come over, and talk to us for a bit.

One time when I was alone in NYC on a business trip, David came out, and we stood chatting for quite a while. Before he headed off on his way, he asked, "When will you be back?"

"Next month," I replied.

"In your usual seats?"

I nodded.

"Okay, great! I'll see you then." He shook my hand, and he walked off.

There was a special bond, a love for each and every person of the cast. Now, they would scatter like fall leaves in the wind, moving on with their busy lives in all different directions. It's possible we could see them again in the future. We're connected with several of them on social media. We will follow their careers and support whatever shows they are in next. In all likelihood, though, January sixth, 2019, would be the last time we would see this special group of performers. We had only one day more.

Honestly, even if the show had run another ten years, we would have felt the same about its closing. It's always too early to say goodbye.

On January fourth, we arrived at LaGuardia airport and took a car to our usual hotel, the Hilton Garden Inn at 8th Avenue right around the corner from the theater. Unlike other trips, we didn't have a whole lot planned. Usually, we have other shows and activities on the itinerary and hardly any down time. This weekend, our schedule was pretty empty.

Trying to make the most of our day, we checked in to our hotel and then headed out to grab a quick healthy lunch at Dig Inn, where it's easy for me to stay on my low-carb diet with a delicious bowl of roasted chicken and lots of veggies. I didn't want to gain back all the pounds Rodrick had helped me release. Rodrick chooses the word *release* because to lose weight or anything at all implies you want to find it.

That day, Dig Inn was packed, and there were no available tables, so the three of us took our food back to the hotel to eat. After finding a place to sit in the lobby, we ate in relative silence, each of us in our own little world unable to lift ourselves above the gloom. Normally if we have nothing planned in the middle of the day, we find some place fun to go even if it's just a walk to Central Park and back, but after eating, we didn't feel like going anywhere. Instead, we stayed in the room and grabbed the books we had brought. Kathy finished reading *Worlds in Harmony: Compassionate Action for a Better World* by His Holiness the Dalai Lama.

After reading for a while and then FaceTiming Jessica back home to check in with her and say, "Hi" to Roo and Rory, we were restless and decided we had to get out of the room. We headed out to Empire Diner for dinner. It was better than sullenly hiding in the hotel the rest of the evening.

Ryan, on the cusp of adulthood, wasn't happy when the hostess handed him a coloring page as we sat down. He's fourteen-and-a-half and getting ready to learn how to drive, but because he's inherited Kathy's small-human genes, people think he's about ten. It infuriates him. In his mind, he's already an adult. I have to admit, despite his physical build, he is an extremely mature kid.

He politely took the coloring page from her and moved it to

the empty spot at the table. Grinning mischievously, he said, "It's for my younger brother."

She looked a little confused as she walked away wondering why we had asked for a table for three.

Throughout dinner, we reminisced about our favorite *Once on This Island* moments: the Tony Awards, Rodrick playing Papa Ge, the time Agwe messed up a line and it came out "Polish up the peasants," instead of "Polish up the Mercedes," the night Rodrick jumped in Ryan's lap, and so many others.

After dinner, we ordered dessert because Ryan had his eye on the vanilla shake with sprinkles. Okay, he's not *totally* an adult yet. Kathy and I shared the apple galette drizzled with caramel sauce.

Later that evening, we had tickets to a small show called *Say Something Bunny* at a tiny little theater on West 20th Street. It was not a typical show. Only about twenty people fit in the small room, and we were each given a "part" to play and a script to read in this historical mystery. We didn't actually have to speak. The actor did all of that for us, but we were the physical manifestation of "our" character, and we were to follow along. Everyone chuckled when Ryan got assigned to play the part of the grandfather.

Saturday was rainy all day, reflecting our somber mood perfectly. We went out for a late breakfast at Rustic Table, which I would definitely recommend. One of the best things about being in NYC was trying lots of new restaurants. We have our favorites that we frequent as well, but part of the fun is exploring new places. Luckily, Ryan enjoys finding new restaurants too. I have a whole list of places on my to-try list. We'll probably never get to all of them.

Afterward, we meandered down 40th Street heading toward the Drama Bookstore, where Lin-Manuel Miranda would occasionally go when he was writing *Hamilton* and *In the Heights*. He recently became a part owner of the bookstore to save it from closing down.

On the way there, we passed a food pantry handing out grocery bags of canned goods and other non-perishable items. Two older women were walking away quickly, each with a cart of food. A rather disheveled man followed close behind them. As we approached, we heard the man swearing and hurling racial slurs at the women. Kathy was disgusted. She wanted to say something, but before she had time, the man hurried off sputtering madly to himself. Kathy shook her head. She was disappointed in herself that she hadn't spoken up, but the man clearly had mental health issues. I reassured her the situation came and went too quickly. Other than words, he wasn't hurting the women. Though words can cut as deeply as a knife, only the scars are borne on the inside.

"Nothing ever changes if we remain silent," she said, still bothered by her inaction.

Inside the Drama Book store, Ryan sat and read a book on the making of *The Book of Mormon,* and Kathy and I browsed the books on producing and writing. We didn't feel like strolling through the streets on a rainy day, so we decided to head back to the hotel. Kathy finished reading *Gmorning Gnight!: Little Pep Talks for Me and You* by Lin-Manuel Miranda. She's a self-described slow reader and never finishes one book on a trip, let alone two. Now, she was out of books. Usually, we don't have any time to read while in New York, but we didn't have anywhere to be. Ryan had finished the four-hundred-page Matthew Reilly book he'd brought, and he got an idea.

"Hey, Mom, download *Ice Station.* I've already read it, but we can read it together."

An action-packed mystery at an ice station is not the kind of book Kathy would normally choose on her own, but she did it to spend time with Ryan.

Just the other day back home, I had noticed Kathy and Ryan

sitting on the couch together, and he was showing her some website that sells shoes. He'd clicked on a model he liked and explained what made it cool. It was a limited edition or a collaboration with some other fashion company or star. She'd asked intelligent questions about it. She wasn't looking at her phone in between. She was really listening, not because she cared to learn about expensive footwear but because *he* cared about it. He must have shown her twenty different styles over forty-five minutes. It didn't matter to her how she and Ryan were spending the time. The fact that he wanted to share something with her meant she wanted to listen.

Now, as I looked over and saw them thoroughly engrossed in *Ice Station* together, I realized maybe I needed to be more like that. It was much easier for me to be a dad when the kids were little. All I had to do was hug them, be silly, and take care of their needs. Now that they were teens and young adults, it was different, and I wasn't always prepared for this new role.

For dinner that night, we went to the West Bank Cafe. Ryan was quiet. I never know if he's tired, in a teenage mood, or distressed about something. He's a great kid. I'm so proud of him, and I probably don't tell him that enough. He is very thoughtful and does well in school, and he's worked hard to be an impressive guitarist. His fingers look like spiders scampering over the fretboard. The fact that he started his own band at thirteen, and they set up their own gigs and practices and are still together kind of blows my mind. I have nothing to complain about except that, like every parent, I think he's on his phone too much. My biggest issue is that I know he's not going to need me very soon. His once tiny hand used to hold mine as we walked, and now, I feel him slipping through my fingers. That breaks my heart. I'm not ready to let him go yet.

Thankfully, I had purchased tickets to see another show this evening after dinner. I hadn't wanted to pack our itinerary, but I knew we would need a few distractions to lighten our mood, which turned out to be good planning because, at the moment, our hearts were as heavy as a boat filled with sand. We paid the bill and walked to the West Side Theater to see *The Other Josh Cohen,* a charming and heartfelt musical that raised our spirits at least for a few hours. Lately, we had been enjoying several off Broadway productions as well and had been trying to see as many as we could fit into our schedule. Most of them are produced with a lower budget, but they are done with so much passion, creativity, and heart.

Passion and heart were exactly the qualities that drew us into *Once on This Island* from the beginning. All musicals should have great music, but only a few leave you feeling breathless and somehow changed. *Once on This Island* brought that to us. In our eyes, it had everything, including an unbelievably talented cast from the principals to the understudies. Over the course of the year, after visiting the Island multiple times, we had the pleasure of seeing most of the cast perform at one time or another. During each performance, they put every ounce of their heart and soul into those ninety minutes. Do they realize the gift they are giving to people every night?

Kenita and Phillip are perfect examples. Every single show, they are crying after they sing "Ti Moune." It takes them halfway through "Mama Will Provide" to recover, and they do it eight times a week. I don't know how they do it, but the raw power and emotion in the music must help. It naturally moves an open-hearted soul.

The morning of January sixth, none of us wanted to wake up. If we stayed asleep, maybe the day wouldn't happen, and the show wouldn't close. My heart hurt. Our journey was coming to an end. I kept telling myself I had to let go, but I didn't want to. No one could hold off the inevitable. I was an arrogant fool to think otherwise.

So many beautiful souls had joined together so that *Once on This Island* could live and breathe again, and now, it was at an end. It was heart-wrenching to say goodbye. The experience of seeing a performance of *Once on This Island,* especially this revival with its intimate setting of natural elements and "found" instruments, was like no other. The world would be losing a very special work of art when it was gone.

Ryan wondered if they would at least make a movie of the stage production and run it one last time for the cameras. If they did, we would be one of the first in line to buy it. A movie of it would be better than nothing, but even that would only be like looking at old photographs of loved ones now gone. It could never be the same as being in the theater, experiencing it live.

Any live performance—a concert, a play, a musical—has its own soul-like energy, an ethereal quality. It's not like popping in a DVD or watching Netflix. No live performance could ever be exactly the same as another one, and that's part of what makes it special.

You have to take advantage of the brief moment that it exists. If you miss it, you can never get it back. Even in the same production, no two performances are exactly alike. You never know exactly what you're going to get. A line might be said slightly off, a step might have just a little more energy, a note may be belted a little differently one night, or your attention might be focused on something else this time. Each performance has its own energy that can be detected by the audience as well as the cast. You have to be present in each moment and let yourself be moved. When it's over, it's over. Its soul moves on and no longer exists. It only lives on in you, in your memory of being in that experience, in that one particular moment and place. Everyone present shares this one moment in time with you.

Celebrating the life of *Once on This Island* was why we were here, and no amount of sleeping in was going to delay the end, so we eventually rolled unenthusiastically out of bed and made our way down to Jack's Wife Freda for our favorite comfort foods: waffles, eggs, and chicken kebabs with endless cups of Stumptown coffee.

That perked us up a bit.

Even though it was a crisp January day, after breakfast, we walked through Washington Square Park and stopped to watch all the dogs play at the fenced-in dog play area thinking maybe that would put a smile on our faces, but today, it only made us miss Roo and Rory more.

"Can we stop at a store to see if I can find a new suit jacket for tonight?" Ryan asked. "The one I packed is a little too small."

Nordstrom Rack was nearby, so we wandered in. It wouldn't be easy finding him a new one on such short notice, though. He's at an odd size at this stage, too skinny for men's clothes and too tall for kids clothes. There was one that almost fit, but it wasn't quite right. Kathy suggested we check Macy's, so we headed over.

"Mom, look at this one!" he exclaimed. It was exactly what he'd been looking for— a sapphire blue velvet jacket, a matching vest, a tuxedo shirt, and a bow tie. Best of all, it was on a big post-holiday discount.

Back at the hotel, we changed and prepared ourselves for the night ahead. Ryan suddenly looked older in his new suit. He's at the age where I simultaneously get glimpses of the man he'll be and flashbacks of the little boy he was. I'm proud and wistful at the same time.

"Can we go to Tacuba? I'm hungry for tacos," Ryan asked.

"Sure," I said.

The wind had come up a bit, but we braved the biting cold and walked a few blocks to have dinner at Ryan's favorite taco place in the city, where they serve authentic Mexican dishes and make their tortillas by hand. Ryan anointed them the best tacos anywhere.

The hostess smiled at him when we walked in. "I remember you! Good to see you again."

We end up there frequently.

Ryan ate his usual two orders of chicken tacos quickly, so quickly that we had to take up extra time by getting the tres leches dessert with a soft browned meringue and fruit salsa. Kathy sacrificed herself for the family and ate most of it, which she thoroughly enjoyed.

Around six-thirty, we headed to the theater. The upper lobby was already packed. Excitement was in the air, though I was not excited. I was having difficulty knowing this was the last time I would ever see this amazing piece of work. Nothing like it has ever been done on stage, and I despaired that, despite winning the Tony Award, it wouldn't be around to touch the hearts of new audiences.

The three of us stood quietly in the lobby. Ryan, while forlorn about the closing, had a big smile on his face. He felt like a million bucks in his chic new threads.

Around seven, they let us downstairs. I looked at Kathy. Her eyes glistened. She struggled to keep it together as well, so she turned her attention to Ryan, which helped keep her mind off her own despair. All we had left was this one last time to enjoy being here.

Standing near the theater door, we noticed Phillip Boykin's wife, Felicia, whom we had met at the *Gettin' the Band Back Together* opening party back in August. I went over and introduced myself again.

When she saw Ryan, she remembered us immediately. Probably the only reason most people remember us is because of Ryan. He's quite recognizable, especially with how engaged he is in theater. She said, "Hi," to Ryan then added, "Wow, do you look sharp in that outfit!"

His smile widened, and he thanked her.

"I can't believe it's ending tonight," she said wistfully.

We empathized with her. Even the usher standing nearby joined our conversation.

Then it was time to go in.

For the last time, we sat in our favorite seats in the sand. It had been just over a year since we'd done the same at Opening Night. How had the year gone so fast?

We saw Diego Kolankowsky come in and sit across from us a few rows up. Of course Ken Davenport was there, as well as Michael Arden and Lynn Ahrens. Then Emerson Davis, one of the original young Ti Mounes who had already left the show, sat right beside Kathy. In the year since the Opening, she had grown and handed off the role to another young Ti Moune.

"Hi!" she said brightly as soon as she saw us.

"Are you working on a new show?" Kathy asked her.

"Yes." She smiled.

Kathy perked up a bit having Emerson sit beside her.

Cassondra was first to come out onto the sand. She took a deep breath as if to ready herself for this last night on the Island. We weren't the only ones struggling with the loss. I can't imagine all the emotions the cast must have been going through. To work with a group of such talented and wonderful people every day for over a year, putting your heart and soul into every performance, crying and celebrating together, and then to all of a sudden have this family be separated and move on to other things... I guess every cast goes through it eventually. We all have to learn to let go.

Cassondra walked mournfully to the fallen "tree" and ran her hand slowly over the pictures that had been pinned to it. From the beginning of the run, cast members had fastened pictures of their lost loved ones onto the pole. Every night, they paid homage to them when they first came out for the pre-show. With tears in her eyes already, Cassondra turned, gave little Ti Moune a hug, and hurriedly walked back off stage.

I looked at Kathy. Her eyes were filling up, but she held back the tide. She knew once the dam broke it would be impossible to stop the deluge.

Papa Ge, played now by Tamyra Gray, came out next leading the goat—I'm not sure if it was Peapod or Sparky—and the crowd cheered. Each time a cast member appeared in the sand, we all hollered and showed our appreciation. This was our first time ever experiencing a closing night show. Maybe a mini ovation happens for each cast member on all closing nights, we didn't know. I wished it had occurred every night. This was one of the most talented groups of people I'd ever seen. Even the understudies we'd seen were just as brilliant as the principals. They all deserved every bit of love they received tonight.

As each cast member came out, many of them spotted Emerson in the front row right away. They rushed over, ignoring any protocol, and hugged her. David came over to us and shook our hands. Kenita, with tears in her eyes, ran over to Emerson and scooped her into a hug. She let Emerson and Ryan pet the chicken one last time. They were all making peace and mourning this loss in their own way.

Daniel Yearwood, who played a narrator and was an understudy for Daniel, noticed Ryan's suit, came over, and asked, "Can I see that suit? Stand up and show it off."

Another ear-to-ear grin emerged on Ryan's face.

Pretty soon, the cast was ready to begin. Kenita took a deep breath steadying herself, barely holding back the tide. Then for one last time, she raised her powerful voice to the gods and began the show with eight simple words, words that for us carried meaning as deep as the sea.

I looked at Kathy. The dam had broken for both of us, and tears flowed like a swollen river. I held her hand in mine. So many emotions coursed through me. I was forever grateful to have been given this opportunity to be a part of this show. I couldn't be prouder and happier for this cast, but my heart was breaking. I couldn't stop the flood, and I didn't want to.

Hailey Kilgore, despite having been sick all week, made her last entrance as Ti Moune running through the water to the left of us.

She held nothing back as she sang "Waiting For Life," and the audience jumped to its feet as soon as she finished. She stood barefoot in the sand, in her flowing red dress baring her soul. Sobbing uncontrollably, Hailey turned to take in this ocean of people standing for her final performance of her Broadway debut role. She had been discovered in Oregon when Michael Arden set out on his international casting search for the right Ti Moune.

We all cried with her.

The night was already going too fast. If only I could have paused time, to stay in this moment just a little bit longer...

Tonight's energy and appreciation for this show and its cast reminded me of the elation I felt at the Tony Awards. I wished they had received this same level of applause every night. Why does it take losing something or someone to fully appreciate them? Why did we take them for granted because they are always there and only realizing what we had after we've lost it?

In previous performances, the first tears for me always came to my eyes when Kenita and Phillip sang "Ti Moune." They had been happy together before Ti Moune had come into their lives, and now, they could not bear the thought of losing her and pleaded with her to stay.

In their hearts, Ti Moune would always be their little girl, needing their love and protection. I feel the same way with my girls. Ti Moune would not listen to their pleadings, and despite my advice, our girls make their own choices, not always following my guidance.

Then, Phillip, in his deep, emotion-laced voice, said that he will let her go.

I break every time.

Accepting and letting go.

Jess and Alyss are leaving us to find their dreams. Will they find their happiness?

By the end of the song in every performance, both Phillip and Kenita are crying. I don't know how to tell the difference between "acting" tears and real ones, but it seemed to me that tonight, their very souls were weeping. Mine was too.

The song earned another standing ovation and a torrent of tears from the audience as we wept along with them.

It was clear that tonight, all of our hearts were breaking, and we would leave this theater cleansed and without a tear left in our bodies. Kenita and Phillip stood for a moment in the sand holding each other, each gaining strength from the other as they let the adoration of the crowd sink in. Kathy reached over and squeezed my hand, both of us on the brink of all out-sobbing.

As always, Alex Newell's big moment singing "Mama Will Provide" lightened the mood and was a welcome relief. Night after night, he used every ounce of his larger-than-life personality to play the role of Asaka with an incomparable sultry sass.

Electrified by tonight's energy, he swayed his hips with more heat than the sunbaked island sand and pushed his voice to divine heights as he belted out the song that seemed to have been written for him.

Tonight, we didn't need to start anything. The crowd was on its feet even before he started his final run. This audience knew they were seeing one of the most extraordinary moments on Broadway. That Alex, a self-described gender non-conformist preferring the pronouns "he/him", was even cast in this traditionally female role was cutting edge. Director Michael Arden had decided that the Gods of this island were all gender fluid and could manifest in any type of human form. This concept of gender fluidity was theologically an ancient idea around the world. In Haitian Vodou, the Iwa of the Gods can possess anyone regardless of their gender, and the Hindi God Shiva is often represented as Ardhanarishvara, a composite of the male

Shiva on the right side and Parvati the female on the left, but it hadn't been done on a Broadway stage before. It was brilliant.

As soon as he hit the last note, the theater exploded with applause. The tidal wave of sound from hands clapping and people screaming and whistling for Alex must have lasted at least five minutes. Overwhelmed by the love washing over him, he broke down, sobbing. Tears streamed down his face as he turned, put his hands on his heart, and took it all in from every corner of this circular theater.

Lea Salonga rejoined the cast for the last two weeks as Erzulie, The Goddess of Love. Like the other three gods, Erzulie only has one big solo, but Lea's otherworldly rendition of "The Human Heart" brought the crowd to its feet yet again. Then, it was Isaac Powell's turn to get a standing ovation after singing "Some Girls."

Next came "The Ball" scene, one of Kathy's favorites. As a figure skating coach, she pays close attention to choreography. The dancing in this scene had a special energy. Every time we saw it, she hoped the audience would give this number a standing ovation, but if they weren't going to stand for Alex, surely a dance number wouldn't get them out of their seats. Tonight, on this final night, Kathy got her wish. The crowd cheered even as Ti Moune began her dance and again as each new palace servant joined in.

Kathy saw the dance as a metaphor. The peasants, for a moment, were allowing their bodies to enjoy the freedom of movement their souls longed for. It was a protest of the inequality they faced in the house of the Beauxhommes simply because of the color of their skin. When Daniel's heart was carried along by the tide of emotion and he rose to join the dance, it became a rebellion. This was the only moment in his life that he had the courage to stand up to his father and the shackles of history. He was finally free when he joined this traditional island movement with Ti Moune and the other servants, so different from the stiff emotionless European style dancing that he was used to. For an instant, his heart dared to dream how the world could be, but he could not sustain it. He was not strong enough to break the chains of the traditions and ignorance that bound him. Even his wealth and station could not set him free. They held him in invisible fetters. He was too afraid to lose his own position of power to stand up for what was right and fight for change. And he, like so many before him, turned a blind eye to justice.

When the dance was done, this audience leaped to its feet.

The worst part of The Ball scene is that it signifies the final turn, that the show is coming to the end. I broke down again. I had to accept what was about to happen. Papa Ge was here to take *Once on This Island* down to the underworld, and there would be no trading of souls to bring it back.

These were the last few moments of its life, the last few moments we had with it, but our hearts had been touched forever. They could never return to their state before *Once on This Island*, especially this production. It would always be a part of us.

Kenita broke the silence in the theater and cried out to her daughter lying in the sand. Her voice was rich with all the agony of a mother weeping for her lost child.

A flash of me tossing my little girls high in the air at our building's rooftop pool in Philly crossed my mind. They laughed, screamed, and said, "Again, Daddy." And then, like my brain changing channels, I saw an older, rail-thin Jessica fighting for her life in the eating disorder treatment center. I sucked in a shaky breath.

Tonight, Kenita paused for an extra second to collect herself, desperately holding the line between all-out sobbing for her own loss of this show and still being able to perform.

Everyone in the theater struggled right along with her. Even

Phillip fought for composure and visibly paused as he prepared to sing his line. I heard sniffling in every direction.

Once on This Island superfan Brianna Simpkins, who we had seen a couple other times, was sitting two seats down from me and had lost the fight. She was sobbing uncontrollably. All 725 of us in that circle were suffering together the loss of this amazing piece of theater.

This is the power of theater. All of our hearts moved as one.

Theater can bring to light what our hearts already know. Love for one another is why we are here. Love, not just for those close to us, but love for all humanity no matter our skin color, religion, sexuality, nationality, or political affiliation. We are all part of this big, beautiful, human family.

We're all striving for the happiness of our families, friends, and ourselves. We simply want the freedom to love who we love and live in peace. If we would only listen to our collective human heart, we could all dance together.

But maybe in order to dance together, we first need to grieve together, and here we did.

As the cast sang the last notes and the lights went out, we were all weeping—cast, crew, and audience.

In the darkness, we jumped up to show our final appreciation, crying, cheering, clapping. It went on for at least ten minutes, maybe longer. None of us wanted to move. As soon as we left the theater, it would be over, so like a child stalling at bed-time, we continued to clap, cheer, and celebrate the beautiful short life of this production.

In total, Kathy, Ryan, and I saw this show over twenty-five times. We never took a single moment in any of the shows for granted, and yet we were still just as devastated when it was over. Even if it had lasted another year, we would have felt the same. No one is ever really ready to say goodbye.

The cast took their bows. They stood in the sand absorbing the love. Then, original cast members and guest cast members like Norm Lewis came down the aisles and joined them on the Island. Camille A. Brown, the choreographer, and other people involved in the show including producers also joined them. I guess technically as co-producers, we could have joined them, too, but we didn't. We had our feet in the sand. That was enough. We still thought of ourselves as fans because first and foremost, that was why we were here. We didn't have any part in the creation or running of this show. We simply loved what these amazing creators, cast, and crew had brought to the world. Can they possibly understand what their work means to those of us lucky enough to experience it?

Rodrick, who had been in the audience, rushed down the steps and hugged everyone in his path. He made his way over to us. Many people were videoing the end, the ovation, and afterward. I kind of wish I had, but I also wanted to LIVE in this moment. I wanted to be present. I have pictures in my mind. We stood and watched the joy and grief of the cast members as they embraced the people who had become family. Maybe they wouldn't see some of them again for a long time, if ever.

I don't know how long we stood there. Time didn't matter. No one wanted to leave anyway.

After a while, Ken Davenport walked around, handed out ziplock baggies, and said, "Take some sand home."

So we did. Ryan filled his bag to the absolute brim. I hoped it wouldn't cause a problem flying home, but at that moment, I didn't care.

Eventually, the ushers told people they had to leave. Kathy spotted Jay sitting on the other side, so we crossed the sand and headed up to see him. He was waiting for Rodrick and talking with Felicia Boykin. He wrapped his arms around us. One of the things that amazes me about both Jay and Rodrick is how special they make each person feel. It's a wonderful quality.

As we sat there talking with them, waiting for Rodrick, we watched the continued commotion in the sand. Camille A.

Brown was coming up the steps toward us. Kathy walked down a few steps. She greatly admired her choreography and wanted to finally meet her and thank her.

That's when I saw Cynthia Erivo step onto the Island making the rounds and talking to people. We had seen her in *The Color Purple* a few years ago. I had never seen anything like her performance. The audience had given her a standing ovation for her rendition of "I'm Here." She had sung with her whole body. The pain and passion that her character Celie had suffered from being abused and losing her children had flowed out of her. It had been absolutely stunning. Ever since, I'd hoped to someday get the chance to tell her what an honor it had been to watch that performance.

My stomach dropped like I'd just crested the top of a roller coaster. She started walking up the stairs toward us. She kept coming closer. If she looked away from us, I wouldn't say anything, but instead of avoiding eye contact, she looked right at me and smiled. My heart almost jumped out of my chest, and a surge of adrenaline rushed through me. Now was my chance. I may never get another opportunity.

I took a tiny step toward her and said, "Ms. Erivo, I have to tell you. We saw you in *The Color Purple*. We see a lot of theater, and we have never seen anything like your performance. It was phenomenal. Thank you so much."

I figured she would smile, say thanks, and then walk away, but she didn't. Instead, she said in her British accent, "Thank you. It truly means a lot, and I wanted to tell you I was watching your family in the front row, and I'm a big fan of yours and how open your hearts are. We need more people like you in theater."

My head spun like a top. What? Did Cynthia Erivo just tell me she was a big fan of MINE? My heart was flitting about my chest like a hummingbird, but I tried to look calm. She still didn't walk away. I could hardly believe I was having this conversation with her.

"This is our favorite musical," I said. "Are you going to be in another show soon?"

"I'm working on something new," she said with a wink.

"We'll be there!" I said.

"Thank you," she repeated, and then she headed out.

Eventually, Rodrick sauntered up the steps to join us. He shouted, "Norm! How are you?"

We turned to see Norm Lewis standing just behind us. They embraced and talked for a few minutes, and Norm moved on to congratulate other cast members.

Rodrick turned to us. "Are you guys going to the party?"

"We wouldn't miss it," I said.

"Do you want to walk with us?" he asked.

"We would love to."

We were some of the first people to arrive. A few other cast members trickled in slowly. We found a table and sat and talked with Rodrick and Jay for an hour or two, but it was getting late, and Rodrick had to teach a five o'clock training session the next morning. We took some pictures with them and then said our goodbyes. Luckily, we would see them again the next morning anyway at CRF for an eight o'clock class.

For us, it was too depressing to end the night already because that meant this amazing journey was really over. In spite of our early morning the next day, we walked over a block or two to the producer's party. We realized the first one had been a cast party. The second one was packed. The guy at the door took one look at Ryan and said, "My man! Look at you! You're the best dressed one in here!" He gave Ryan a fist bump.

Ryan smiled and said, "Thanks."

It had been just over a year that we had been at the Opening going around mingling and meeting these same people. What a year it had been. Now, this was our last chance to hang out with all the people whom we had met on this amazing journey. The mood wasn't quite as somber as the get-togethers after a wake, but in my heart, that's what it felt like. We reminisced about all the many wonderful aspects of its short life and the shock and surprise we'd all had at the Tony Awards.

The three of us made our way around the restaurant, and just like at the Opening Night party, we thanked any cast member who went by. Everyone complimented Ryan's fashion choice. Daniel Yearwood stopped us, asking if he could get a picture with Ryan, dubbing him the best-dressed guy in the room.

Not only was the entire cast incredibly talented, but everyone we met was warm-hearted and sincere. We'd had that impression on Opening Night, but now after spending a year on the Island, it had been confirmed. I was incredibly grateful to have had the chance to get to know them even a little bit.

It was getting late and weariness began to set in. We had to say goodbye to Kenita before we left and went to look for her. As soon as she saw us, she smiled and opened her arms to embrace us. This might be our last time seeing her, though we hoped maybe someday, our stories would weave us back together.

"You guys feel like family to me," she said, tearing up. "I'm really going to miss seeing you."

A lump formed in my throat.

"Oh, we will miss you too!" Kathy said.

"We just love you so much," I finally was able to say.

"Can we get a picture with you?" Kathy asked.

Kenita turned to someone nearby and handed them our phones. She took several pictures of the four of us. We all embraced, but before we said our final goodbyes, she asked Ryan if she could give him a kiss on the cheek. Of course he said yes. What a beautiful soul.

We searched for Cassondra to tell her goodbye as well, but unfortunately, we must have missed her. We looked around at the thinning crowd. It was now time for us to let go. There was nothing left but memories to hold on to.

With heavy hearts, we headed for the door and walked back past the doorman, who again complemented Ryan for his suit. We told him, "Goodnight," and headed out the door. Without a word between the three of us, we walked as if in a somber slumber back to our hotel.

I fell asleep first.

Kathy and I awoke around six forty-five the next morning to get ready for Rodrick's class. "Last night, after you fell asleep," she said, "Ryan plopped face down on his bed and uttered one word, 'sad,' and drifted into sleep. It broke my heart."

By seven-thirty, we headed down to SoHo to Core Rhythm Fitness. In the afternoon, we flew back home to Cleveland, leaving a bit of our hearts forever at the Circle in the Square Theater.

EPILOGUE: "WHY WE TELL THIS STORY"

October 23, 2020
Cleveland, Ohio

ATHY

"*C*ome on, honey, hurry up! It starts in five minutes," I
call out to Jesse.

"I know. Get everything set up. I will be right there."

This has been our daily routine now for almost the last
seven months. With yoga mats in hand, I run past our little
shrine to *Once on This Island* in the dining room. A decorative
glass bowl filled with the Island sand from closing night sits on
a small end-table in the corner. Next to the bowl of sand is a
two-foot chunk of the telephone pole that acted as the "tree."
Pictures of the casts' loved ones are still affixed to it, and the

metal pegs which Ti Moune used to climb it are still protruding. I put my free hand on it, taking a moment to breathe in the memories and emotions of our year.

Then, I rush into our living room and lay out the mats so we're all ready. The weights are where they are easy to grab, and then I run back to the kitchen for a big glass of water. Jesse hurries in with his laptop and clicks on the Zoom link.

We sit side by side, waiting for the connection to go through, and then we hear that delightfully familiar scream "AHH! JESSEE! KATHYYY!!" He stretches out each name like he's vocally hugging us. Then, that smile brings a ray of light into our home and our hearts even in these bleak and anxiety-ridden times. Rodrick checks in with everyone as their faces pop up on screen. Most days, it's the same fifteen to twenty of us. Sometimes, thirty or more join the class, but today only ten showed up. On screen, we can see the other two Jesses, Mary, Jenny, Lori, Eric, Capathia, and Vivienne. We are all here to sweat our stress away. But it's not just the High Intensity Interval Training (HIIT class) we're here for. This is about mind, body, and soul.

With his virtual CRF classes, Rodrick has brought a community together, people from all over the world: Atlanta, Cleveland, New York City, Los Angeles and even Mexico. We log in every morning because at least for this one hour of the day, we feel lifted, like we've just been to church. His words ground us and bind us together as a family even while we're in our own spaces jumping off our mats.

It's ten o'clock, and it's time to begin.

"Mary," Rodrick says and pins her screen so we can all see her, "what is this month's mantra?"

"Surrender," she says, taking herself off mute.

"Yessss! And what does surrender mean to you, Mary?"

She thinks for a moment. "It means to let go of things I cannot control."

Rodrick puts his hand to his heart, and we all nodded, thinking about what surrender means to us.

"Let's get started. Lie down on your mat, legs straight at a forty-five degree angle, heels together, toes apart, arms six inches off the mat and pulse." Rodrick leads us through the pilates warm-up.

By the time we're done with the first five minutes, my abs are in a knot and on fire. I hope that means I'm pushing myself harder because even though we've been doing this six times a week for almost a year, it never seems to get easier!

Only forty-five minutes left to go.

Rodrick starts up the playlist, usually a mix of popular rap songs—the non-explicit versions—and some pop tunes all with a rhythm that makes you want to move.

Today, the first exercise is side lunges into a squat. Only sixty seconds of each exercise, but my legs already feel heavy. The stresses of the world outside have taken a toll on my sleep and I don't think I'm going to make it through today. Twenty-five seconds left. I suck in a deep breath.

Somehow, Rodrick senses my waning stamina through the screen and calls out, "C'mon Kathy, just a few more!"

I dig deeper. I breathe and keep pushing.

Doing the virtual class is not the same as being in his NYC studio on Mulberry Street, but for us, living in Ohio, this is almost better. Before, we could only take his class about once a month whenever we were in town. With CRF LIVE, we are blessed with seeing Rodrick multiple times a week. It also gives us the opportunity to meet and get to know more fellow CRF students than we ever would have. Previously, in the studio, after class, everyone rushed off to work or whatever other responsibilities they had for the day. There wasn't really time for more than just a quick "Hi," and we hardly ever saw the same people. The new platform actually allowed for more inter-action, and we saw the same people every day.

The workout is just as hard in person or over Zoom.

The next exercise is cardio, a simple three steps down the mat and three steps back, with high knees, but today, he adds a "bonus" dance-off during our rest. I feel a moment of dread, as I try to think of some dance move I can do. I dance worse than Elaine on Seinfeld, but it is all part of the fun, and I surrender to my insecurity. When Rodrick shifts the screen from Eric, who is moving effortlessly to the beat—he's probably a professional dancer—to Jesse and me, we flail our arms and legs around and start laughing. I'm getting better at being out of my comfort zone.

We ended on abs, with scissor kicks with our head off the ground. Jesse has a hard time with that one.

"Jesse, straighten those legs and point the toes!" Rodrick playfully yells at the camera.

All three Jesses pause, look at the screen, and straighten just a little more.

And then Rodrick says the word I've been waiting for. "Rest."

Somehow, I've made it. Jesse and I lie on our mats sweating like pigs in a steam factory. Rodrick changes the music to soft, soothing yoga-type music. His voice, so full of energy just a minute ago, is now comforting.

"Put your left hand on your heart, your right hand on your left. Breathe." He pauses. "We have spent this month surrendering, letting go of all those things we can't control. This has left space and openness, room for something new. Share in the chat what you've surrendered and what new opportunities it opens for you. While you're thinking, bring your knees to your chest then right ankle over left knee..."

Jesse has to run upstairs to shower so he isn't late for his first meeting of the day. I lay there thinking and stretching. I feel like this year, 2020, has forced us all to surrender to a new way of life. A new way of thinking about what is important. For me, I have thought a lot about how I want to spend the rest of my time on this planet and what I should be working toward.

I've had a lot of time to reflect since the closing performance of *Once on This Island* on January sixth, 2019, especially in the last eight months as the world has been turned upside down by the COVID-19 Pandemic.

One day, we were all going to work, planning trips, meetings, and nights out with friends. The next day, the whole world stopped. I'm sure most of you remember the last thing you did before everything shut down. For me, it was taking my theater on ice team to competition. The very next weekend, Ohio and most of the world closed.

As of today, October twenty-third, 2020 over two hundred thousand Americans have died according to the World Health Organization, and the numbers just keep going up.

In March 2020, we were ordered to shelter-at-home, to only go out for necessities and stay at least six feet from everyone because *anyone* could be a carrier unknowingly. About a week later, I went out for groceries. It was eerie. People who normally smile and interact were hastily going about their business, looking down and making it a point to not make eye contact. Several shelves in the store were empty. There was no milk, beef, chicken, or bread left.

I remember stories Gramps would tell me of his growing up in the Great Depression. He was born in 1921. He was often sent alone to the butcher shop as a child. Not to buy meat, they couldn't afford that, but to see if there were any bones left. If he was lucky, the butcher would give him a bone or two. Then, he would run home to his mother, who would boil it and make soup, adding a few stray vegetables to the pot so they would have something to eat for the week.

I always thought it was sort of a sad but charming story of his resilience and the hardships he faced growing up in the twenties. Of course, he told that story to remind me how good I had it, but for me, growing up with privilege in the United States, food was relatively plentiful and cheap. His story was almost like a legend to me, difficult to fully understand because it had no relevance in my life. I was thankful for my dinner each night but not in the same way he was. He had lived through real hunger.

For me, there has never been a time when food wasn't available. There were times when Jesse and I couldn't afford more than rice and diapers if we wanted to still pay rent, but the shelves at the grocery stores were not bare.

Today, our local store has mostly been restocked, but there are still some items that aren't available. Depending on how long this pandemic lasts, we could be facing real shortages, just like my grandfather did. Hopefully, we won't have to.

I know many are struggling. I'm lucky. Being quarantined in my house with Jesse, our kids, and our dogs is not such a bad thing, though for several months, I was out of work, and I missed all of my skaters dearly when the ice rinks closed. Jesse, at least, has been able to continue to work remotely, and I'm surrounded by the people I love.

What else do I need? The people around me, the relationships I hold dear, and the memories we've made together are the things that make my life full.

I've always been a hopeless romantic. I've always believed that love is the strongest force in the universe, that love can conquer anything, that all we need is love. Maybe it's a naive cliché thought.

Some people speak out against *Once on This Island,* saying in this time of advancing women's rights: Do we need Ti Moune's story? Do we really want young girls to follow Ti Moune's example?

This is complicated. I don't think our young girls should believe finding a rich "Daniel Beauxhommes" is the answer. What I do believe is that each of us needs to make our own decisions about what we want and the direction our life needs to go. We need to let go of societal expectations and hierarchies and find our own wholeness, whatever form that takes. Being empowered means following our own hearts, whether it's becoming a teacher, performer, a NASA scientist, a lawyer, or a myriad of other possibilities. Ti Moune did this. She didn't settle for what was expected of her. She didn't listen to her parents or society. She set out on her own for what she wanted, rather than what her parents or even *we* wanted for her. This example, our youngsters would be wise to follow.

Without Ti Moune challenging the island's traditions of class and color bias, nothing would have ever changed. In her own way, she was standing up and rebelling against oppression. Is it unworthy because it was in the name of love?

I don't think so.

She followed her heart, decided her own path, and stood against all odds to break the chains of the system which held her people. She was willing to sacrifice her life for that cause. Change may not have come soon enough for Ti Moune, but it was she who began the conversation.

Stories can begin the conversation, especially when threads of reality are woven into the tales. I say we need Ti Moune's story of racial and class oppression. I say we need more stories like hers, stories that move the heart and reveal truths about ourselves that maybe we have ignored for far too long. Everyone walks away with a unique perspective when they experience art, and maybe some won't like it. That's okay. We never know who will be moved by our stories and our songs. When we tell authentic stories that come from the heart, people will be moved, and that is how change is eventually brought about.

Jesse, Ryan, and I weren't the only ones moved by *Once on This Island*. It touched the hearts of thousands. They were changed forever after experiencing its love and forgiveness, just as we had been over twenty-eight years ago.

When I was a young twenty-year-old woman waiting for my life to begin, *Once on This Island* gave me the strength to see that, as a woman, I was free to choose my own path no matter where that path led. Yes, the harsh world around me may create mountains that are far too high to climb and I may never get to my destination, but that is okay as long as I am the one leading the expedition.

Against my parents' wishes, I chose Jesse. In my heart, I always knew that we were not two separate beings but two halves of the same heart. We were separated by space and time for a while, but as the tide always comes back to the shore, we were bound together.

After Jesse and I were engaged, my mother-in-law-to-be, Reiko, told me that her mother from Japan used to draw one image over and over again throughout her life. It was an American girl in a skating dress with ice skates on. Reiko's mother had passed the year Jesse and I met, and I was never able to meet her.

That doesn't mean Jesse's and my life together has always been blue skies and sun. We weathered the storm my parents whipped up. It was through love that my parents found the courage to come to Jesse, admit they were wrong, apologize, and sincerely ask for his forgiveness. The fact that he forgave them still stuns me to this day, but he did it because of his love for me.

Love has the power to conquer anything, to bring people together despite their past differences. They all did this because of their love for me.

We survived our biggest tempest, and other squalls have blown our way. We've had our share of disagreements, disappointments, and difficulties, but a long time ago, I realized that none of that mattered. I knew no matter what we argued about, the bottom line was that I wanted him on this journey beside me, forever.

We lost most of the money we put into *Once on This Island*. Investing in a Broadway show is not an investment strategy I would recommend, but somehow, our lives hold more because of the year we found ourselves on the Island. The friendships and experiences that grew from our time there are priceless. Each person who has touched our lives is like a single strand in a tapestry, weaving in and out of our story to form an exquisite design. We wouldn't trade that for anything.

There is one trade that maybe we would make. If Papa Ge gave us the choice, we would trade that Tony Award displayed proudly on our dining room cabinet with Jesse's name on it to sit in the Circle in the Square Theater and experience *Once on This Island* one more time.

Like a Tibetan sand mandala, *Once on This Island* only existed for a brief moment in time and was swept away. It was beautiful, partly because of its impermanence, but only eternal in our hearts.

I finally open my eyes, still laying on the mat, sweat dripping from my body, my muscles still vibrating from the exertion. I sit up and look at the screen. Rodrick and all the other CRF members are in thoughtful meditation. They are now family, without whom I'm not sure I would make it through the stresses of quarantine, the political climate, and the heartaches of systemic hatred and racism. Every day for the last eight months, these beautiful people have been here.

I type in the chat on screen: *I'm surrendering to endings bittersweet and happy, without which I could not come to new beginnings.*

I'm not sure yet what will be written in this new chapter of my life. I can't change the world and bring love and peace into everyone's hearts. As David Mitchell wrote in *Cloud Atlas*, "... your life amounted to no more than one drop in a limitless ocean...yet what is any ocean but a multitude of drops?"

I can't even make my three children get along all the time, but what I *can* do is change myself. I can't change what the universe throws at me, but I can choose how I react to it. I can walk into this new chapter with intention, with attention, with kindness, with love, love for myself and all those around me. Maybe kindness is as contagious as COVID-19. Maybe if we take down the walls from around our hearts that distance us, we can spread love and kindness faster than the wildfires that rage through California. Maybe it only takes a spark.

This time of quarantine, of pause, brings to light that most of all, I want to spend my brief time on this planet in a way that I choose, writing the words on these blank pages that I want to be written.

Once on This Island gave me the courage to live my dream, the courage to choose my own path in spite of what anyone else thought. If that's not girl power, I don't know what is.

I tell this story because I'm the only one who could tell it. Jesse and I chose love and forgiveness from the beginning of our life together. Seeing *Once on This Island* in that year when our own lives were following that same path only strengthened our resolve to choose love over everything.

I tell this story because I hope and believe that we can emerge from quarantine, from grief, and from fear, with a little more gratitude, a little more forgiveness, and a little more love in our hearts.

December 23, 1994
Maui, Hawaii

ATHY

esse and I, finally on our own as the newly married couple Mr. and Mrs. McKendry, raced up the winding mountain road in our little rental car on the Road to Hana, the rainforest on one side of us and the deep blue Pacific sparkling in the sun on the other. I looked over at Jesse as he turned up the CD player. We both took a deep breath in preparation. We waited. Then, at the top of our lungs, we did our best to belt out, "Provi-i-ide!" to the birds and trees.

We laughed. I looked at him and drank him in. We were the only two people, Jesse and me, in this moment.

We had no worries, no past, no future. Just simply now.

His eyes brightened, and he smiled as if an idea had just hit him. "What is the craziest idea or project you would like to work on?" he asked.

"Hmmm." I thought for a moment. I was almost embarrassed to say it out loud, maybe it was a stupid idea, but I had been dreaming about it for a while now. "Okay, this is super crazy." I paused. "But someday, I want to choreograph a full musical on ice…not just a Disney On Ice-like show, but a real musical, like *Les Mis.*"

I felt myself blushing. It wasn't just crazy. It was probably impossible.

He steered the car around a hairpin turn on the side of the mountain. My breath caught in my throat at the sight before us. I tried to snap pictures of the lush mountain valley disappearing into the sea, but the lens could never capture the feeling of being there.

"What about you?" I asked.

I hoped his answer would be even more insane than mine.

The Island breeze played with my long hair, and the sweet earthy perfume of the rainforest filled the air as I sat next to my favorite person in the world.

He took his green eyes off the winding road and glanced at me. "I have no idea if it's possible or even how I would do it…" He paused. "…but some day, I would love to help get *Once on This Island* back on stage, maybe a local production, or who knows…"

ACKNOWLEDGMENTS

WALKING WITH OUR OLD FRIENDS

This story would not be without *all* the beautiful people we met along our journey. This is my attempt to thank them all, though words can never say enough. Thank goodness I have more than ninety seconds to thank everyone, unlike on stage at the Tonys.

First, I want to thank all of the cast and crew of the original *Once on This Island*, the touring cast we saw way back in 1992, the creators and writers of the show, especially Lynn Ahrens and Stephen Flaherty, and Rosa Guy the author of *My Love, My Love* the book from which the musical was based.

Thank you to Nina Silbergleit, Jesse's boss at the Wharton Center, who scheduled him to work that fateful November night.

Thank you to all the beautiful cast and crew of the revival of *Once on This Island* on Broadway for bringing this beautiful story back into our lives. Every night, you performed your hearts out in the sand, and we truly love and miss all of you.

Thank you, Camille A. Brown, for creating stunning choreography for the whole show, utilizing movement to take the story to a deeper realm, telling the tale of oppression and breaking the chains of bondage.

Thanks to Michael Arden for having the vision to create this unbelievable revival production with gender-neutral gods, using the real elements of sand, water, and fire yet keeping the original production's simplicity.

A special thank you goes out to those cast members who gave freely of their time: Kenita R. Miller, Cassondra James, Phillip Boykin, David Jennings, and Darlesia Cearcy.

Thank you to Ken Davenport without whom this journey never would have happened.

Thanks to Valerie Novakoff, who kindly answered all of Jesse's questions.

Thank you to J.L. Woodson, who created a gorgeous cover for this book, and to Nicole Zoltack for her superb editing. This book has been much improved because of her expert suggestions.

Thank you to all the incredible casts and creators of all the musicals who touched us on this journey. They hold a special place in our hearts.

Thank you so much to Ashley Benedict of The Big Picture Communications Consulting, who was pivotal in helping me navigate the licensing aspect, and when things didn't go our way, you stood by me anyway. Without your support, I may not have made it to the end with a complete book.

A very special thanks goes out to Victoria Weinberg and Tobi for your wonderful friendship! It means the world to us. Love you so much! Can't wait to see what is next and to hang out in the city with you both.

Thank you to *all* my students past and present whom I've cherished teaching. You have all made my life so much more full. And a special thank you to all the very talented skaters on my theater on ice team who have given so much of their time and talent to creating works of art on the ice. Sometimes, it's crazy out there at our practices, but I love every minute of working with you. I can't believe some of you have stuck with me six years or more! We haven't yet created full musicals on ice, but we're getting there. Ennika, Michelle, Emma, Lexi, Maegen, Faith, Matthew, Gabby, Katie, Rita, Carolyn, Jess, and Alyss, you are all so special to me. I was so unbelievably proud of all of you skating our *Hamilton* program in NYC! Love you all!

And thanks to Elisa, who let me run with my crazy theater on ice ideas!

To Rodrick and Jay Covington, I don't think I have the words to fully express all the ways you both have impacted our lives. You are truly a light in this world, and we are so blessed to have met you. Love you both!

Thank you, Lori Rapposelli, for being my best friend and coaching partner—I couldn't have a better one—and for having incredible patience with me as I finished this book.

Thank you, Melody Champion, for supporting Jesse and I so many years ago and making my beautiful wedding dress. I am grateful for your friendship.

Thank you to Jesse's parents, Dave and Reiko, for welcoming me into your family from the beginning and loving me like your own daughter. You are the best in-laws a girl could have! Love you so much!

Thank you to my parents, Sandie and Paul. You gave me an amazing childhood filled with love, and thank you for opening your hearts and asking forgiveness. You have been a constant well of love and support for us ever since. Mom, you're still my best friend, and I cherish our time together. Dad, I miss you already, and I'm thankful that Paul, Dave, Mom and I were able to be with you when you took your last breath. Love you both with all my heart!

Thank you to my two amazing brothers, Paul and Dave and their families: Paul, Bonnie, and Georgia, and Dave, Denise, Belle, and Matt, who are eternal sources of love, laughter, and support.

Thank you to my grandparents, Paul and Catherine, for being wonderful examples of hard work, resilience, and love, and for teaching me to follow my heart. Your love will always be with me.

Thank you to our children, Jessica, Alyssa, and Ryan, I will always see you as those little kids laughing and chasing turkeys in the rain with me. You have made our house crazy and crowded, but our lives hold so much more because you are in it. Love you with all my heart. And thank you, Jessica, for your expert editing of the final draft and helping me to write a better story!

Most of all, thank you to Jesse. You have made my life everything I ever dreamed of and more (except for maybe the rafting down the Ganges). I can't wait to see what our next chapters hold.

Love you with all my heart.

Kathryn J. McKendry

APPENDIX

SHOWS ALONG THE WAY

The original version of this book had lyrical quotes from *Once on This Island* woven throughout the narrative to give the reader the flavor of the language in the musical. In addition, after each chapter title, I had carefully selected one quote from other musicals which touched us on this journey and holds a special place in our hearts. Unfortunately, I wasn't able to secure the licensing to include the *Once on This Island* quotes. In the end, I think it worked out for the best. While it delayed publication considerably, it forced me to dig deeper to create a better book that hopefully still puts the reader in the sand at the Circle in the Square theater while not relying on lyrical cues to do it. I am a little sad, however, that I was unable to highlight some of my most favorite lines in the show. The only reason I had originally included them was to pay homage to the incredible beauty of Lynn Ahrens's work. Hopefully, you have taken my advice and listened to the cast album to hear the genius of both her work and Stephen Flaherty's.

Because I had to remove the *Once on This Island* quotes, I also took out all the quotes from the other musicals that introduced each chapter as well.

The entire reason for writing this book was to pay tribute to all that Broadway has given us. Therefore, I am compelled to list by chapter these musicals and the songs which I had originally quoted here in the hopes that you will listen and that your heart will be touched by them as well. Each song chosen has lyrics that fit perfectly with the mood of the chapter it introduced. As a challenge, see if you can pick out which lyric I may have quoted and let me know! Some of these musicals are from Off-Broadway, and some were just about to head to a larger venue when COVID shut everything down, so there are a couple you may have a challenge finding.

I would also love to hear which musicals have changed your life and how!

Chapter 1: "Life Support," from *Rent* by Jonathon Larson

Chapter 2: "Dust and Ashes," from *Natasha, Pierre and The Great Comet of 1812* by Dave Malloy

Chapter 3: "A Sympathetic Ear," from *A Strange Loop* by Michael R. Jackson

Chapter 4: "Campfire Song," from *The Lightning Thief: The Percy Jackson Musical* by Rob Rokicki

Chapter 5: "Not My Father's Son," from *Kinky Boots* by Cindy Lauper

Chapter 6: "The Lesson," from *Syncing Ink* by NSangou Njikam

Chapter 7: "Dear Theodosia," from *Hamilton* by Lin-Manuel Miranda

Chapter 8: "Forever Young," from *Girl From the North Country* by Bob Dylan

Chapter 9: "Ordinary Sunday," from *Tick Tick Boom* by Jonathon Larson

Chapter 10: "I'm Here," from *The Color Purple* by Brenda Russell, Allee Willis, and Stephen Bray

Chapter 11: "If I Had My Time Again," from *Groundhog Day* by Tim Minchin

Chapter 12: "The Field," from *Octet* by Dave Malloy

Chapter 13: "Sarah Brown Eyes," from *Ragtime* by Lynn Ahrens and Stephen Flaherty

Chapter 14: "It Won't Be Long Now," from *In The Heights* by Lin-Manuel Miranda

Chapter 15: "Omar Sharif," from *The Band's Visit* by David Yazbek

Chapter 16: "Stop the World," from *Come From Away* by David Hein and Irene Sankoff

Chapter 17: "Champagne," from *In The Heights* by Lin-Manuel Miranda

Chapter 18: "It's Okay to Remember That," from *Maybe Happy Ending* by Hue Park

Chapter 19: "Road to Hell (Reprise)," from *Hadestown* by Anais Mitchell

Acknowledgements: "For Good," from *Wicked* by Stephen Schwartz

BIBLIOGRAPHY

"Forever Yours"

The MILEPOST, edited by Valencia, Kris, 2021,
  https://themilepost.com/routes/alaska-highway/.

"The Sad Tale of the Beauxhommes"

Plato. *Symposium,* 360 B.C.E., translated by Jowett, Benjamin
  http://classics.mit.edu/Plato/symposium.html.

"Some Girls"

Andrews, Evan. "9 Things You May Not Know About the
Oregon Trail," History Channel, October 28, 2018,
  https://www.history.com/news/9-things-you-may-not-
know-about-the-oregon-trail.

"One Small Girl"

Ferri, Joshua. "Tony Nominee Dane Laffrey Shares the Secrets and Stories Behind His *Once on This Island* Revival Set," *Broadway Box*, June 5, 2018,
https://www.broadwaybox.com/daily-scoop/dane-laffrey-shares-the-secrets-of-once-on-this-island-set/.

"Some Say"

Green, Jesse. "Once on This Island, Revived and Ravishing," New York Times, December 3, 2017.
https://www.nytimes.com/2017/12/03/theater/review-once-on-this-island-revived-and-ravishing.html

"Mama Will Provide"

Mejia, Zameena, "Parkland Teacher Who Hid 65 Students, Got a Prize Worth $10,000 at the Tony Awards," CNBC.com, June 11, 2018.
https://www.cnbc.com/2018/06/11/parkland-teacher-melody-herzfeld-who-hid-65-students-got-10000-prize.html

Spears, Jared. "'The Joy and Pain Combined': Morisseau-Leroy's Haiti." Asymptote, 2021,
https://www.asymptotejournal.com/special-feature/jared-spears-on-felix-morisseau-leroy/.

Two Different Worlds

Anderson, Jenni and Ferri, Josh. "Broadway Replacement Stars That Left Us Stunned: The Heart of Once on This Island, Darlesia Cearcy," Broadway Box, November 6, 2018,
https://www.broadwaybox.com/daily-scoop/broadway-replacement-stars-that-left-us-stunned-darlesia-cearcy/.

Other articles about *Once on This Island*:

Ahrens, Lynn and Flaherty, Stephen. "Breaking Down the *Once on This Island* Revival Cast Album Track by Track," *Playbill*, May 23, 2018,
   https://www.playbill.com/article/breaking-down-the-once-on-this-island-revival-cast-album-track-by-track.

Vine, Hannah. "Get Up Close With the Set and Props of Broadway's *Once on This Island*," *Playbill*, June 3, 2018,
   https://www.playbill.com/article/get-up-close-with-the-set-and-props-of-broadways-once-on-this-island.

NOTES

3. "WAITING FOR LIFE"

1. https://www.playbill.com/article/exclusive-broadway-aimed-once-on-this-island-tests-new-sound-in-workshop

4. "FOREVER YOURS"

1. https://themilepost.com/routes/alaska-highway/

5. "THE SAD TALE OF THE BEAUXHOMMES"

1. http://classics.mit.edu/Plato/symposium.html

8. "SOME GIRLS"

1. https://www.history.com/news/9-things-you-may-not-know-about-the-oregon-trail

11. "SOME SAY"

1. New York Times Review https://www.nytimes.com/2017/12/03/theater/review-once-on-this-island-revived-and-ravishing.html

14. "MAMA WILL PROVIDE"

1. https://www.cnbc.com/2018/06/11/parkland-teacher-melody-herzfeld-who-hid-65-students-got-10000-prize.html
2. This poem was inspired by reading the poem Natif-Natal by Felix Morisseau-Leroy a Haitain born writer and activist.
   https://www.asymptotejournal.com/special-feature/jared-spears-on-felix-morisseau-leroy/

16. "TWO DIFFERENT WORLDS"

1. https://www.broadwaybox.com/daily-scoop/broadway-replacement-stars-that-left-us-stunned-darlesia-cearcy/

Made in the USA
Middletown, DE
05 September 2021

47673332R00170